Kindness and Compassion

The inspiring aftermath of the tragic
Amish Schoolhouse shootings

BE INSPIRED

Bruce Becker

Kindness and Compassion
The inspiring aftermath
of the tragic Amish Schoolhouse shootings

FIRST EDITION

Cover Art: Bruce Becker
Author's Photo: Timothy Becker

To acquire your print of *Kindness and Compassion* and learn more about Bruce Becker and his work, visit *www.beckerartist.com.*

ISBN: 978-1-60126-121-2

Masthof Press
219 Mill Road
Morgantown, PA 19543-9516
www.masthof.com

"Be as a star, shining brightest
when surrounded only by darkness."

- Bruce Becker

Contents

CHAPTER 1

It's All Connected

O CTOBER 2, 2006, began as peacefully as any other day in the small Amish community of Nickel Mines, Pennsylvania. The sky was a clear, beautiful, cerulean blue. A cool breeze was attempting to brush the last hopes of summer completely into autumn. The Amish children attending the Nickel Mines one-room schoolhouse were at their desks. Their parents were hard at work in their shops, fields and kitchens. As for me, I was just in from an early morning run and already at the easel painting. I am a full-time artist. The path leading me to this life was well lit from an early age. Guided by hard work, the courage to follow my heart and the diligent belief that all our lives are connected by a power greater than our own, has led me to make a living at what I love, painting.

On a day as beautiful as this, no one could have imagined the event that was about to occur. An event that would drastically change the beautiful color of that late summer day to black. An event so tragic, so horrid it's nearly unspeakable. Those young children (ranging in age from eight to twelve years old) while seated attentively in school, would come face to face with an evil more grave than their innocent minds could have ever imagined. Many of them would be injured and an unfortunate few would die. All of this would happen as unexpectedly as a lightning bolt from that clear sky. The events triggering this nightmare would begin and end in less than an hour. Yet the effect would be so great that tears would be shed and thousands, even millions, would feel its pain. The innocent of the innocent were about to experience the unthinkable.

But that would be the story you have already heard. The story most of you are familiar with. The story the newscasters reported. The one in which a man of the English community (that's how the Amish refer to anyone that is not Amish) would storm into that tiny school. How he would terrorize the children, their teacher and those visiting the school that day. Eventually he would shoot eleven young girls, killing five of them then killing himself. Tragic doesn't even begin to describe that event.

But this story, the one about the people in that community only begins with that event. What I will tell you is the rest of the story. The hours, days, weeks and months that followed. This is a story of people responding to tragedy in a way that made all the difference. A story of awareness and action. It's about recognizing life's coincidences, connections, spiritual intervention, call it what you will. But it's about seeing it unfold before you, recognizing it and acting upon it. A story of seeing the goodness in others . . . of responding with kindness and compassion even when faced with the most terrible loss.

Saturday, September 30th, two days prior, was a gorgeous day. Like many other weekends, I found myself at one of the local flea markets. I enjoyed the time spent on the hunt for that perfect find. The antique I was looking for yet never realized, until I found it . . . The item that was out there waiting to be discovered and longing for its proper place in my home . . . A treasure from days gone by, waiting to be rejuvenated to new life. Waiting to be dusted off and have the light of a new day shine on it again. Sounds like how most of us approach flea markets, right? Well, this day one of those treasures found me.

The subjects of my paintings do seem to find me. There are times when I am not certain of what my next subject will be, or what I will paint next. In that respect, this item was like the others. It found me. When that occurs my role is simply to be open and aware that it is happening. You see, I've been an artist all my life. Until about six years ago I was doing other things for income . . . but always painting. Six years ago I took the leap of faith and said no to other forms of work and no to a steady income. Those things just distracted me from my true passion, painting. This is a passion that stretches back as far as the earliest years of childhood. My earliest memories are those of sitting on the floor, drawing and coloring (always outside the lines). I knew then that I wanted art in my life.

Let me explain to you some of my background. Some of the groundwork laid earlier in my life that brought me to be on this journey and telling you this story. Growing up I was the middle child in a large, primarily, Irish Catholic family. Along with my eight brothers and sister, my parents and my grandmother, the house of my childhood was a full one. By no means were we a wealthy family. But we certainly weren't starving either. The hard work ethic of my parents drove them to provide, as best they could, for all of us. Dad always had at least two jobs and I never knew a time when mom didn't work. She was a waitress. But more than that being a job, it was her social life. Everyone knew mom. She was the woman who would always greet you with a smile and say something positive to help lift your spirits. People loved her for that. Once I became an adult and realized how special that was . . . I did too. Mom was the first-born generation in this country, from Ireland. Her parents came over on the boat, as they say. Being a very strict Catholic, meant mom had us in church at least once a week. The morals and values of Jesus' teachings were prominent in our lives. Mom did her best to not let any of us stray from those ways . . . not even dad. In her wise and strong ways, she knew how to lovingly control even him. The kids in the neighborhood knew not to cross her too. Mom was not one to be fooled with. She had no trouble setting anyone straight if they wronged her, her family, or anyone unjustly. Perhaps without realizing it, she was a groundbreaker in the approach to raising children with tough love. With dad always out of the house working, she was the front line for care taking, feeding, guiding and disciplining for nine children. Not a task for the weak of heart. But heart is what she had plenty of. In a most affectionate way I suppose I could sum up my mother like this: Mom was a woman who could love you with a strong hand. Strong enough to help you, guide you and hold you up when you needed it . . . or strong enough to put you in your place when you deserved it.

Dad had his own struggles that brought him to manhood. His upbringing was filled with tough times. His father, one of my two grandfathers that I never knew, was not the best role model for a young boy. He was a vigilante in the coal mining towns of northern Pennsylvania. Most of his time was spent away from home, dealing with business. The business of setting people straight in his own way. You might say he worked outside the law, while enforcing the law, illegally. Dad was left alone with his mother and family to fend for themselves. Times were tough. One time dad told me of how he most remembered encountering his father, after not seeing him for months. He would show up at the door, throw a new white shirt at my dad (as a token of being away for so long) and say, "Here this is for you. You doin okay?" Then before dad could even answer him, his father would tell him to shut up. He didn't really want to hear it. Then he'd leave again, not to be seen for another few months. Dad, as a young boy, found himself on the street much of the time. He became streetwise and street tough. His mom didn't fair well with this life either. To help care for her, he left school after the eighth grade. Caring for her was a practice he continued well into his adulthood. I remember as a child going with him to visit her. Quite elderly then, she was still an ornery, chain-smoking, drinking and cursing stubborn woman. There wasn't much good she had to say about anything or anyone. Least of all my mom, a woman with very different values than her own. But nevertheless dad was always there, the son that cared for her.

As a boy, dad lived through the struggles of a household that seemed to be in constant erosion. As a man, and now the father of his own family, he vowed not to let that happen again. He and mom instilled in all of us the importance of family. They kept us together by building a home based on love and care. They taught us to watch out for each other, and do what was good and right, no matter what the consequences. We were taught to stand up for each other and ourselves. Help each other and use our heads and hearts before our fists. Don't get me wrong we weren't perfect. With nine kids there were plenty of knock down, drag outs, between us. But for every one of those battles, I'll bet you could find one where we stood together against outside forces as well.

In this explanation of my family background you didn't hear much about the art world, did you? No, while growing up art had no place in our house. There were no distant ties to gallery owners. No wealthy relatives that were collectors. No famous painters, sculptors, dancers or musicians in this family tree. Not even my brothers or sisters had an interest in art. My interest made me an enigma. In a meat and potatoes upbringing like this one, I had to fight to hold my ground. You see my dad didn't see art as being a valid career. He didn't really see it as work. He would say, "Work should be just that. Why do you think they call it work? Art isn't work." Realizing now, the hard life he had I suppose I can't blame him.

So holding my ground is exactly what I did. The art world was the light I could see shining from the other end of the tunnel. It was out there. That light was emanating from somewhere. I didn't know exactly where. But even at a young age it had reached me and I was engulfed in it. I just needed to find my way to it. Drawing all the time, drawing everything and anything in front of me, eventually led me to painting. One time I even ordered one of those art tests you see advertised on TV. The one that says "See if you have what it takes to be an artist." I finished the test and sent it back. They responded by sending someone to my home recruiting me for their school. I'll never forget sitting at the kitchen table with that man and my parents. You had to be at least eighteen years old to enter their school and only then did this man find out I was only eleven. That gave my parents cause to take a second look at my choice. Maybe I did have a gift.

By the time high school came around I suppose my drawing skills were getting pretty good. I was the guy everyone asked to help them with their school projects . . . drawing up posters for science projects, do lettering, creating signs. All sorts of things like that. I even sold my first drawing at the age of twelve. My high school offered no art classes. None. There was no art department, not even a drawing class. That of course did not sit well with me. Perhaps it was the determination instilled in me by my parents for standing up for what I wanted and what I thought was right, but I wasn't about to settle for being deprived an education in the arts.

As a freshman, I marched myself into the principal's office, told him of my interest in the arts and requested they offer an arts program. As well intended as I was, he wasn't impressed. He simply told me it wasn't in the budget and it wasn't going to happen. Not satisfied with that, I found a teacher from another school who offered to give two or three other students and myself, lessons at her school. Classes would be held at night for no credit. It was a start. We did that for several months then went back to the principal and showed him our progress. He still wasn't impressed enough to initiate a change. After seeing him again, once a full year of classes was under our belt, he said we could continue classes and receive credit for them. Well, to shorten this story, eventually that class grew in numbers and we did so well that my school hired an art teacher. Classes were offered for credit and twenty years later they had me back to speak at the now well-established art department. I was holding my ground and not losing site of the light.

After high school I went to college and studied fine art, leaving there on the Dean's list. Had it not been for the academics I was forced to take, I would have finished top of my class . . . all A's in my art studies.

After college I started showing in galleries and filling in the empty blanks of income with odd jobs. Exhibits were happening for me in various parts of the country. Then came another stage in my life. It wasn't long before I was getting married. Shortly after that children were on the way. The life of an up-and-coming artist is one of struggling for an income. That made it tough to raise a family. So much of my design skills were turned to the commercial art field, advertising, marketing and such. At least during the day, that is. At night, on weekends, whenever I could, I would paint and continued to exhibit my work. That was my way of life for about fourteen years. I was an artist dad and loved it.

But some things never do seem to stay the same, do they? After fourteen years of marriage, the woman I thought I'd be spending my life with wanted a divorce. I was devastated. This hit me like a brick I never saw coming. Being raised by the loving parents I had, married for more than fifty years, divorce was not in my game plan. Almost unbelievably it's been ten years now since that happened. It was a total start over for me. I was living alone and unfortunately spending a lot of the time without my kids. The two incredible kids I had read to every night before bed and helped daily with their homework now were seeing me on weekends and special occasions. For so many years not having them with me everyday was devastating. Divorce was something in my life that I had never seen coming. But I pushed on, as so many people do these days. Jobs, most of them good, have come and gone. Living on my own was something . . . I guess I just got used to.

Now I'm a single father in his mid-forties, of two wonderful children. Young adults really. As this journey begins my children are both in college. Timothy is 22 and Molly is 20. In some respects they are as different as night and day. Molly is the academic athlete. Yes, she always had both those elements very strong in her life. She was always a tower of strength, self-confidence and determination, even though she was always the smallest one on the team . . . any team, and she was on every team. Tim is the emotional deep thinker. He's so personable. This guy can find the good in any situation and would do anything to help anyone. He's the x-games kid with the big heart. Such a joy they are. I love them both more than they may ever know. You know what I mean? As a parent you hope your kids realize how much they mean to you as you struggle to make ends meet and keep them on the right track. As a single parent that challenge is even greater.

Another passion in my life, one that may trump the importance of my art, yet I don't discuss often, is spirituality. Have you ever felt as though you're on a path or journey perhaps one of spiritual and philosophical awareness. I've felt like that all my life. Like being in a constant state of openness. No, that description makes it sound too sedentary or implies being fixed in space. It's more fluid than that. Perhaps it's better stated, as being in a state of constantly being opened and made more aware of higher levels of consciousness. This is not a solid, singular state of being.

This path has led me to explore many schools of thought, religions and philosophies . . . of course due to my childhood there was Catholicism, but also many other religious beliefs caught my interest: various delineations of Christianity, Judaism, Buddhism, Taoism and more. Just the importance and power of religion itself over the state of humanity and its social structure has always fascinated me. This path has also led me to examine the sciences. I find myself intrigued by the likes of Physics, Psychology and Biology and others. Through my observances and experiences I have grown to appreciate how all people are joined by the things we share in common. That these are the things to be celebrated and built upon. Rather than be focused on the ideas that separate us, keep us at war and in battle, sometimes literally. Throughout my life I have stayed open to what God (whatever you perceive Him to be) has presented to me and always tried to move in the direction of kindness and goodwill toward others. I have no doubt this is working hand in hand with my art. I'm not always sure where it will take me, how I will get there or even where I'm going. But somehow they work together.

Remember I told you of the leap of faith I took to make my painting my sole income. Well, I was actually helped along a bit with that decision. There I was a single dad, very much in need of the good job I had. Because even though I was divorced, I was still very much supporting the kids, their mom and myself. One day, totally without warning, the company I was working for decided to "downsize." Yep, and it started with my office. Just like that I was out. No notice, no severance, nothing. That day, as I sat alone at home wondering what to do, it came to me. I knew it was time. What I had always wanted to do was literally at my fingertips: paint. No more wasting my time in offices and making money for someone else. I had a passion and I wanted to live it. Right then and there I made the commitment to dedicate my time and energy to the things that truly mattered to me: My kids, my family, my painting and my spirituality. How's that for a combination of concerns to focus your attention on everyday? This was the right decision and I knew it.

This news didn't sit very well with my family and friends. They unfortunately didn't share the same enthusiasm for my passions. For years I was asked things like, "When are you gonna get a real job?" or "So, you still painting? . . . How's that workin' out for ya?" No one took me seriously. If someone needed a favor done during the daytime "regular" working hours, I would hear comments such as: "Ask Bruce. He can help. He doesn't have a job." or "He's not working." Not working? Do they realize how difficult it can be to totally change direction in mid-stream, just to do what you love . . . and try to make a living at it at the same time. Trust me that's work. Perhaps they just didn't know how to react to such a departure from the norm. I went from seventeen years of a business suit, in the advertising and marketing field to torn, tattered, paint-covered, clothes. No office. No boss. No daily grind . . . and no weekly paycheck or health insurance. But I was happier and freer than ever.

Don't get me wrong it was tough and sometimes still is. But it was the life I always wanted. To all you wanna-be artists out there, remember this, you won't find jobs listed in the paper asking for artists, painters and sculptors. You need to find your own way and you need to have the skills and creativity to back it up. But along the way, if you find your way, it's so worth it. So, I was determined to make it work. All those years of marketing and advertising continue today to come in very handy. For all those years I put my efforts into promoting someone else's business. Now it was time to promote my own.

My work quickly became widely accepted and admired. Exhibits, sales and requests for my work came in from all across the country and eventually from parts of Europe as well. To this day it can still be a struggle. I never know what will happen from month to month. But I push on. Following my heart, following that light. Walking the path.

I'll never forget the day that was a turning point in my life and career. The day I was let go from the company and made my decision to follow my heart. As difficult as it was to find myself without work that day, it paled in comparison to the news I received that very same evening. You see, that was the same evening I learned my father had cancer. At this point in time, dad lived alone. Mom had passed away about six years prior. She had been mis-diagnosed with an illness. Then incorrectly medicated. It was a series of mistakes made by a group of doctors that had fatal results. This vibrant, loving, energetic mother of nine, wife of fifty years, hub of our large family, was taken from dad and all of us much too soon.

Now it was dad who was ill. This shed an entirely new light on my situation. I now saw my loss of a job as freedom. Not just from the ties binding me in the financial rat race, a pursuit we all find ourselves in at times. Not just the freedom to follow my dream. But right then, more importantly, it allowed me the freedom to care for dad over the course of the next year. My time and schedule were mine to make. So care for him is what I did. In fact, the entire family cared for him in every way they could. Those of us that are local shared in seeing to his personal needs. Others living further away made special trips to visit, lots of extra phone calls, sent e-mails, prayers and support. Twenty-four hours a day, seven days a week, he was our priority. My days were spent painting when I could and caring for dad whenever he needed me. Hospital visits, feedings, changing of bandages or just sitting and talking. I realized the importance of not just caring for his physical well-being, but attending to his mental, emotional and spiritual pains as well. There were times that all he needed was someone to talk to, or watch the game with, or not do anything at all . . . just be there. After so many years of him having to be away, working and toiling to support us all, now, while he was home, I could be there to support him. His work was done. After a year of his uncomplaining battle, he did pass away quietly. But not before he and I shared the closest year of our lives.

His entire life dad was a workingman. A meat and potatoes type guy. What mattered to him was working hard, caring for his family and keeping them together. Having him understand and relate to my lifelong desire to paint and my attraction to the arts was not an easy task. It was not until his last month of life that he truly gave me his blessing. He saw my paintings. He saw people showing an interest in them and buying them. I'll never forget that meaningful conversation, simple as it was. I was driving him to a chemotherapy treatment. In his now quiet voice, raspy from cancer and the treatments, he said to me, "I heard you been selling your paintings." I simply smiled and said, "Yep." "I heard what you been selling them for," he mentioned, referring to their selling price. People were buying my paintings for more money than dad may have spent on his first car. I responded and smiled, "Nice isn't it." Then he said it. The words I never thought I would hear him utter, "You oughta keep this up. You could make a good living with this." There it was. Perhaps some of the most inspirational words ever given to me came from dad. He said, "Find out what it is you enjoy doing. Then find a way to make a living at it. You'll be doing it for the rest of your life." Forty-seven years into my life, with dad perhaps drawing some of the last breaths of his own . . . and he used them to give me his blessing.

I was with both my parents when they died. I mean right with them. Next to them. At their bedsides, even holding dad's hand when that exact moment came. As awkward as it may sound, I suppose that was a blessing in itself. These two, most important people in my life, gave me the basic values and principals that guide me today: The importance of family, compassion for others and following the dreams that make you happy.

The very next painting I did after dad died was of his birdhouses. He loved to feed and care for the birds. A good friend and supporter of my work wanted to buy it. It held so much meaning for me because of the subject. But remembering what dad said about making a living at this, I sold it. From that point forward I always thought of my best work not as the pieces that were already finished, but rather always looking to the next one yet to be painted. For the next few years I carried on, painting and following the light.

So, that brings me back to telling you, now years later, about this flea market and the next subject for my painting. A subject that would change my life. It's September 30th, 2006, two days before the tragic Nickel Mines Amish schoolhouse shootings. I am at a local flea market enjoying the beautiful weather, the food and of course the hunt for that perfect find. Strolling through this collection of antiques, I am in the midst of the woods. Yes this market is actually a series of dirt paths that connects the stands filled with goods. Towering trees are everywhere. The sunlight dapples the ground through their leaves, which provide welcome shade in the heat of summer. I roam the grounds and look over the cluttered, weather-beaten tables full of trinkets, tools and assorted junk. That's when the subject of this upcoming painting found me. Peaking out through the dusty assortment of collectables, discarded by someone who once cared for, or loved each of these items, was an object that caught my eye.

It was a small, unassuming, white porcelain bell. When picked up from the table, it dangled from the black wrought iron hanging mechanism it was attached to. Inside the bell was an old wooden clacker, hanging from an old piece of rope. The entire bell and hanger was no more than eight or ten inches tall. Small as it was, it had a sense of power to it. I was drawn to it immediately. Its simplicity was in keeping with much of the subject matter I enjoy painting. This would be the subject of my next painting.

Through my inquiries to the stand owner, I discovered it

was owned by an Amish woman. She got it off of a one-room, Amish schoolhouse. Her intent was to use it as her doorbell. Later she realized she wasn't happy with its sound. I can't say as I blame her. The wooden clacker against the porcelain doesn't ring quite like any other bell. Its sound is quieter, more reserved, almost intimate. Throughout history the ringing of a bell has symbolized the proclaiming of a message. Their sounds would boom across the fields and towns telling people of many things: Freedom, liberty, a calling to prayer. This little bell sounded its message much more humbly. As if while you're ringing it, its sound, its message, is just for you. Being used as a doorbell was not the use for this little bell. The Amish woman decided to sell it. Little did I know that in a very short time the message this bell proclaimed would have the power to be heard around the world.

A quick bargaining session later, as is the case at a flea market, and the bell was mine. Never could I have imagined the journey I was about to begin by owning this bell. The remainder of my stay at the market was pretty much like any other. A few more finds of interest. Perhaps another snack to eat. A little color from a day in the sun and it was soon time to head home.

Throughout the day my anticipation to work on this next painting was building. Upon arriving home, I removed the newspaper wrapping from the bell, dusted off the dirt it collected through the years and began contemplating my next composition. I could pretty much visualize the painting right away. But as I normally do, I sketched it out with one or two variations. After seeing them, I determined my first instinct was the correct and best one. I had my layout. Now all I needed was to have it hanging in the direct sunlight on a clapboard wall. That's how I saw it: Shining and reflecting light off its curved, snow white surface. The black of the wrought iron hanger was stark against the simplicity of yet another white surface, from which it hung. The shadows cast in blue and purple created a shape of intrigue. Even the shadows were filled with light.

As the next day began, Sunday, I went for my morning run. All the while I was looking for the clapboard to be used as the backdrop for my painting. I ran by house after house, studying the siding. There was brick, wood, stone, everything but clapboard. I arrived home and as usual I paced a bit along my house to cool down. That's when I noticed the clapboard on my next-door neighbor's home. There it was, right in front of me. Often that's where the answers will be found, right in front of you. If I simply stay open to all possibilities, the answers will come in ways least expected. This is one of the beliefs by which I live. That philosophy was going to be more and more evident in the days to come.

After knocking on my neighbor's door and asking her if I could use that piece of wall for my painting, she agreed. Some of my neighbors know I am an artist. She is one of them. Others may still wonder what goes on in my house. There can be music and lights blaring at all times of day or night. I never keep regular hours. Painting either by day or at night is normal for me. But not for my neighbors who mostly have set schedules and 9 to 5 jobs.

I hammered a small nail into the side of her house, being careful not to split the wood. Carefully, I hung the bell on the nail and straightened it. There it was, perhaps hanging much like it did on the schoolhouse it came from. Stepping back, I saw the sunlight strike it just as I had imagined. The white bell was shining brilliantly, casting a glow of color around it. The black wrought iron hanger strongly contrasted in value against the white slotted wall with a vibrant purple and blue shadow. I was very happy with this image and photographed it for reference. Then I removed it. After I carefully pulled the nail I headed into the studio.

My studio is in my home. It actually takes up the entire basement of my home. Now, many people think it a bit odd to have a painting studio in the basement. "How's the light down there? Isn't it dark?" they ask. Well, let me tell you, I can light that place up like a baseball field if I want. Or, I can get the light as dim and soft as a summer evening just before nightfall. The key here is that I control the light. There are no big windows with ever changing and moving sunlight. Anytime of day or night, rain or shine, the light can be just as I need it to be. The fifteen foot by forty foot room is both functional and comfortable. In addition to the portable lights that hang everywhere, there is an easel that stands next to a very strong hand-made wooden worktable. On it is my palette for mixing paint. It's a rather big palette, bigger than most. It's about four feet across and two feet deep. It's surrounded by paint tubes, paper towels, painting mediums and brushes. Lots of brushes. Even though I have about three hundred brushes, I still seem to always be looking for just the right one. I can never have too many brushes. Any artists reading this will know what I mean. The rest of the room is filled with a desk, a couch, some chairs, rolls of canvas and some old frames and paintings hanging from the rafters. Along one wall is an eighty-gallon fish tank that was my grandmothers. She gave it to my father and he in turn gave it to me. That's a treasured item. There's also some workout equipment that gets used regularly, including a one-hundred pound punching bag that hangs in the middle of everything. And remember this is a basement, so the washer and dryer are tucked away in one of the corners. I live here. I work here. The space works for me.

The next step in creating this painting was to prepare the canvas. I had done this hundreds of times. Canvas gets rolled out on the floor, measured and cut to size based on the proportions from the initial sketch. It might seem silly, but it has always been important to me to cut the canvas with scissors that belonged to my parents. Mom always kept "the good scissors," as she called them, for special uses. Well, it didn't get more special than this for me. Once the canvas is the proper size, a coat of gesso, a painting ground medium, is brushed on and allowed time to dry. Then a second coat is applied. Once it's dry, the prepared canvas is stretched onto a painting board. Large flat pieces of wood I use for this purpose are stacked in the corner of the room. Then the board, with the canvas taped and stapled to it, goes on the easel. With the lights brightly shining down on it, the blank white canvas awaits being brought to life with color. The remainder of my work that day would be sketching the image on the canvas. This would be the image I envisioned when first conceptualizing this painting the day before, and the same image I saw when the bell was hanging on the wall that morning. For several hours I worked on the sketch. Finally I had it complete to a point where I could see, in black and white, the image that would soon be blanketed with light and color. Enough visual information was now on the canvas for me to start applying paint. That would happen tomorrow morning, October 2.

As that Monday morning rolled around, I was staring it like any other, either with a workout or a run. Today it was a run. As I passed by the houses of brick, wood and stone, all I could think about was the image of the bell hanging on the clapboard wall waiting in my studio. My pace quickened. I returned home to shower and change into my paint clothes. I have drawers filled with clothes I wear just for painting: long pants, shorts, T-shirts, long sleeve shirts, shirts with sleeves cut off, all of them torn from use and covered in paint. My kids love them. I do too. When I am in those clothes I feel I am at my best and ready to paint.

Color is very critical in my work so once I got in the studio that morning I mixed twenty or more colors before even applying one to the canvas. When I was happy with this beginning set of colors, it was time to put brush to canvas. I paint faster than most artists. I allow little or nothing to interrupt me. At times I don't answer the phone or the door. I may not stop to eat or even sleep. The intensity of the moment is over-powering. It feels as though the image is rising up from within me until it reaches my skin and fingertips. I can't get it onto the canvas fast enough. Once I get started, it's not unusual for me to finish a canvas, of an average size of four feet by four feet, in about twelve hours. The planned finished size for this painting was much smaller than that, less than two feet by two feet. My painting is not solely a thought process. In fact I seem to do it without thinking at all. It's so much more than that. It's a combination of heart, hand and head, working as one. There are times when I'll work on a piece for hours. Then stand back look at what I've done, smile and ask myself, "Where did that come from?"

This day's work began around 8:00 a.m. By 10:30 I was well into the flow of painting. The image was taking shape and I was pleased with how it was going. That's when the phone rang. For some reason, unlike other times, I answered it. It was my brother-in-law, Jerry. This was a Monday, one of his days off from work. Jerry is married to my sister Claire. They've been together for 30 years so I have known him most all my life. To say he's my brother-in-law isn't enough. He's my brother. We are that close. He's only a few years older than me and having known him for so long, we almost grew up together. He too has a strong sense of his spirituality. Often our discussions are of the state of humanity, religion, world philosophies and incorporating your beliefs into your daily life. For the past few years we've also been workout partners. Meeting on a regular basis to lift weights and run gave us even more opportunities to grow closer. We've been through a lot together, both hard times and easy. We talk about and share everything. No topic is off limits. The conversations can be deep and very meaningful or simply full of laughs. Either way they are always welcomed. So, it was good to hear his voice. Although this conversation would be brief, it would set in motion a very unexpected change with this image.

"Have you heard what's going on?" he asked. Of course I hadn't because I had been busy working. Music was playing in the studio, as usual. In my studio you could expect to hear anything from Vivaldi to Country, or Brazilian guitar to Punk. I chose the music in the studio to reflect my mood. And I certainly wasn't watching the news on TV because I had pulled the plug on my TV set about two years prior to that. No TV in my house. It was another distraction from my work . . . beside the fact that for a while I couldn't afford it. To actually pay for that distraction to be in my home, where my studio is, was ridiculous.

Generally, Jerry's a very positive, upbeat, individual. He is a talented musician and plays guitar very well. Although he doesn't play much anymore . . . we all wish he would. He has always had a love of motorcycles. In all the time I've known him, he has never been without one. I think the sense of freedom he feels when he rides may be much like I feel when I'm painting. His tone as I picked up the phone was serious, indicating to me that something was certainly wrong. He told me that just miles from both our homes (he and Claire live just about two miles from me) an Amish schoolhouse full of children had been seized by a gunman. Not much more was known just then, as the tragedy was happening right at that moment. He suggested that perhaps I should listen to the news. The last time he made a call to me with that sense of urgency in his voice was when he called me to tell me of the attack on the World Trade Center, in New York. He was my original contact source for that tragedy as well.

It was simply his concern regarding the importance of this tragic incident that initiated his call. Because neither he, nor anyone else, knew that I was painting a subject of Amish origin. So, at first I was a bit taken back by what he said and its coincidental attachment to this subject. It seemed surreal somehow to listen to his words. I literally stood there with the phone in one hand and brush in the other . . . looking at this Amish schoolhouse bell in a sudden shock of near disbelief. So, I said nothing to him about it.

After hanging up the phone, I went directly to the radio and tuned in a news station to listen. As I listened, the reality set in that this was truly happening. I was painting a subject that seemed connected to this terrible tragedy. In fact, as I'm writing this it has occurred to me that although I have been painting all my life, I have never painted anything related to the Amish. Nothing. This was the first Amish-related painting I had ever done. "How strange," I thought. Suddenly, that elated feeling I always have while painting had taken a drastic turn. It turned to one of concern and sadness for all those involved.

The broadcasts continued on and off for hours. There were reports of children being shot. Some believed to be dead. The gunman shot himself and dies by his own hands. The Amish community is finding itself in sudden, never before imagined, turmoil. This never happens in the Amish country. Not to these people. Not to these children. The Amish community has always been only peaceful. Growing up here and visiting the Amish community was always comforting for my family and me. Shootings don't occur in Amish country. Baking, farming, quilting, children running, laughing and playing, that's what happens there. Not killing. To say it was all disturbing and confusing is putting it too mildly. This was unheard of. This was an event that was truly sad and tragic. My heart ached for these people.

I was upset to the point that painting this image, one so closely related to these people, was out of the question . . . at least for now. There was no question about that. Right then I couldn't continue. Throughout the day I would listen as the broadcasts came through . . . "The name of the gunman is not being released" . . . "it's believed at least three children are confirmed dead at this time" . . . "reasons for the killing are not yet known." Speculation was rampant. Sadness was in the air. The community was in disbelief. A white, Englishman (meaning non-Amish) had invaded and violated the trust of that community and the trust of everyone, in a way that was unthinkable. These peaceful, innocent, neighbors of ours were in the midst of a living nightmare.

At one point, my curiosity overcame me and I went to my sister's home to watch the coverage on TV. Claire was still at work; so Jerry and I watched news footage of the choppers, state troopers, coroners, EMT personnel, grieving Amish and blood. The blood of innocent children. Images such as these, of this once tranquil community were now being broadcast across the country and around the world. But those watching were not seeing the community, as we knew it. The world was witnessing a truly uncommon horror in this pastoral setting. This community, whose main street traffic are the horse and buggies, bicycles and scooters, was overrun with ambulances, police cars and helicopters. Media crews were everywhere. Satellite dishes and news vans are totally foreign here. Yet they were lining the streets. This was a joining of the Amish and English worlds like never before.

This was the first and last of the TV news coverage on this topic that I would watch. Over the next few days and weeks, an occasional glimpse of the news in a restaurant, or on a set in someone's home while I was visiting, would present me with as much footage as I needed to see. But never did I sit down and bombard my mind and heart with those tragic scenes again. I felt the devastation. I felt the pain and sorrow of loss. Seeing it was not necessary, nor did it hold any positive input for me. I stayed abreast of the facts as they developed. Radio played a major roll in that process.

That night I went to bed with mixed feelings: A prevalent sadness and a sense of confusion. Wondering why someone would do such a thing. And a strange connection to it through the subject I was painting. Why should I feel this connection, I wondered. I didn't know any of these people personally. I just happened to be painting an Amish schoolhouse bell when this took place. Coincidences happen, right? I prayed that night for the comfort and well being of all those involved. Then I prayed the same prayer I do everyday, tragedy or no tragedy: "How may I be of service?" Then I slept.

As I woke the next morning, I was of course very aware that the scene in Nickel Mines, just minutes from my home, must be chaotic. Yet I had a sense of calm about me. As the day moved forward I listened to a few reports. But I was back in the studio, once again painting. The painting of the bell would be finished today. When I paint, I bring everything that is me to the canvas: The positive. The negative, all the events that are going on in my life. The things that are molding the person I am. My work comes from deep enough inside, that without effort all of me is present when I'm in front of the canvas. All of it comes out. This morning the influences were much different than any other day. Somehow the feeling that normally accompanies my work was different. It was not the elated feeling of needing to rush. Nor was there the high-energy type of excitement. Instead it was one of respectful awareness. I'm not sure how else to put it other than to say, there was a presence of heart. A calm presence of spirit and life in the studio that day. There always is life in the studio. But this was different.

Hours passed. Maybe I ate that day, maybe not. I'm not even sure. I just know I worked through the day. The only reason I was even aware of the time was because I had to teach that night. So I all but finished the piece before going off to class. I say, "all but finished" because it's common for me to have a painting sit for a day after it's complete, then look at it again with fresh eyes to determine if any changes need to be made.

Just before I left for class, I was looking at the painting and wondering if there might be a way this image could be of some help to the situation.

By now, talk of the shootings was everywhere. It was the lead story on every news broadcast, both radio and television. It was across the front page of all the newspapers and it was what people talked about wherever I encountered them. During class it's common for all of us to discuss whatever is on our minds that day. I have taught students from the age of eight to eighty, from people who never touched a brush to professionals of twenty-five years. So what gets discussed in class always varies. We share all kinds of things about our kids, work, and so forth. That night my students and I spoke about the shootings. When I shared with them the topic of my painting and the unusual timeliness of it, they also seemed to feel a unique connection. I suppose many people felt connected through the feelings of loss and despair shared with those involved directly. Feelings of sympathy or empathy will do that. But this was different. I couldn't explain it. I had a feeling of involvement. But I hadn't been involved. At least I hadn't been involved yet. What was ahead would have me more involved in ways that I could never have ever imagined.

CHAPTER 2

The Message

I N THE FOLLOWING days, this tragedy was more than the lead story of the news. It was the news. The Nickel Mines area was overrun by media and on-lookers, curious to see firsthand just what went on. People came from all over to drive by the site. Gifts of candles, stuffed animals, cards, flowers and much more were placed at a designated memorial area, near the school. State troopers were posted at the school around the clock. The community was still in disbelief.

As for myself, the idea of still feeling connected to it all was so prevalent. But why? What could I do to help? How does this "coincidence" connect me to it all? Perhaps it was because using my work to help others is something I have always done. Many organizations have asked me to use my art in benefit of their causes. Aids research, Juvenile Diabetes, Literacy Council, Boy Scouts, homeless and impoverished children's organizations are just a few that I have been involved with.

One of the most powerful experiences, of offering my working assistance, was when I was asked to help the victims of the 9-11 attack. When the first tower fell I was on the phone within minutes calling everyone I thought of, offering my help in any way they may need it. I called local police, Red Cross, State Police, National Guard, any organization I thought might be involved in the rescue and recovery. Working for myself, my time was my own and I would go if they needed me. All I had to offer was an extra pair of hands and a willing heart. I got turned down with each phone call. They wanted people with medical experience and I didn't have that.

About four months later, I woke up to a phone call. It was my brother Kevin. At the time he was the director of a medical team that was assisting a group of three hundred survivors deal with the trauma they had lived through. These were people who actually escaped from the burning tower. The survivors were due to be released from care and the trauma team wanted them to have an inspirational, motivational, visual reminder that life goes on. They were asking me to paint this image. Being asked to do this was an honor. Of course I said yes and offered to donate all the work, in the hopes of simply being able to help.

In the following weeks, I went to meeting after meeting in Boston and New York with the trauma team. We couldn't decide on the appropriate subject of the painting. Then on the night before the last meeting it hit me. The painting they needed to have was already complete and hanging in my dining room. It was a piece I had done with similar intent to their request . . . symbolizing that life goes on. I painted it when my mom died. It was my own personal inspiration that life goes on. At that last meeting we began to discuss ideas for a subject. One of the women attending described an idea that was so close in its description to my completed painting you would have thought she was looking at it.

She was presenting the idea of a painting that depicts something representing growth. A young tree perhaps lush with green leaves. Conveying the hope of a new day, a new start and projecting the feeling that life goes on. She was describing my painting. It is an image that's a bit more abstract than some of my other works. But the image represented is of a young tree, lush with green leaves. It appears to be lit with brilliant light, even though its surroundings are of a cold dark night. Snow covers the ground and the elements around it signify a world not conducive to new young growth. Yet there it stands, thriving, healthy and persisting against all the odds. This woman, never having seen my painting, or ever talking to me about it, had no idea what an introduction she was giving me.

That's when I knew I had to offer this piece. So, just then, I did. I showed them pictures and told them of its original intent. They loved it and accepted it. The deal was done. We set a presentation date and two weeks later I was headed for New York. The trauma team asked me to speak to the survivors and tell them of the symbolism behind the image. The gift of this painting was a surprise to these people. I hoped they would see its special significance, as I did.

The presentation in New York was being held at a federal building just blocks from Ground Zero. I had to drive my car, with the painting, through extensive security checks. Finally I was in the underground parking garage beneath the building. Federal workers assisted me in getting the piece to the twenty-seventh floor for the presentation. After setting the painting on an easel and draping it with a cloth, the room began to slowly fill with the survivors. I was in awe of the situation and humbled to find myself in this circumstance. There I was in New York City, just months after this tragedy, surrounded by these survivors. The view from the window was of Ground Zero, as close as two blocks away. At that point, it was in the beginning stages of cleanup. And I stood, waiting to present my painting to these survivors. Humbling for sure.

This was a lunch meeting so everyone had served themselves some food and taken their seats. Kevin, the trauma team director, said a few words and introduced me. Simply attired in my jeans, work boots and black pullover shirt, casual as usual, respectfully I took the microphone and began. Now, Bruce Springstein had just played New York and his presence must have still been in the air. Because as I stepped up to the mic, the entire room began to chant my name, as they do his name,

at a concert. "Bruce . . . Bruce . . . Bruce . . . Bruce . . . " How
surprised and relieved I was to get this lighthearted welcome.
We all laughed and they applauded as I stood next to the painting. This piece measured approximately three feet wide by four
feet tall. It was draped with a cloth to be kept from view before
the unveiling. I thanked them for having me there and spoke
for a few minutes about what I was asked to create. Then I gave
them the background of the painting, telling them its original
intent and how it seemed appropriate that it now be theirs.
As I stood there and spoke the realization of something rather
special occurred to me. So, I shared it with them. This painting, which had been created as inspiration to carry on after my
mother died was being presented to them on the exact anniver-
sary of seven years, to the day, of her death. It was exactly seven
years ago, to the day that she had died. That was the last thing I
said to them before unveiling the piece. Their response to it was
one of a collective gasp and sigh. They were extremely moved.
I remembered this was a lunch meeting, but just then no one
was eating. No one was even chewing. They were all motionless. And then, as one, they all clapped and stood and cheered
in approval.

Following my presentation, I left the building for about
half an hour. As they conducted other business, I walked over
to Ground Zero to be outside and get some air while collecting
my thoughts. I was careful to return to the building in time
to greet everyone before it ended. Once again through all the
security checks, I was crossing the lobby and heading for the el-
evators just as the doors opened. The crowd exiting the elevator
surrounded me. Then the same thing happened from another
elevator. Fifty, a hundred, then two hundred or more people
were surrounding me. It was the survivors I had been speaking
to. The meeting ended a bit early and they were on their way
out. I was inundated with thanks, handshakes and hugs. Some
told me stories of how they lost their parents and stories of

what they went through on September 11th. It was exhilarating. It was humbling. I was grateful nearly beyond words that I could help.

Several weeks later I received a letter and a photo from the group. The letter stated they were in their new building. The photo showed their placement of my painting. It had become the inspirational centerpiece and focal point of a self-help center located in their new building.

Life will unfold and its pieces will fall into place, as they will. As I continue to be aware of the forces greater than my own and greater than any of ours, present in this unfolding process, I find my life is continually enriched. This enrichment is very fulfilling. Through this awareness I know that utilizing my work to enrich the lives of others is what I have always wanted.

But with this painting of a simple bell, I was coming up short. Prayer, contemplation and staying open to possibilities were all I had. Things like this are not something one can will into action. Only be aware when the door opens and the answer comes. The coincidences that led me to this point . . . finding the bell and knowing it once hung on a one-room Amish schoolhouse, painting it as the tragedy was happening . . . were only just the beginning . . . I simply had to stay open as this journey unfolded and the answers would come.

It was exactly one week to the day since the shootings and the idea of finding a way to help was still very strong in my mind and in my heart. I was in the studio. The radio was playing a local country station, WIOV. Their coverage of the incident was the most caring and compassionate I had heard. About 10:30 that morning Casey Allyn, one of the morning DJ's, had asked for a moment of silence for all of those involved. Then she asked a question that sparked something in me I will never forget. Just as I was asking, once again, for guidance in this matter, she said, "I'd like to ask that all the bells in the area be rung in unison, symbolizing our support for all those involved, especially the girls that lost their lives." There it was, another bell connection. Now maybe it seems I'm reaching here to connect her request with my painting. But to me this was the answer I was asking for . . . to me it was as clear as a bell. I immediately picked up the phone and called the station. Why exactly was I calling them? I didn't know. I had no plan. I wasn't even sure what I would say. It simply felt right. I told them who I was, what I had painted and expressed an interest in helping. I told them if we could work together and find a way . . . I wanted to do whatever I could to help. This conversation lasted all of five or ten minutes. The person on the other end of the phone was quite moved by it all. She asked if I would write the story in an e-mail and send it along with a photo of the painting. Within half an hour that mail was sent. Now I waited.

WIOV's broadcast station is located very near the scene of the tragedy. The people who work there felt the pain of the Amish community perhaps more than any other media in the area. It was their coverage that was my main source of information. By this time I knew national and international coverage was taking place. I just hadn't seen much of it because of having no TV. Furthermore I had no interest in filling my mind and memory with the gruesome images being repeatedly shown. It was primarily through WIOV's broadcasts that I was beginning to learn something miraculous was happening. Something no one in the English community could have even imagined. The Amish were not responding to this evil act with reciprocal hatred, anger or negativity. They responded with kindness, compassion and even forgiveness. Yes that was their response to all involved: the victims as well as the gunman and all of his family. This was truly an expression of their faith put into action. They were living out their beliefs under the worst possible circumstances. Beliefs that guided them to lead the simple life of trusting in God's will. The circumstances they were now in, of having their own children held hostage, shot, maimed and killed, is as tragic as it gets. What more devastating event could a parent, a family, or a community, go through? But rather than feed the fire of violence or encourage the anger over this dreadful act, they responded with kindness. If prayers were being said around the world for all of us to find peace in this madness, those prayers were being answered. Astonishingly, the answer was coming from the victims themselves.

Later that day I received an e-mail response from Casey, The WIOV disc jockey. She expressed the feelings she immediately had upon seeing the image of the painting for the very first time. As she told me, I was unaware that I was hearing the same response that was to come from thousands upon thousands who viewed this and felt exactly the same way. She said it gave her a feeling of calmness, a sense of peace and it brought some awareness of stability back into her life. She said she couldn't really explain it. She simply felt it. Her interest in having the radio station and myself do something positive with this image was immediate. As soon as possible, she would talk with her boss and bring him into the loop on taking some action. What action would that be? Neither of us knew.

I had never met Casey, but I knew of her. Many people in this area know Casey. Especially if you're a fan of Country music. She is the co-host of the very popular morning radio show. One time, years ago, I may have seen her at a book signing or some radio sponsored event. I'm not sure what it was. She's an attractive woman about my age, married with several children. Her personality is one that you would wish for if you could choose who would be your neighbor. By that I mean she seems like she would do anything to help anybody. She's a very generous person that was always involved in activities benefiting the community. Her outlook is always bright. I suppose you could even describe her with a word I rarely use, but I'll use now in a most respectful way, bubbly. This is a woman with a good heart.

In the next few days she and I would e-mail and talk by phone regarding the positive responses the painting received from people at the station. Here is the transcript of a letter I sent her on October 10, 2006.

Casey,

Nice to hear from you. Thank you for your compliment on the painting. It's always a pleasure when my work affects people in a positive manner.

I also would like to compliment you on your sincere concern for and positive approach to handling this tragic situation. Just as many people right now are learning a lesson of forgiveness and compassion from the Amish, many in the media could learn a lesson of how to approach a story like this without capitalizing on its shock value, or the promotion of negativism, by taking note of yours and WIOV's attitude.

My work has always been about helping others. I hope I/we can find a way to utilize this image in the spread of goodwill and compassion, for those affected by this incident. Let us not focus on the horror of the actions taken, but rather focus now on responding to it in a positive, caring, manner.

Keep up the good work.

All my best,
Bruce Becker
www.beckerartist.com

Without realizing it, this letter may have been what began to determine the message associated with this image. Even at this time, so early in our discussions, you can see I was aware of the response of kindness by the Amish. My focus now was squarely on recognizing the positive in this negative act.

Casey was in fact so moved by the painting she asked if I could make a print of it for her own keeping. There was the idea I had been looking for. I knew what we had to do. The next step on this journey had become clear. From the letter below you will see how, from this point on, the message attached to this image was one of compassion. I didn't even know this woman (Casey). We had never met, never spoken prior to two days ago. But I sensed that with her help we could take some positive, influential action. The following is an excerpt from my letter to Casey on how to utilize the painting:

> *. . . That's very nice of you to want to have me on the air. It's not necessary, but I'd be glad to accommodate. Perhaps we could talk off the air as well. I could share an idea I have for utilizing this piece to raise money for the victimized children. Here's a thought I had: If inexpensive prints could be made (perhaps the printing could be donated by a local printer) the prints would be given to contributors, very inexpensively, with the profits going to the children. It could be promoted not as an image commemorating that day. But rather as a reminder, to those purchasing it, to always be compassionate to those in need. The bell could symbolize never allowing goodwill and compassion to be silenced . . .*

The idea went straight to her heart. She loved it. She would run it by the production manager and determine just how the station could help. Her energy about this was so positive it actually caught me a bit off guard. But I knew this was a good thing.

At this point in our conversations I made it very clear that in no way did I want this image to represent the terrible tragedy of that day or be commemorative of that day. Rather it would be a reminder to all of those receiving it and viewing it to always respond to others with kindness and compassion. No matter what the circumstance. That is what the Amish community was doing. That is what was so inspirational and positive to me about this awful tragedy. That would be the message of this image.

Stop and think about those words for a moment and realize just how powerful that message is. "Always respond to others with kindness and compassion." For instance, put yourself in the recipient's position of such a response. Would you not always want to be treated kindly, no matter what? The responsibility of acting that way toward others rests with each of us, as individuals. The most extreme example of how that can be done was happening, right here, right now, under the worst circumstances possible, by the Amish community.

My explanation of this message to everyone at WIOV completely sealed our bond. Everyone at the station was one hundred percent on board. By now, all of them had taken the opportunity to visit my website, read up on my background and review my paintings. The respect they were showing for my work was greatly appreciated. It was made very clear to me that they understood painting was my livelihood, my profession and my passion. Due to this understanding they also stated to me, more than once, that they recognized this image was a product of that passion and what we did with it was entirely up to me. This station, that organizes large media events all the time, was turning the reigns over to me.

But I was not seeing this image as part of my professional work. This image held much deeper meaning than that. What I would do with this image would be based on the beliefs that guide my life. That is to be of service to others. My thoughts and intentions, in my daily life and in my work, are always of shedding positive light on any darkness.

As for the message, I felt that wasn't solely mine either. I am simply a messenger, recognizing the incredible kind and forgiving actions of so many others. This painting became a way of delivering that message. Now our challenge was to determine just how to do that. How would we get the prints and its message to the people?

After much consideration, having a print signing seemed to be the best idea. We would need to have prints produced, find an appropriate location and make them available to whoever wanted them. WIOV was offering to promote the event on the air. The task at hand was to now put all the details together. Realizing that the DJ's would be talking about the painting on the air, Casey asked, "How will we refer to it, what do you call it? What's its title?" Now this was an interesting question to me, because I only ever titled my work descriptively. A bowl of lemons was *A Bowl of Lemons*. A violin and bow was titled *Violin and Bow*. You get the picture? But this represented more than a bell. It had to be made clear what it represented. If the titles of my paintings simply stated what they represented, then this had to do the same. The answer seemed obvious to me. I simply told her, "Its title is *Kindness and Compassion*." I remember hearing her repeat it back to me as a question, "*Kindness and Compassion* that's it?" "That's it." "I said, "That's what it stands for. That's what it represents. That's the title." Right then she got it. She understood and said, "*Kindness and Compassion*, of course, that's great. It makes perfect sense. That's what we'll call it when we talk about it. This is wonderful." The excitement in her voice was so evident that I could almost feel her smiling over the phone.

That feeling I had of being connected to this incident was manifesting itself. I felt myself becoming more connected. But I had no idea what was ahead and just how much further this would go. Now that connected feeling had spread to include everyone at the station also. We were all now becoming involved and taking an active role.

There were a lot of things that had to happen to get this done. All of which none of us were sure how they would get done. No one knew how the prints would get produced or who would pay for them. And how would we distribute the prints, once they were produced . . . and where and when? I figured I would handle the payment part. Not like I had the money to do that . . . but somehow it would come. Just as everything else had fallen into place so did the prints. The next day, while at the station, Casey received a phone call from a local printer. They told her they wanted to be involved with the food drive that the station was sponsoring. This was a bit baffling to Casey, because they weren't having a food drive. Thinking on her feet, she informed them that there was no food drive . . . but there was another project being discussed . . . one that required the production of prints. Casey explained all the details to the company owner, an understanding woman who was quite moved by the idea of this project. So much so that she responded very generously. She offered to produce one thousand prints, free of charge. We had a printer! The company even asked to remain anonymous. No one was involved in this for financial gain. Not myself, the station and no not even the printer. But all of us were gaining more emotionally and spiritually than we could have imagined. At this point, Casey and everyone at the station were seeing and experiencing firsthand how this was meant to be. We were all caught in the flow of this powerful event. The light was spreading.

Choosing a location wasn't very difficult. Since this print and message was about responding with kindness and compassion, we thought, "What group of people do that on a daily basis? What group of people responded first to those suffering on that tragic day? The ambulance crews." These first responders were there that day giving all they had to assist those in need. Their response of kindness, compassion and care is evident everyday and never more so than during this tragedy. We specifically looked to the EMT centers around the Nickel Mines area. So many of them were instrumental and did all they could on October 2, that choosing one location wasn't easy. So, we decided to split the day between two locations. We would be at one location in the morning, south of the site and one in the afternoon, north of the site. Each EMT station asked was very willing to participate. I felt that coordination of these sites was best left to the radio station personnel. These folks were popular in the area. Everyone knew the on-air personalities and would be more willing to oblige them, as opposed to working with me. It was the right decision. In a day or two the locations and date were set. The signing would be Saturday, October 21. That left us about a week to finalize all the preparations, including the print production and on-air promotions.

While we were busy organizing, this tragedy was still very heavy on everyone's hearts. Barely more than a week had passed now since that tragic day. That was all, only a few days really. In this community, the ill feeling of that day hung with us. It gnawed in the pits of stomachs and ached in the hearts of everyone. Activity was still at a peak around the schoolhouse grounds and throughout Nickel Mines. Media continued to swarm the area. Funeral services were being planned and held for the five girls who died, as well as the gunman. He was a neighbor to these families. He was a man who many of them saw everyday. He was a milk deliveryman who was trusted on many of their farms. His family lives across the road and next to families directly affected. So his funeral would be held here also. These facts are part of what makes his horrendous acts incomprehensible. Why would this befriended Englishman turn on these innocent children? No one was really sure. But that didn't make the pain of it any less. In fact it may have made it worse.

These Amish families' lives were in turmoil. Everything changed from the moment of the shootings. The extreme intermingling of the Amish and English worlds had never been experienced like this before. Parents and siblings were being driven back and forth to hospitals, caring for the children. The uninjured children, who remained at home, were dealing with the emotional crisis of it all, while finding themselves surrounded on a daily basis by hundreds perhaps thousands of English media and onlookers. State Troopers, EMTs, media crews, curiosity seekers, people in cars, people on foot, or motorcycles, or bicycles. The English were in the Amish community like never before. Sounds like tremendous pressure for the Amish doesn't it? Well, I'm sure part of it was . . .

. . . But believe it or not, as time was passing the response of kindness, originally generated by the Amish, was spreading. The people of the surrounding community were finding any way they could to show their support through acts of kindness. This evil act of an Englishman had penetrated the Amish community and in response their actions of kindness were now penetrating our world. The sense of kindness to others was almost becoming infectious. I could actually feel people wanting to be kind, not only to the Amish but also to one another. No one was certain just how to deal with such grief over the pain and loss felt for our peaceful friends and neighbors. But concern for them and for each other was everywhere.

Things were a bit different though in my personal life. Surprisingly, I was finding little support for the involvement I was undertaking, from my family. They had seen me use my art for good causes before and they were always supportive. But this time the majority of their responses to what I was doing, when there was a response at all, dealt with their concern that I was overstepping some boundary. "Are you sure you want to get involved in this?" "What a nice gesture you're doing, just be careful." Or more often than not, there was no talk or mention of it at all. As this journey began to unfold, this was the response from all but one member of my family. The exception was my nephew, Stefan.

He is one of my brother Dennis' children. Dennis is the oldest sibling in the family. He has lived and raised his family in the Boston area for the past forty years or so. He settled there and started his own business after acquiring his PhD in Speech Communications. Now he and his wife Paula, head the most prominent speech coach company in the world. Yes, the world . . . but more about that later. Stefan is one of their four children. He's a great guy. He's the kind of guy who doesn't know he's thirty-seven. He think he's still twenty-seven . . . or younger. I mean that in a good way. He's young, both at heart and in his actions. He keeps himself aware of what's current in many aspects of our society: Music, movies, politics, electronics, medicine, and much more. I didn't mention medicine just by chance. One of the things Stefan is known for is to seemingly always be battling some kind of physical issue. You'd never know it to look at him. I mean he's a good-looking guy. But behind that handsome facade hides the sleep disorders, migraines, vision problems and such. His migraines have always been the biggest challenge. This guy has such a good heart and means so well. But so often his physical self deters his emotional and spiritual self from being actualized.

Perhaps he's a perfect example of how the experiences we all encounter along the path we walk, guide us in ways that are not always immediately apparent. What I mean is this. His battling migraines for instance have opened his mind and heart to ways of dealing with the human thought process and how our minds interpret certain stimuli. That in turn directed him on a path of studying Psychology. Now he uses that to help troubled teens. That's great stuff. Perhaps his struggles have also been a motivator for his examining and researching religions and philosophies from around the world, particularly from both the Native American Indian and the far east. This in turn has opened his mind and heart to be a very conscientious and caring individual. His awareness of those philosophies could be one of the reasons he and I relate so well. He and I have had a deep bond for many years. We talk about everything. We are there for each other through the highs and the lows. When family gathers here in Pennsylvania, siblings, aunts, uncles, cousins, nephews and nieces, he usually crashes at my place. One time he even came to PA and stayed with me through an entire summer. So, it didn't really surprise me that he was the family member first taken by the importance of this journey right from the start. He understood the power of what was happening. He recognized the influence of kindness and the large scale scope of what was going on here . . . he got it. Looking back on it I now realize that everyone I was encountering since the day I started that painting had a role to play on this journey. At this point, I didn't know Stefan's role, other than that of being supportive.

As for the rest of the family, perhaps things were happening so quickly that no one quite realized the message of kindness and forgiveness that I was seeing. For some in my family, the tragedy hit them so hard they couldn't even talk about it. Most of them have children of their own and the pain of such a deadly tragedy made it too great to even focus on for too long. Then again, many of them live in other states, so they were much further from this ground zero. For me, the schoolhouse was thirty minutes away and it felt like it was in my own back-yard. We all have things in our lives that take our attention: jobs, children and so forth. I understand that. Let's not forget also, that I was constantly being reminded of this tragedy through my painting and all the personal experiences connecting me to it. As time would move forward I had no idea just how deep those connections were about to become.

During the week of the print signing, WIOV was of course reporting on the latest developments in Nickel Mines. In addition there was considerable on-air talk about the painting, the message, the print signing and myself. Eight or ten times a day they would bring up my name. It seemed a bit unreal to be hearing this so often. Several times they had me live on the air. I was asked questions about the painting and its message. Then we would talk about the time and dates for the print signing. I was very grateful to have their support.

These radio spots and the on-air interviews began to stir interest in the community. I was getting phone calls at home and comments on the streets from people who had heard them. Strangers were expressing well wishes, prayers and support. One evening I even cancelled my painting class because a local TV news team wanted to come by the house and studio for an interview. They called me saying they heard about what I was doing with my painting and wanted to cover it on the nightly broadcast. After hanging up the phone with them, I barely had enough time to cancel my class and they were knocking on my door. We set up in my studio—lights, the cameraman, the reporter, the original painting and myself. The reporter had questions about the bell, the timing of when I was working on the painting, the message and the use of my work for other causes. One of the points I made very clear in that interview was this: "This is not a painting commemorating that tragic day, but rather it symbolized the response of kindness and compassion shown by the Amish community and surrounding area. It's a reminder to all, to respond to others with kindness and compassion." That message took top priority with me. The spot ran on the air that night and the next day. Of course I never saw it because I didn't have a TV. That didn't matter. The message and I were now on a journey and the message was being delivered.

When the night before the print signing was upon me, an uneasiness began to edge its way into my being. Questions of "What if?" surfaced in my mind. What if no one showed up tomorrow? What if people misunderstood the message? What if I was overstepping some boundaries? But I know better than to listen to the worries of "what if." Like my grandmother always used to say, "Worrying is like a rocking chair. It gives you something to do, but it doesn't get you anywhere." So rather than allow my time to be stolen away by foolish worries, I dismissed them. Instead I thought positively. People will show up. It doesn't matter how many. Some people will always misunderstand a message. No matter what it speaks of, there will be those that dispute it. As for overstepping boundaries, no way. Kindness knows no boundaries and kindness is what this is about.

Those worries were replaced by my search for the proper words that I would use to sign each print. It had to be concise. Nothing lengthy, this had to be right to the point. Several pages of paper were filled with words I jotted down that held meaning in this circumstance. From those words, I formulated sentence after sentence, groping for the appropriate combination. I wanted the statement to be humble, like the Amish. Yet strong in its conviction to the overall message. Nothing flowery or showy would do either. Clearly stated, simply, easily understood and meaningful, that's what these words had to be. Much like I do with my paintings, I was chiseling away the excess, leaving the essentials of what makes something beautiful. Something that now shines as though it lies beneath a strong, warm light, radiating with beautiful color for all to see. Now separated from anything surrounding it that can cause undo judgmental responses.

About an hour into the process, I found it. The violent act, at the school that day, was met with forgiveness and compassion. So my handwritten reminder to those receiving prints would need to reflect that, as well as help deter additional violence. On every print given out I would hand write, "Peace through kindness."

I now had no doubt about the message of the print or the message I would add to it. The remainder of that night was spent praying for guidance and relaxing which then turned into sleep. Falling asleep wasn't a problem because my mind and body were at ease about what I was doing.

In the middle of the night, I was awakened from a sound sleep by noises in the house. The kids were off at college most of the time, so basically I lived alone. When the kids were in town, they spent many of their nights at their mom's house. Hearing noises in the house, especially those loud enough to wake me up, was startling. Only half awake and eyes blurry, I stumbled out of bed and into the hallway. It was pitch dark. Before me, in the darkness, I saw what seemed to be small floating lights coming toward me. They were about four feet off the ground, small and moving in an erratic motion as they approached. White, blue, red, the colors seemed to vary as they moved. Not knowing what was going on and still half asleep, I tried to say something like, "Who's there?" A voice came back from the darkness saying, "Dad it's us." It was Tim and Molly, my son and daughter. With a sigh of relief, I fell back into bed, still not a light had been turned on. The lights I saw in the hallway were their cell phones. They were using them to light their way through the house. I rolled over and looked at the clock. It was 3:30 a.m. By the time I rolled back over, the kids and one of their friends, were in my bedroom. They flipped on the light and proceeded to sit on the bed like it was the middle of the afternoon. "Why didn't you turn on lights when you came in?" I asked them. "Being so late we thought that would startle you. So we were going to just come in and wake you." These two are young adults, but they are very much still kids at heart. It turns out they were out with friends, got hungry and stopped by to raid the refrigerator. They also wanted to wish me well for the next day. Perhaps it would have been more thoughtful if they had done that while the sun was still shining. Even so, I love them dearly and was grateful and glad to see them. After a short chat, while I was back under the covers, they were off to raid the fridge. I was headed back to sleep. Hoping to catch a few more hours rest before the big day.

CHAPTER 3

Drawn Together

N INETEEN DAYS HAVE now passed since the shootings. Virtually the entire world knows of the tragedy. Newscasters, both national and international, have been on the scene in and around Nickel Mines. Reporting on the initial, horrid, act is what makes up the bulk of their broadcasts. Only a handful of reporters are noticing and reporting the miraculous actions that are occurring. I am of course referring to how the Amish and this local community have dealt with the situation and responded with kindness and forgiveness.

Many of the reporters and concerned individuals now in the area have never been here before. Their knowledge of the Amish is perhaps limited to what they have seen or heard about this area being a tourist attraction. Trust me this is much more than a tourist attraction. You are about to find out that as different as we are from the Amish, we share more in common than is first recognizable. That's something I've known by living among them all my life. Granted my home is about twenty-five or thirty minutes from "Amish country." So my interaction with these people is unlike those who live right next door to them. But I grew up knowing that Amish country was all around me. For many years I have been visiting their shops, buying their produce and goods and encountering these people in a variety of ways. It's never been uncommon for me to see or run into Amish just about anywhere. It's a normal accepted part of my life. I've had friends that lived right in their community. While visiting these friends, it was as common for me to hear the clapping of horse hoofs going by the house as it may be for you to hear the roar of a car engine go past yours.

These peaceful people first came to this country escaping religious persecution. They were in search of a place to live out their days according to their beliefs. The Amish are a devout Christian based community, living off the labor of their own hands, literally. Tilling the earth, sewing, baking, building, gardening and then selling the fruits of their labors is mainly how they sustain themselves. What we in the English world most associate with them are things like their modest dress and non-use of many contemporary conveniences, such as cars and electricity. As I understand it, it's not that they dislike or find these things to be evil. But rather, before they permit conveniences such as these into their lives they ask themselves, "Will having this in my life and the life of my family strengthen or potentially diminish my or our relationship with God?" That's how important their faith is to them. If it's not seen as strengthening that relationship, they simply dismiss it. Doing this has kept their lives simple and uncluttered. The focus then remains on their core beliefs. Less distraction allows for more time and attention to be given to prayer, God and promoting a peaceful existence between themselves, the world around them and all people. The Amish ways may be plain, but I have always had nothing but respect for a people that can live such peaceful lives, in such harmony with the earth and according to their spiritual beliefs.

While the Amish community now struggled with their grief, many of its members found the strength to visit with the family of the gunman. His wife and children were victims in this incident as well. No, they were not in the schoolroom that day. But they also would be feeling the pain of loss, shock and sadness from this tragedy. These visits began on the very same day as the shootings. This immediate response of kindness for his family's well-being shows strength of character and stead-fastness to the beliefs of their faith. Right from the very beginning, the response of the Amish was distinctly different than what one might expect from the English community. During the first two weeks, after the shootings, funeral preparations were being made and carried out for their own children. The injured and hospitalized children were being visited daily. Just imagine preparing funeral services for your children, or children of your friends, while simultaneously caring for the surviving injured children and still finding a place in your heart to visit the family of the gunman. Amish, who never drive or even own cars, were finding English drivers to take them hours away to care for these innocent victims. Emotional trauma was stirring within all of the children in the community. The parents who were consoling them were in need of being consoled themselves. Even through hardships like these nearly one hundred Amish attended the funeral of the gunman. They were searching for and finding forgiveness for him. They would not add to this evil. They fought it with peace in their hearts.

Acts of forgiveness and kindness like these were unheard of in the English community. Locally, nationally and internationally, on-lookers watched in near disbelief. These were the actions I was witnessing in amazement. This God-like response of the Amish is the driving message of my painting. This is the story that all of us need to hear. This is what has set me on this journey, experiencing things I never imagined.

I woke on the morning of the print signing with a bit of fuzziness in my head, perhaps due to the late night interruption, from Tim and Molly. It only lasted for a few seconds, because as soon as the realization of what day this was struck me, my thoughts and emotions were clear and focused. The energy was so great that I nearly jumped out of bed to begin the day. It was coffee . . . a bowl of cereal with some fruit . . . a quick shower and into my clothes. I had done print signings before at gallery openings, so I knew to prepare the night before. The previous night, my choice was made as to what I would wear and all the things I would need were gathered and waiting. Bottled water, two boxes of Sharpies, the directions and, of course, the original painting, all sat waiting to be loaded into the truck.

As that morning started, a thought came to me, "Except for a few friends, no one had seen this painting. Would people show up to receive a print of a painting they had never seen?" Well, it's too late to be bothered by that. Nothing could be done about it now. I put everything in the truck and was about ready to leave the house. The print signing, at the first location, was to begin at 9:00 a.m. I had never been there before, so I was allowing about an hour for the drive. At 7:45 the phone rang. It was Casey. She said she had just gotten a call from someone at the first EMT station, where I was headed. She told me what they said to her, "We hope that Bruce is bringing his good writing hand because people have been outside waiting in line since 7:00." "What?" I asked. "People are waiting in line?" Her excited words came back, "Yes. They started showing up two hours ahead of time. Isn't that amazing?" As she told me this, her words were filled with an exhilaration that made it evident to me; she thought this day held great promise.

I took a few minutes to sit quietly out back, think about this and again ask God for guidance. A few minutes were all I had if I was going to leave and make it there on time. Although I already felt the excitement of a big crowd, I was more over-come by the fact that these people were showing up because of the message. That was wonderful. As I sat there on the step of my deck, I noticed how chilly it was. I was wearing a leath-er jacket and still I felt the uncommonly cold fall breeze. My thoughts turned to those people, waiting in line, outside, in the cold, anticipating my arrival. It was time to leave.

My estimation of the drive time was correct. Winding my way through backcountry roads, with directions by my side and coffee in hand, I made the last turn. There it was The Manhiem Ambulance Station. What I saw on the street before me, left me awestruck. The line of people was out the door, down the block and around the corner. I could hardly believe my eyes. Ambulances and police cars were parked on the grass. The lot where the EMTs usually park, day after day without a problem, was overflowing with cars. The surrounding streets were also filling up as I watched more people arriving just as I did. I drove past the front entrance and headed for the parking lot, hoping to find a space. Finding none I parked on the grass, as the ambulances did. People were watching me as if they knew me. I thought that perhaps they were wondering, "Is that him? I think it is." There was no way I was going in through the front door. I found what seemed to be a back entrance, opened it and let myself in. I had walked directly into a classroom and class was in session. It seemed to be EMTs in training. I excused myself, told them who I was and why I was there. The instructor, not too pleased that I interrupted his session, simply pointed in the direction I should be heading, which was out of his classroom. It was the door at the opposite end of his room. That direction meant I had to make my way through the desks and passed his entire class, which I did in a rather hurried manner. Again excusing myself along the way. Not the most graceful entrance.

Upon entering the ambulance bay, finally I saw a familiar face. It was Casey. We had met once or twice while preparing for this day. But just then, what came to mind was the first time I had seen her. It was a time I couldn't fully recall prior to this. It was from a distance, years ago, at one of her cookbook signings. She's famous for her cookbooks. They are collections of recipes from her listeners. Casey develops a theme and her listeners write in with their favorites. She had been doing this annually for more than a dozen years. Perhaps it was seeing her in the midst of the forming crowd that sparked the memory.

The ambulance bay was empty of vehicles, so we could make use of it. It's a large clean room. Surprisingly clean for a garage. Essentially that's what it is, since this is where they keep the ambulances. The morning light was streaming in through the bay windows. It lit the rescue and safety equipment that was hanging from wall hooks. I couldn't help but wonder if this was the same equipment used as these EMTs assisted at the schoolhouse that awful day. There were two long tables set up near the big bay doors. The doors were closed. Just on the other side of them is where the line of people were waiting. Right there, in the cold, is where they had been for the last two hours.

The radio station personnel were in charge of seeing that the prints arrived safely and on time. They assured me that all was well with them. At one end of the two tables I saw a stack of prints and a very modest collection box. The tables were draped in a brilliant royal blue cloth. Chairs were positioned on one side for a few of us to sit. On the floor was a radio, playing music broadcast from WIOV. EMT personnel scurried around making final preparations. One of them offered me a cup of coffee. I gratefully accepted it and took what would turn out to be the last sip of anything I would have for the next few hours. I made sure to greet everyone in the bay: the radio people, EMTs and anyone who was helping out. There were lots of hugs and smiling faces. It was good to see smiles generated by this event. Because without it ever being spoken, we all knew that just beneath the surface of those smiles were the memories of the event that brought us together. Those memories were especially present for the EMT people. These were the folks that were on the scene that day, giving all they had to help. So, keeping this in mind, we respectfully all went about taking care of the last minute details. Very little was in need of being done, as the EMT workers had prepared so well. I positioned the easel and the original painting at the end of the two tables. It sat just next to where I would be seated. This was the first time that anyone in that room had seen the original painting. To this point only a handful of people had seen it in person. To say their comments were complimentary would be an understatement. It became evident from their remarks (and even from the few people that had seen it earlier) admirers of the painting began to view it as being a product inspired by a greater power. Due to the modesty I've always had about my work and my life, it's hard for me to even write those words. But that was the nature of the unexpected and surprisingly exalting comments I received.

All of us were aware of the people waiting outside, so we didn't waste much time getting underway. The last thing I did was sign a few prints for the workers at the station and the folks from WIOV. Now it was time to open the doors and begin. The large bay doors were lifted allowing the cool morning air to rush in. But with it came the sunlight flooding the room with its warmth. The light and warmth also radiated from the hearts of those good people waiting to share their concern for our neighbors. From our vantage point there was no end to this line. It now stretched as far as we could see. There must have been several hundred people waiting for those doors to open. I sat behind the table, took a deep breath and began greeting and signing.

This is the first point in my recapping of these events that the proper words are hard to find. How do I explain the feelings? How do I describe the care and concern these people felt and expressed and how that affected me? The emotion in the air was palpable right from the start. Remember the connected feeling I previously had . . . well, it was like someone had just increased the intensity.

People immediately began streaming in. They were directed to the far end of the table. There they received a print, gave whatever amount of contribution they wished and were directed toward me. Everyone contributed whatever they could. No set amount was required. All the proceeds of this event were going to the victims of the shootings. Any amount that anyone wanted to contribute would be accepted and turned over to assist the victims in the Amish community. No one would be turned away, even if they could give nothing. This was a message I wanted everyone to have. This was more about the message going out than it was about the money coming in. One homeless-looking, elderly man, in tattered clothes, a baseball cap and a face that had been unshaven for days, reached into his pocket and dropped what he could into the container. The few coins rattled as they hit the sides. He approached me with tears in his eyes and as he reached out to shake my hand in approval, he said, "If I had more I'd give it. What you're doing is a wonderful thing." This was the type of giving that went on that day. People from all walks of life came through those doors, farmers, lawyers, truckers and doctors. You name it they showed up. People came alone, with their kids, their neighbors, their boyfriends and girlfriends. WIOV personnel anticipated that we might have a large turnout. So when they promoted this event on the air, they announced that only one print would be given per family. Not one per individual. We only had about a thousand prints and we wanted them to go as far as possible. It was looking as if their foresight was correct.

It would be impossible for me to tell you every comment said to me, or every comment I made to everyone else. As good as my memory of this event is . . . it's not good enough to recall every word. But I will tell you, that I was very aware of the importance of every single individual that showed up that morning. Each of them got my full attention when they were in front of me. There was eye contact and an exchange of questions and comments. Then I personalized and signed their print. Every one of these people that showed up was there in support of our neighbors. Each of them deserved the most I could give them, even if just for a minute, that person in front of me got all I could give. These people were a living, breathing embodiment of the kindness and compassion message. Their very presence was an expression of their concern for the victims of that tragic day. Not only did these people understand the message, they were living it by being here.

One after the other, people thanked me, telling me that they were praying for me and were so pleased I was doing this. While all the time, I was thinking, feeling and telling them, "It's you who are doing this. It's you who are making this good thing happen. You are here, expressing the kindness and compassion. My painting is simply reflecting how you and our Amish neighbors are living."

Hour after hour crowds continued to stream in. The line never let up. In fact, at times it got longer than when we started. Cups of hot coffee were periodically placed next to me, by thoughtful workers at the station. One after the other each got cold and was taken away. None of them touched, because I had not even a few seconds to drink them. Truly, I was that busy. Pausing for even a few seconds to drink seemed like an interruption.

One woman went through the line and came to the table twice. Each time she waited in line for more than an hour. Both times she was acquiring prints for those affected directly by the tragedy. One print was for the teacher at the Amish schoolhouse and the other was for the children attending class that day. Her intention was for both prints to hang at the soon-to-be built new school. As she approached the table for the second time, I recognized her from when she first came through. When she told me who these prints were for, she asked me if I would personalize them. I thought this was a wonderful gesture on her part, very thoughtful. But how did she know these people, or how to get the prints to them? It turns out that Kym was very involved with this tragedy right from its start. Kym, that's her name. I learned that from a brief exchange of comments we had for each other while she was at the table for the second time. It turns out that Kym lives within walking distance of the Nickel Mines School. This caring and thoughtful neighbor of theirs heard about this print and its message on the radio. She immediately knew that the Amish community would appreciate such a gesture. Due to her concern for them, she had now been waiting in line for several hours. Not for herself, but for them. These prints would go to her Amish neighbors. In fact, when I realized that she had none for herself, I offered one to her. Her expressions and actions of such kindness indeed represented its message. This is an image I wanted her to own.

Even with the few words spoken between us, an immediate bond of friendship between Kym and I was formed. Neither of us knew at the time how our paths were soon to join in this cause. But it was obvious she understood and supported the message.

Periodically throughout the morning, Casey's DJ partner Murph, who was on the air that morning, talked about what we were doing. It wasn't your typical "live on location" broadcast. There was none of the fast talk, bells and whistles, and hype attitude. Murph simply and with humility discussed the morning's event, as he and Casey both had been doing throughout the past week. The attitude from both of them was one of calm reverence and respect. The painting and its message were talked about as an inspirational creation, carrying a message of healing for all to hear. This was a message that would fill the empty void felt by so many. Being a country station in a community that is strong in its faith, they had no problem referring to this painting as being directly inspired by God. Love of God and family are things people still talk about here . . . and they live it here. By now comments referring to this painting as being inspired were heard everywhere. This only added to my present sense of humility. My head was level. Never was I looking for, or even imagined, that comments like this would be generated. Nothing they said could cause me to puff my chest or feel proud about my painting. In fact, as this kind of talk increased the more humble I became. I was constantly looking for and asking that attention be given to the message. I was only the messenger.

We were scheduled to be at the morning location from 9:00 to 12:00 and the second from 1:00 to 4:00. As 12:00 approached the line was still down the street. Casey had to ask if some of these people could meet us at the second location. We had to leave, if we were going to get there on time. Even after asking this, I signed prints until 12:30. At that time we gathered everything together, said a grateful thank you to the station personnel and we were off. On my way, I stopped for a quick sandwich and drink. As I was eating, my cell phone rang. I didn't recognize the number. But these days that meant nothing. The way this journey was unfolding, I was taking just about any call. I could never be sure who would be on the other end. This one was from a TV news station in Philadelphia. The reporter introduced herself and told me that she heard of what I was doing. She was calling to confirm its truth. They were enroute to cover the event and were an hour away. I asked, "How did you get this number? My cell phone is not listed anywhere." She answered, "We have our way. See you soon." With that, I finished lunch and was headed off. Even with the size of the crowd and now the reporters on their way, I still felt the same sense of calm as when I started this day. I was ready for whatever lay ahead. But I had no idea how incredible things were about to get.

The second location was the Ephrata Ambulance Station. It was just minutes from where I was having lunch. As I pulled up, the scene of a waiting crowd was much like the morning . . . only bigger. Cars were everywhere. The line not only went around the building and down the block, but it also stretched into the parking lot of a neighboring business. Yellow caution tape was everywhere. Police vehicles were directing traffic. I was later told that people had been waiting in this line for more than two hours before I was scheduled to show up. That meant these people were in line here while I was still signing at the first location for an additional hour and a half. But even in the midst of all this energy and anticipation, there was a wonderful sense of calm. Everyone was respectful of why we were there.

So, first things first . . . where was I to park? I mean really, cars and people were everywhere: On the street, the sidewalk, in the station lot and in the parking lots of the surrounding businesses. Where was I to go? As I approached the front of the station, still on the main street, the police recognized my vehicle and me. I suppose they were told when to expect me and keep an eye out. They stopped traffic for me and directed me into the ambulance parking lot. There I found a parking space had been saved for me, right in front of the station. That was a very thoughtful gesture. I pulled in, being careful of the yellow caution tape, red cones, cars and the crowds of people. I was parking right next to the tables, where I would do the signing. These tables were outside, in front of the station. The table set up was much the same as it had been that morning—two tables, draped in blue cloth, a few chairs, the prints and the collection box. Everything was set up and ready to go. As I got out of the truck, I noticed the weather had become beautiful. The sun was shining and warm. The sky was blue and a slight breeze was blowing. As was the case at the first location, I was greeted with lots of warm welcomes. Handshakes and hugs from everyone. But we didn't waste much time with greeting each other. The people in line had been patiently waiting, they could see that I was now there and it was time to take care of them. I took my seat and started right in with more signing.

People approached the tables in the same fashion as the morning. The line was directed to the far end of the table. Any contribution amount desired was dropped into the container. They received a print and brought it to me for signing. One after the other, they came to me with well wishes, thanks and prayers. Pen in hand I would thank them and ask, "Would you like me to personalize this for you? Perhaps put a special name on it?" Many of them told me they were picking up the print as a gift for someone else, such as their mother, father, school groups, co-workers and such. I was so pleased to hear that these people thought enough of this image and its message to give it as a gift.

It was shortly after we began that my kids, Tim and Molly, showed up. They were working their way toward the table when the police and EMT personnel stopped them. These EMTs were simply directing people to the end of the line. They didn't know Tim and Molly. "Could you please go through the line to get to the table?" they politely asked. "Oh, we're trying to get to our dad. We're Bruce's kids," came the response. Hearing this, of course, they were allowed to be at the tables. That's how tightly things had to be watched. There were so many people. I was thrilled to see Tim and Molly. But had so little time to greet them. Quick hugs and smiles, then it was right back to signing. They were amazed to find the crowds and excitement in the air. They had seen me in the center of crowds before, at my openings and such. But nothing like this. None of us expected such a turnout.

Little encounters, like the one between Tim and Molly and the EMT security, were told to me later, once the crowds had left. People told me stories of experiences that they were having and would remember for the rest of their lives. Memories from this day would be kept forever. So many people were doing their part to make things run smoothly . . . and they all did so well. Including the crowds themselves. The people that turned out were so patient and caring. I will always be grateful for the roles that each and every person played in making that such a memorable day.

The people showing up at both these locations were those who live close to where the tragedy happened. This was home for them. These people were the neighbors of the Amish. These people grew up with the Amish next door or down the road. These people saw them differently from the visitors to our area. To them, the Amish are not a tourist attraction. They know the Amish as the kind souls they are . . . a quiet, simple people, with jobs, children, families and striving for happiness, just as we all do. Yes, the Amish ways and the ways of the English may be different, but through this event, we were finding common ground, that being . . . we care for each other.

Less than an hour had passed from when I began signing, when the most unexpected thing happened. No one involved with this day could have ever imagined what was to come next. Murph, who is the morning DJ partner with Casey, was off the air now and at the ambulance station with us. He noticed that several Amish had shown up. There were maybe six of them. I had not seen them as my focus was fixed on whoever was in front of me. There was not a moment's break. I signed and greeted and signed and greeted. The Amish had gotten in line as everyone else did. The line at this time was so long there was a wait time of nearly two hours. Curious as to whom the Amish might be, Murph asked a few questions. He talked to the EMT people and perhaps the Amish themselves. It turns out they were family members who had children at the school that day. These were family members directly involved with the shootings. Amazing that they would show up. Just wait, it gets better.

Remember Kym, the woman who came through the line twice at the morning location? The Amish were here because of her kind and thoughtful actions. She was so moved by what this image stood for and overcome by how many people were turning out in support of it, that she knew she had to do something. When she left the first location, earlier this morning,

Kym drove to each of the Amish households who were affected that terrible day. She explained to them about the print, its message of kindness and what she had witnessed that morning. She impressed upon them the kindhearted message that was being spread and the tremendous response it was getting from the community. Then, this wonderful woman offered to drive any of them that wished to come to the station and see for themselves. Many of them were in the middle of work, some were in the fields, some were with the children. The few that could make it climbed into her SUV and now they were here.

This is the kind of person Kym is. She works from her heart and her gut. If action needs to be taken you can bet she'll be first in line. If something seems wrong she will right it. Kym has lived among the Amish for many years. She and her husband Paul have a buffalo ranch and a dog kennel just outside of Nickel Mines, in a town called Paradise. Many people in that area helped when this tragedy struck, including Kym and Paul. Kym assisted the families in several ways: She organized and distributed gifts of food to the families. Lots of food and gifts. Nearly a warehouse full. She is the person who cared for the "commemorative site," if I can call it that. It's the place where flowers, prayers, candles and such were left. There's so much more she took care of. With the passage of time you will see how her and my role on this journey became tightly intertwined.

So, as everyone was becoming informed of the Amish's presence, I still had no idea they were here. The end of the line was so far away I couldn't see it. Word spread to the station crew of our special guests and they were formulating how to handle the situation. This was indeed unexpected and extraordinary.

Now, let's slow down here for a minute and grasp what's happening here. It's important because the arrival of the Amish at this location gives you a good indication of how moved they were by this event and this message of kindness. These were family members who had lost their own children in this tragedy. These people had stayed clear of all media and attention of the English. The Amish don't want to be photographed or draw attention to themselves. Throughout all of the media coverage, broadcast by so many TV and radio stations from around the world, very few Amish had submitted themselves to any of it. But here they were, showing up in the middle of all these people in the English community. Humbly they positioned themselves at the back of the line, prepared to wait, like everyone else. Truly an expression of the humility and quietness these people live by. It was their expression of kindness and compassion that had drawn me to them. Now, it was my acknowledgment of their kindness and compassion that has drawn them, to me.

So, still unaware of their presence, I sat, signing and talking with the folks that approached me at the table. Murph quietly came up behind me and softly said a few words. Understand, speaking softly is not Murph's way. He is a burly guy with a deep, strong radio voice. But as he spoke, to tell me the news, he was soft and respectful. He leaned over from behind me and said, "Bruce, members of the Amish families are here. They showed up and got in line for prints." Surprised by what I was hearing, I stopped all I was doing to give him my attention. He continued, "It's not right they wait in line. So we are letting them know they didn't have to wait. They asked if they could meet privately with you. They're being escorted to a room inside the station. Would you like to meet with them?" Just then I looked to my left. I saw maybe six or so Amish being lead into the building. They were no more than twenty feet away. The black of their clothing in the bright sunlight stood out in contrast against the colorful clothes worn by the line of English that stretched out behind them. What Murph had told me was now confirmed with my own eyes. At that moment it was as though the compassion being expressed for these people had been amplified. A change was in the air. It was as though the feeling of compassion itself had actually manifested into a physical state and replaced the air around us. It was that present. With the intake of each breath, I became more filled with the moment. With the release of that breath, I was sharing this feeling with the crowd gathered around me. I could physically feel its presence. This air of compassion completely encircled me. Like a cool breeze on my body, it brushed across me and seemed to raise my spirit to the point of saturating my skin.

Murph then told me that he and others from the station were going through the line, letting everyone know the families were here and telling them, "Signing will be halted for a few minutes because Bruce is going to be meeting with the Amish families." At this point there seemed to be more people in line than there had been all day. Policemen, EMTs, children, adults, elderly, they were in line and on the streets around me. The concern they felt for these families was evident on their faces. Suddenly, it was as though I could sense the caring concern of the entire community, the nation, even the world. I was feeling the responsibility beginning to rest squarely on my shoulders, to express the condolences of all these people, to these grieving souls. This was my opportunity to express how so many felt, directly to the afflicted families. The amount of respect shown by the crowd, here this day, was so admirable. It's a feeling that can move you beyond words. But in the midst of all this reverent silence, words were exactly what I needed. In the next few minutes I would find myself face to face with these grieving families.

Somehow this news, as powerful as it was, did not send a jolt of excitement or nervousness through me. Rather, my sense of calm was the same I felt throughout this entire journey. This was simply the next step on my path. I turned to Murph and said, "Of course I'll meet with them. Tell me when they're ready." I calmly went back to signing the prints for the people in front of me, giving them my attention until I got the word to go inside. It didn't take long, only a minute or two. There was Murph letting me know the families were inside, seated and waiting. He looked at me and said, "I don't know how you can do this, man. I know I couldn't handle it." In an instant I had thoughts such as this: "What if they didn't approve of what I was doing. Maybe they misunderstood the message or thought I was commemorating that tragic day . . . they would hate that." NO. Those thoughts left as quickly as they arrived. I had no doubt. Not even a little. My whole sense of being was now overcome with the notion of my task at hand. A big task? You bet. But that calmness was there, as it had been all along. I was ready. I had no pre-planned words and no idea just what I would say, when Murph asked me, "What are you gonna say, man?" I looked at him and said, "If my heart is in tune with my mouth the words will come." With that, I got up and walked toward the building. I entered through the open garage bay doors and was led just outside the room in which they waited. The door to the room was closed. Opening it would be a step further on this journey. The journey of following that connected feeling I had since that first day. This is a big step. Perhaps it would even bring me full circle and the journey would end. I didn't know, but none of that mattered. I was simply following my heart and reaching for the doorknob.

I turned the knob, gently eased the door open and walked inside. It was a small room. All the walls were white and the furnishings sparse. This was a building where serious, traumatic, business was dealt with and the room reflected that cold seriousness. Even though there were only a few of us gathering here, the smallness of the room caused us to sit shoulder to shoulder. Around the conference style table sat the Amish visitors: Two young men, appearing to be in their late twenties, maybe thirty years old. Their clothes still marked with the dirt from the field they had been working in earlier that morning. Their hands were like the hands of most Amish, rough and strong from a life devoted to the labor of building whatever they needed with these two God-given tools. Those hands were now resting calmly on the table before me. Two women sat across from them. One woman seemed to be nearly the same age as the men. She also portrayed the presence of hard work. Yet, as I walked in, she was looking at me with a smile that included her entire face. You know the kind of smile I mean? The kind that comes from deep inside. Her eyes were bright and with them she expressed an acute level of pleasant alertness. The other girl was a teenager, maybe fourteen or fifteen years old. Such innocence filled her eyes as she looked at me through the glasses she was wearing. Behind those eyes may have been the memory of she, herself, sitting in that schoolhouse room not more than a year ago. At her current age, she was now through with her schooling. In the Amish community formal schooling ends at about the age of fourteen. In between these two young women sat an elderly woman. Her eyes were not expressing such innocence. This was the face of a woman who had seen hard times and now was grieving from a great loss. Her granddaughter had died that terrible day.

Kym was seated with them also. As was appropriate. It was, after all, the strength and independence of her actions that had gotten them here. She had the foresight to recognize that they would appreciate this day.

There was a seat left empty for me, just inside the door. With all the eyes in that room now fixed on me, I stepped through the doorway and sat down. Perhaps it's the artist in me, but I remember colors again. The darkness of the black Amish clothing seemed to fill the room. Its stark contrast against these white walls seemed to exaggerate the difference of these two worlds, now brought together. I was wearing black this day. At no time more than now, was I more grateful for that. Black to me is simply a color I sometimes wear. But black is the color the Amish choose to wear always. Their black is another way of not drawing attention to, or placing importance on, their dress. Keeping their clothes plain allows them once again to keep their focus not on things of this world. But rather on their spiritual beliefs. Maybe in some way, be it ever so small, it may have put these visitors just that much more at ease.

Kym spoke first, starting by introducing me to our guests. Names, smiles and nods of approval were all that were exchanged. There was not a word or a handshake at this point. It was all very casual, yet with a sense of mutual respect. She explained to them that I was the person who painted the image of the schoolhouse bell. The Amish lifestyle is so different from ours that even the concept of me being a professional artist (making a living by painting images) was difficult for them to grasp. It quickly became obvious that Kym was very comfortable around the Amish. As difficult as the original circumstances were that brought us together, she handled this situation well. She continued by recapping how and why she got them here. She told us all how moved she was by this message of kindness and compassion and the response of the community. She felt very strongly that the Amish needed to be made aware of it. Then she asked me if I would tell them in my own words why all these people were here today.

Knowing that the Amish had no TV sets or radios, I started by talking to them about how the world was learning of all they were going through. "The story of what happened to your children that awful day is being heard around the world. So many people are grieving with you. I have heard firsthand, from so many, that they are praying for all of you. All these people here today, this community and thousands, even millions around the world are praying for you and your children."

I told them how my niece, Hilary, is a pediatric nurse in the emergency unit at Children's Hospital of Philadelphia. "Hilary was the nurse holding the hand of one of your girls that had been shot. She was consoling her, as she became conscious and told her story to the police." At this point the grandmother and young girl were moved to tears. Perhaps the EMT personnel suspected this might happen and had tissues ready and waiting at the table. Kym, already clutching one, with tears in her eyes, handed them to both the grandmother and the young Amish girl.

I explained to them how I had witnessed their acts of forgiveness and kindness in the face of such devastation, "Your acts of kindness moved me to the point of wanting to help. That's when I decided to produce these prints and make them available to anyone wanting one. Contributions made for these prints are going to be given to your community, to help in this time of need. The message associated with this image, the message of treating each other with kindness was generated by you and your community. I'm doing this in the hopes of spreading that message."

"Do you have any questions for me? Can I do anything for you?" I asked. The questions they had for me were simpler than I expected. "Where did this bell come from? Where did you get it? And you were painting this as the shootings happened?" they asked. Mainly their questions were about the bell. "Why was it white?" they wanted to know, as bells used today are black wrought iron. It would not be until much later that any of us would learn why this bell was white. I explained how I came to own it and confirmed, "Yes, I was painting this piece at that exact same time of the shootings."

This seemed to be the perfect time for me to express the message to them directly. "I assure you, in no way do I want this image to be commemorative or in memory of that terrible day. What I do want it to stand for is the way all of you, all of the Amish community, responded with kindness and compassion to everyone involved. I saw that response spread through the community, the nation and around the world. That's what this image is about, treating others with kindness." I knew right then . . . they understood. They knew what I meant. Their lives were centered on the importance of this message. I could see it on their faces. They were pleased.

Kym asked them if they would each like a print. Remember they had trouble understanding what a professional artist was. Grasping the idea of what a print was did not come any easier. I briefly attempted to describe what a print is. These folks had no idea about how the photographic or printing process worked. Several of the prints were on the table in front of me. I picked one up and explained, as simply as I could, how the print was an image made from the original painting. How I painted it one time and reproductions were made to look like the original. Everyone in that room seemed to understand that we were in the process of bridging a gap between our two worlds.

This realization was one that was pleasing to all of us. It brought smiles to all of our faces. In this circumstance, brought on by the initial act of terrible violence and everyone trying to console each other, smiles were welcomed by all. Our visitors agreed to each have a print and I would personalize it for them right then.

But just as that got under way and I began to sign prints, they began talking to each other in Pennsylvania Dutch. That's the language they speak most frequently. It's a combination of German and English, all made distinctly their own. Kym could understand some of this and began to ask them some questions in English. They were realizing that others, more family members, might like a print also. Kym began making a list. A list containing the names of other family members. In minutes the list grew from the few in the room to twenty, then thirty, then more. In fact, those present realized there might be still others they wanted to speak to about this, before giving me a total.

We decided I would simply hold onto the list made right then and wait for further instructions. Kym would be in touch with the families and finalize any additions. All of the prints would be delivered at a later date. With that gesture, this brief, moving experience was coming to an end.

We all stood and prepared to leave. I thanked them for showing up here today and expressed again that we are all praying for them. They in turn thanked me for what I was doing. How gratifying and humbling it was to hear that. In the course of this twenty-minute meeting, my feeling of being connected to this tragedy and these people had reached yet another fulfilling plateau.

As we left the room, tears were replaced with soft smiles. This was a good thing that had just happened and we all felt it. I stood back and allowed the Amish to leave first. As one by one they passed by me, I shook an outstretched hand from each of them. Knowing their ways are so demure and modest, I hope shaking the hand of the women was appropriate. It seemed just fine with them. In fact I felt that hugs were more in order here, but I was not about to overstep my bounds. We genuinely wished each other well and I assured them they would get their prints. Together, we walked through the empty ambulance garage and exited the building. Just a few steps later we found ourselves back in the bright sunlight of this beautiful day. The Amish, escorted by Kym, headed directly for her vehicle and departed as quietly as they had arrived.

I, on the other hand, having been through one of the most emotional times of my life, was faced with hundreds of people. Media crews had shown up while we were inside and there was still plenty to do. I was thankful that the media had not gotten there in time to capture all this on tape. The Amish were gone before the reporters knew the full extent of what was going on. None of this special time would end up as a headline on the evening news.

Under the intently watchful eyes of the crowd, I proceeded directly to the table. I stood for just a minute sipping water from a bottle, placed there for me earlier in the day. I remember looking at the crowd. The eyes and faces gazing back at me were filled with respect for the moment. Although I'm sure their curiosity was overcoming them, the respect reined the moment. There was no shouting of questions or comments from any of them. In fact there was more silence than there was noise. This crowd of hundreds stood in reverent silence. Then gently nodding in approval and calmly smiling to them, I took my seat. Murph approached me and stated, "I don't know what you said in there, but the look on their faces as they left was much better than when they showed up. You must have done good." Without going into much detail I told him, "What we are doing here is a very good thing. They understand it and they approve." Then I asked him to hold back about sixty or seventy prints for the Amish.

Throughout the afternoon I must have seen a thousand faces. Some were familiar, like Eric and Marissa, two good friends and students of mine. There were friendly faces from my neighborhood that showed up. Even the reporter from the local TV station, who was at my home to interview me a week ago, came out for a print. Strangers were making friends with each other in line. The elderly or disabled were escorted to the front of the line, so they wouldn't have to wait as long. Positive feelings of kindness were flowing through everyone. The united feeling generated by everyone here and now the Amish, who visited with us as well, solidified the righteousness of this message even further.

It didn't take long for the TV and newspaper reporters to be active on the scene. For a time, I was hooked up with a TV network microphone while I was signing prints. Cameras were just a few feet from my face as I greeted people. Photographs and videotaped interviews of the crowd were being taken. This event was becoming news. I held my attention on the people standing right in front of me having their print signed. They were the special ones this day. By showing up, by expressing their kindness and compassion, they made this day happen.

This went on for several more hours. Now 5:00, an hour longer than we planned on being there, I was signing the last print of the day. As we were packing up the last of our belongings, a few more people ran up. They asked if they were too late to contribute and receive a print. Of course they weren't too late. Any time someone expresses kindness is a good thing. I saw to it that they too got a print. The day was coming to a close. I had signed prints for nearly eight straight hours. I was exhausted and exhilarated all at the same time. We all were. The day ended with lots of hugs and handshakes, just as it had begun. But now the feeling was different. We had done more good today than we had ever expected.

To our surprise, there were a few prints left over. Which was a good thing. Because very soon I would learn that I needed each of them . . . and more. Soon, everyone of us involved here today would find out just how large of an impact this event, this print and this message was making. This was just the beginning.

CHAPTER 4

Building a New Normal

THE MESSAGE OF responding to tragedy with kindness was spreading in ways none of us had imagined. This was not a message that moved with the power and speed of a jet in flight, passing by with noise and smoke, demanding your attention because its discourteous interruption was noticeable simply due to its mechanical nature. That type of power would only be present for a moment, then gone. Leaving behind only a disruption to your prior focus. No, this message was moving more like it had the power of a giant ocean liner. The engine was now running, wheels and gears were in motion. It was now underway with its tremendous power. Beginning slowly at first, this dynamic message was on the move. Yet with all its might, it remained almost silent. To onlookers of such a powerful, gradual move, it may feel as though they and the very ground they stand on are slipping away, as though the Earth itself is shifting beneath them. When something as large as this crosses closely before your eyes, it can be disorienting, putting you off balance at first and causing you to question what seemed stable just a moment ago. Then you realize the ground beneath you is not moving. Your feet are still planted. All you need to do, to retain your stability, is become consciously aware of what is happening before you . . . look at it . . . understand it . . . act on it. Through experiences like this, we come to realize that some things are bigger than us. Encountering them closely is humbling.

The Amish who initiated the message through their action, those of us involved in recognizing and spreading it, as well as those who understood it, were now on board. We were all headed to a destination unknown. There may not even be a destination to this journey. It may be unending. This is a journey of living.

Immediately following the print signing, much to the surprise of all of us involved, the painting and the message it carried were becoming news items. None of us expected this, perhaps me least of all. But as long as the media stated the message of kindness and compassion correctly, I was okay with it. It meant that more people would hear the message and the more that heard it the better. That's what was important.

The night of the signing, TV news stations covered the event fairly extensively. Footage from the day of the signing was intermixed with footage from the day of the shootings. Interviews with others and myself were shown. The crowds that waited in line were spoken of kindly. Comments were used describing this event as a gesture of goodwill and how it gave the community a way of expressing care for the victims. That night, this type of coverage ran on both the evening and nightly news. Everyday for the next week, coverage such as this was showing up on stations across the state.

Numerous newspapers covered the story, also. For nearly a hundred miles in every direction this was front-page news. Photos of the painting and myself accompanied articles that talked of this painting as being everything from an instrument of healing to a public sensation. They explained how crowds came out to show their support for our Amish neighbors. They reported the details of how the money contributed is going to assist the Amish families. The statements were kind and that promoted even more kindness. News of the print and the message were moving across the land like the light of a new sunrise.

This media coverage generated attention such as I never expected and it began immediately. The morning after the signing, the phone awakened me. It was a young mother who was made aware of the painting by this coverage. She explained how moved she was by its message and asked if there were still prints available. She very much wanted an image representing that message in her home. This I was not prepared for . . . someone calling my home asking for a print. I thanked her, took her contact information and told her she would hear from me if prints became available. The distribution of prints, on the day of the signing, was put together as a one-time thing. None of us were prepared for additional requests. We had no idea it would generate the response that was to follow. Aside from those we set back for the Amish community, there were only a few prints left. I didn't even know exactly how many and we had no plan for distributing them.

That day and for many days to come, calls came in one after the other. These calls were coming in to my home and studio. My phone number was not made available to anyone. I didn't give that information out. These people were seeking me out, driven by their attraction to the message. Calls first came from around the state, then from neighboring states: New York, New Jersey, New Hampshire, even as far away as Kentucky. People were calling from their offices, homes, and cell phones. Requests for individual prints and multiple prints came in. People wanted to give them out at work or to friends and relatives. They wanted to hang them in their places of business, schools and homes. Stories were told to me of how the tragedy affected them and how this message was something good, found in the midst of such terrible times.

Responses didn't arrive solely by phone. The Internet is a method of communication I use daily, for both personal and business purposes. It's not uncommon for me to check my e-mail several times a day. Over the course of the next few days, e-mail requests and responses were as steady as the phone calls. Each time I checked my in box, there were more kind words to be found. The same expressions of concern were now in written form. People were praying for both the continuation of this important message and for me, personally. As you can see in these few examples of e-mails received, people were deeply moved.

> *"Our prayers are with that community and with you and your family for what you're doing to help. Thank you for your work and for listening and following as your work chooses you. May you be blessed always with peace and contentment."*

> *"I am always impressed with the Amish and their way of life: their response to this tragedy has really made people think about forgiveness. The Amish community members you are interacting with are wonderful role models for everyone."*

> *". . . withholding forgiveness in our lives will cause a bitter root to grow, that becomes a spiritual cancer in us that will destroy our inner being. Yet to put forgiveness into practice, even in small offenses let alone an incomprehensible tragedy like this one is beyond most of us."*

> *"While I have already donated to one of the funds, I feel that a bigger honor would be to own one of your prints, not only to contribute more money, but as a way to honor all 10 brave girls and their teacher."*

> *"I was particularly touched by your painting to honor the Amish community following the recent tragedy at the schoolhouse. I am interested in acquiring a print of the painting for my wife as a gift. We are both of the mind that we will not hang anything in our home that does not have personal meaning."*

"Do not let anything discourage you with these prints. When we step out and do something good, sometimes negative forces seem to try and hinder it."

"I'm sure you have made a difference in the lives of many people and helped to bring healing to the community."

"That print resonates with hope."

"Your consciousness of others' distress, with the desire to help alleviate the unexplainable suffering and then acting upon those feelings, is compassion in action."

Hundreds of letters like these came to me, letters that were incredibly moving to read. Not one of them went unanswered. I spent hours, day after day, late into the night, writing back to each and every one of them. The only disappointing fact was that I had no prints for the people writing and calling. As mentioned, prints going to the Amish families were set side. Those were accounted for and their purpose was known. But in addition to those, we had a few more prints remaining. The exact number unknown. The printer had overruns and an extra hundred or so were produced. Making the total we had right from the start about twelve-hundred. Now there were maybe a hundred. As much as I wanted to, I couldn't bring myself to give them away. I had this constant feeling that they would be needed for a special purpose. I had no idea what that purpose would be or even why I felt it. I just knew they would be needed and I had to hold on to them. So they sat, quietly waiting. But for what? I was soon to find out.

I remember now what the production manager of WIOV had said to me about the print-signing day. He is a man who has been involved in the radio business for twenty-two years. It

was less than two years ago that he took this position, coming
to the Lancaster area from New York City. He summed up the
print-signing day like this: "In all my radio experience I have
never been involved with an event that generated such community emotion as this. This is an experience I'll never forget.
Thank you." As complimentary as he was, he may not have
realized how true those words were. Because it seems that what
we did that day, was to strike the spark and light the flame that
would spread like fire through people's hearts. This message
and image now gave them some direction. All the care, concern
and sadness they felt previously had no place to be channeled.
There was no specific outlet. No memorial ground. No ground
zero here. This image and its message were becoming a beacon
of hope in an otherwise very dark situation. It was a way of
finding good where there seemed to be none. And everyone
was in need of that.

Perhaps none were more in need of finding some good in
this tragedy, than the first responders: paramedics, ambulance
crews, policemen, state troopers and coroners. These were the
brave men and women who were on the scene that day, dealing
with the harsh reality at arms length. These people were the
first to extend their helping hands, in kindness, to physically
assist the victims. In their memories lie the images of this inhu-
mane devastation.

It didn't take long until I heard from these groups. Within
days after the print signing, the Lancaster County Coroners
Office contacted me. Dr. Kirchner, the Lancaster County Coroner, had been made aware of the prints and the message. He is
an ex-military doctor, who has seen the bloodshed of battle for
many years. He told me, "Throughout all my career I have never been on a scene as horrific as that of October 2." The wounds
of damaged emotions inflicted on the community and those on
the scene that day were deep. He knew they needed attention.
Those wounds had to be dealt with. He felt that finding this

positive message in the midst of such turmoil shed the light of hope. It was a step in the healing process. Dr. Kirchner was requesting prints for all of his staff. He said repeatedly, "This image and its message are an act of healing for the community."

Following our phone call a deputy coroner was sent to my home, with a list of 30 names. Each was a staff member who was personally involved and affected that day. Each was to receive a print. Before long, I was sitting at my dining room table with the woman sent by Dr. Kirchner. She worked in this field of assisting others for more than a decade. She was on the scene that tragic day. With a heavy heart and eyes watering with tears, she recounted events that happened the day of the shootings. Her job was to care for the bodies of the girls who had been fatally shot. I was intently listening, as she told me that no other scene in her career even came close to the misguided sense of aggression and violent disregard for life that had taken place that day. To see firsthand the gruesome death and destruction in a place of childhood learning was unthinkable. Where moments ago these children had been smiling and eagerly attentive with their friends, now lay the blood-soaked remains of young lives, senselessly lost forever. The discipline of her training and motivation to assist in this grave hour, were the forces that galvanized her focus in this worst of situations. The trauma of that day was so disturbing, that for the first time in her fifteen years of experience, she was seeking help through therapeutic guidance. After living through the nightmare of that crime scene, she shared with me, like many others have, how she was overcome with a sense of calm and peace found in the image and message of this painting. For some unknown reason this simple school bell painting, even before its message was known to the viewer, struck a chord of hope. Then once the message associated with it is learned, the reason for hope is confirmed. That in turn was motivating people in the forward process of healing.

Our visit lasted perhaps thirty minutes. As it ended and she was leaving, she left behind the list of first responders requesting their own copy of the print. But more than that, she left me with yet another personal contact and shared experience of how another soul was recognizing light in this darkness.

It's hard for me to put into words how humbled, yet pleased I was that this image and its message were helping those in need. I saw the affect it was having on the general pubic. That, itself, was incredible. Then to have the Amish families express approval was a totally unexpected experience. Now this image was providing positive affects and a sense of peace to the people assigned the task of dealing with the deceased. It all seemed nearly unbelievable.

It was just about this time that I was contacted by a representative of the state troopers on the scene that day. Not just any representative, the sergeant in charge contacted me. He told me that he had received a print. Someone who was grateful for his efforts, on that tragic day, gave it to him. He, like many others, was touched by its meaning. The other officers, upon seeing the print, wanted to know if more were available. They were moved, that through the madness of that day, I had recognized a message of good. Each of them was looking to own a print as well.

These brave men and women were struggling with the difficult emotions that day had put upon them. One of the officers who had been on the force for more than fifteen years, said he had never been on a crime scene as horrific and gruesome as this. He was fighting with his thoughts and emotions trying to make sense of it all. There was no quiet place within himself to find rest from this disturbing senseless act. But once again, as others had said to my amazement, he told me that he felt a sense of calm, rational peace when seeing this image and learning of its message.

How thankful I felt to be in a position of providing comfort to those who provide it on a regular basis. These men and women are the ones who put their lives on the line to assist and protect. Now here they were finding solace in an image created in my studio. Having my work and all aspects of my life generate and promote goodwill and all things positive in this world is the motivator I wake with each morning. But I was always conscious of the fact, that it was only an image created in my studio. I did not create the message. That message of treating others with kindness, in this case, was initiated by the Amish. Yes, associating the image to the message was a combination developed in my studio. Finding that combination put me in the position of simply being a messenger. A messenger through living by example. I have aspired to that all my life

It seemed the group of prints I was certain would find a purpose, just had. They were going to the first responders.

My days were becoming filled with talking to, writing to and meeting with an ever-growing number of those touched by this tragedy. We were attracted to each other through the message of kindness. Paramedics, state troopers, coroners, neighbors from down the block to strangers across the country. The message was spreading.

While all these new contacts and important people were entering my life, I still had the list, given to me by the Amish on the day of the signing. Remember, the list of families that were going to receive prints? That needed my attention also. I was waiting to hear from Kym with the final total of names. I didn't have to wait long for that update. Only two days had passed after the signing and I received her call. She had been in touch with the families and the list had been revised. In fact, it had nearly doubled. All the family members were spoken to. Some gathered together to discuss this as a group. Others dealt with it individually and among their family members. The important thing was that they all understood I was acting with the best of intentions: That of recognizing and spreading a good and positive message, emerging out of this terrible incident.

The night when Kym and I spoke by phone, she told me what each family wished to receive. Each family with children in the school that day, would receive one print for the parents and one print for each set of grandparents. In addition, several extended family members wished to have a print, as well. For more than an hour, Kym carefully read me the list of names. It contained the names of each family and the names of the children in school that day. Painstakingly I checked and double-checked the spellings of all the names. The Amish recipients for each personalized print requested specific wording. Prints going to the families with daughters who died would have handwritten messages that were worded very lovingly and gently. Those going to families with surviving children would be worded a bit more generally, mentioning Nickel Mines School. All were extremely heartfelt and done with respect and care. Nearly sixty prints in all were requested.

I certainly didn't want to be signing these prints while on the phone. So I made a list and planned on doing all the signing at a later time. That is a very special list. One of several lists gathered on this journey, that I still have and will always own. I needed to sign these at a time that was quiet and peaceful. At a time when I could reflect on the importance of each and every one of these names. That signing would come later, on another evening. The rest of our phone call dealt with sharing stories of what was happening since October 2. She told me of all she was doing to assist the community, which was a lot. Kym has a big, kind, giving heart and it was being put to use through this tragedy. She was driving and coordinating events for the Amish. Helping in any way she could. As I previously told you, she was collecting and distributing food that was donated for them. She was also trusted by the Amish community to the extent of being chosen as the person who drives the children's temporary school bus. Normally the children walked to school. But due to the crowds of English onlookers now in the area, they felt being driven was a wise move. Kym delivered the children to and from the temporary school each day. Assisting the community is not something new to Kym. For years, she was associated with one of the fire, ambulance and rescue teams in the Nickel Mines area. Every one of those emergency personnel were dedicating so much time, day and night, to assist. Their kind gestures were abundant in this time of need.

As Kym and I finished talking that night and our phone call was coming to an end, both of us knew that we were becoming friends through this event. We felt that there was more for us to do, but had no idea what. We felt good about trying to find and express something so positive in an event that was so intrinsically negative. It was getting late by the end of our discussion, after 11:00 at night. When I hung up the phone, the awareness of that moment was overpowering. I sat quietly, looking at the list of names, sensing the calm connected feeling I had to all this. The realization came to me that the Amish, who don't hang artwork in their homes, were requesting this print. This image had a message so substantial that it was being accepted into their homes. There was also sadness in me for the loss of life these families were dealing with and for the struggle each child left behind was living through. If recognizing and reflecting back their acts of kindness could help or heal in any way, I was willing to do whatever I could. That calm sense I had all along, of knowing this was a good thing, was very present. The Amish understood the message being expressed and the importance of it. They were living that message. By their requests of prints, they were encouraging its expression. This was another forward step on the journey. With approval such as this, from the affected families themselves, I was ready to go wherever this path would take me.

Over the course of the next few days, interest in the print was continuing to grow. More phone calls and e-mails were coming in. Live radio interviews were done on WIOV and TV news reporters were asking for more interviews as well. Surprising and amazing things were taking place at this time. Many of them were wonderful expressions of gratitude for this print and its message. I was invited to attend the Bart Fire Company Breakfast, scheduled for a weekend, less than two weeks away. Bart Ambulance Station is the fire and ambulance team located closest to Nickel Mines. Its headquarters are only a mile or two from the school. They were undoubtedly the first to arrive on the scene when the shootings took place. It was arranged that at the breakfast, I would present prints to the state troopers and the Bart crew. To have my presence requested and provide these expressions of kindness to those so closely involved was an honor. I was more than willing to attend.

Just a day or two after talking with Kym, she called me again. This time she would be giving me news and extending an invitation that would elevate this journey to an entirely new level. It was morning. Breakfast and e-mails were filling my time, when the phone rang. She said she had been with the Amish families, delivering things to their homes and discussing how everyone was doing. They had been talking about receiving their *Kindness and Compassion* prints. How that was exactly going to happen we didn't know. We hadn't really talked about how to get the prints in their hands. We only discussed that they wanted them. This phone call would change that. This phone call would change everything. Kym was calling to let me know that the families wanted me to deliver the prints personally. At first they didn't know if they should gather all in one location, perhaps in the temporary school, or have me meet with each of them separately. Meeting individually is what they determined was best. I was being asked to deliver all of the prints to the families and meet with them in their homes. Let me just state that again. Kym was letting me know that each one of the Amish families, those who had children at the school that day, were inviting me to their homes to deliver their prints and meet with them. In fact, they were asking if that would be something I would be willing to do.

"Willing to meet with the families?" I asked her. "It would be an honor to meet with the families." These were the families who kept their distance from the media and the English. These were the families who were caring for their children, shot and injured. These were the families with daughters who lost their lives that day. These quiet people didn't invite English strangers into their homes, especially during a time as hard as this. I was overcome with a sense of humility and honor. These simple people, while grieving in the midst of this turmoil, had heard the message of kindness and compassion reflected in this painting and were asking me to deliver it, personally, to their homes. This meant I was not only going to meet with the parents and grandparents, but I was also going to meet the children themselves. No one from the English community had been allowed to do that. Can I possibly express to you how overcome I was? Can I express the racing emotions I felt? The connected feeling I had from the day I was painting this image was manifesting in ways that were overwhelming.

This astonishing type of news continued, when Kym told me I was also permitted to meet with the teacher and present a print to her as well. Now listen to how special this part is. I was not going to meet with her at her home. But at the new, temporary school . . . while school was in session. Yes, in session, with the same children who had been put through the horror of that terrible day. The temporary school was in an undisclosed location. No one was even permitted to know what property it was on. Let alone what building it was. No media. No English. No one. Kym was the exception to this rule, because of driving the school bus she knew of this secret location. This trust they felt in her, is further testimony to her good heart. This woman had only their best interest in mind. Aside from her, the only others who knew were the state troopers watching over them. That was it. The secret was well kept. No one knew where it was. I would soon be keeping that same secret. These people trusted me, an Englishman, to be in their homes, in the school and with their children. This truly was an honor and I was not taking it lightly.

Kym also was aware of how special this invitation was. Having had almost daily contact with the victims since the tragedy, she knew firsthand of the fragile and private state of mind they were in. But she also knew and saw them as the real, genuinely kind, people they are. She recognized that this was out of the ordinary for them. It was the message of my painting and my recognizing it and spreading it that had touched them. This was drawing us together.

By this time Kym, Casey, Murph and I had become close and shared with each other how this extraordinary event was affecting our lives. It was not uncommon to get a call from Casey anytime of the day with updates from the station, or for me to call her and let her know of the latest unexpected occurrence. This being the case, Casey learned of my visiting the Amish, either through myself or Kym, or both. She was just as amazed and asked if it would be alright to mention it on the air. She and Murph had been reporting the latest details on an almost daily basis. During the morning show the next day, Murph and Casey discussed how moving this invitation was. How important it was in the healing process for both the Amish and English communities. Suddenly, literally overnight, the painting, the print, the message and myself were thrust into the public eye again. This time in an even bigger way than before. Now I was about to be the only Englishman to breach the barrier between our two communities, at this most delicate time. Only weeks had passed since the schoolhouse tragedy and wounds, both physical and emotional, were still raw. Media reporters were now contacting me for additional interviews. Friends and family were now truly taking notice. Total strangers were stopping me on the street and wishing me well. The encouraging e-mails and phone calls increased.

But all the attention was not positive. Surprisingly some people talked to me about my involvement with a sense of hesitation, concern and disdain. "Who are you, to go see these people?" "What will you say to them?" "You're getting pretty deeply involved in their lives. Are you sure you want to do that?" I would even hear comments where people would insinuate that there should be some sort of payoff in this for me. Things like, "Don't do this. What's in it for you? What will you get out of it? Why do you want to do this?" In addition to bringing hope to many people, this message was also now encountering negative repercussions trying to halt its progress. Some people were expressing doubts that I should be involved at all. I was not going to be deterred. What was in this for me was much greater than anything financial. That was never a concern of mine. In fact, if anything, this was pretty severely hampering my finances. But that was the least of my concerns. The wealth found in these actions can't be measured in dollars. This was a matter of spirit. This was about doing what was right and beneficial for people who were hurting. That's all.

Even my family was reacting this way. I think it made them feel more strongly that I was in too deep. Maybe following some artistic drive that was engulfing me in my work, or overtaking me to the extent of being entangled in what was now an international news tragedy. I, on the other hand, knew I was simply following my heart, just as I had done all my life. Finding the good in people, recognizing it and acting on it. Purposeful, meaningful uses like this, of my work and my life are how I choose to live. Following that light, the one I've always seen is how I live my life each day. I was calm about this situation. My head was level and I was following the positive feeling that kept me motivated. Trust me, there were lots of prayers, times for reflection and guidance and lots of answers that helped along the way. There still are.

One person I could talk to, that understood the importance of this message, was Stefan, my nephew. He was open to the reality of this message having a positive impact on those who heard it. In addition to discussing the media, the public recognition stuff, my growing closeness with the Amish and such, he would ask me the straightforward questions that reassured him I was fine. "How's your ego? You keeping that in check? This isn't going to your head is it? Are you eating? How are you sleeping?" My brother Kevin, a well-established psychologist, would ask the same type of questions. I knew they were asking out of concern for me. I was doing fine. Three meals a day and sleeping soundly every night. All because the message that was being spread was one of positive influence and I knew it.

The invitation to visit the Amish came with only a few days notice. There was a lot to be done. I was still answering mail each day and taking phone calls. Signing the prints for the Amish families held paramount importance. Signing those prints would have more meaning and be more special than any artwork I ever signed. These were not just names on a piece of paper. These works of mine, were going to be presented to and hang in the homes of these devastated victims. Each print represented something good, found in what was the most tragic and heart-wrenching time of their lives. I wanted to get this right, give it the attention it deserved. I set aside special time for this task. The evening chosen was a quiet one. Quiet surroundings and quiet inside myself. I cleared my long glass top table of everything currently on it. Then laid out the list of names given to me by Kym, the stack of prints held back especially for this purpose and a few Sharpies. The only things that would get my attention, for as long as needed, were these few simple items before me. As is often the case in my house, candles were lit and burning. Music was playing very quietly. It was almost undetectable. Just loud enough to override any outside noise that tried to enter by riding in on the breeze of the open windows. Pen in hand, I began. Careful to get spellings of names correct and the appropriate personalized statement on each, I spent more than an hour at the table. Names of the girls, family names, carefully worded messages, all written out with care. That's an hour I still remember vividly. The finished prints were then gently, safely placed aside.

Having these prints framed was something else I wanted to do. The families shouldn't have to be bothered by that detail. Many phone calls went out to frame shops in the area. It wasn't easy finding someone who could get all these completed in the next few days. Being a painter and having run several frame shops in the past, having this job done properly was important to me. They had to be simple and unobtrusive. Nothing flashy or fancy would be appropriate for these plain people. No matting, clear glass and a simple, small, black, wooden frame, as quiet and understated as the message itself and the people receiving it. A small shop just miles from Nickel Mines obliged. They knew of the print and wanted to help. I was very grateful for that. They only had two or three days to complete the job. They understood the importance of these pieces, worked diligently, and the job was completed on time.

Having the prints ready, I wanted to make sure that now I was ready. It was time to reflect on what was happening in my heart and head. The opportunity of meeting and talking to the Amish at the print signing, was honor enough. But now I was about to meet each and every one of these families, including the children, in their own homes. I was about to be face to face with the grieving parents. The children, still injured, both physically and emotionally, would be sitting next to me. Grandparents, who have suffered the loss of life from two generations younger than themselves, would be seated at the table, discussing this trauma. All of them free to ask any question of me that they wanted. Free to tell me any stories of the children, or stories of that tragic day. Or even, free to not say a word. Simply sit in silence and look at me perhaps wondering what I had to say. No matter which of these scenarios, or others I would encounter, I was ready. No preset or contrived statements. This would come from the heart. As I had said to anyone asking me, "What will you say to them?" the answer remained the same as I had given Murph, when the Amish visited us on the day of the print signing. "If my heart is in tune with my mouth, the words will come." The words did come on the day of the signing, and I was certain, without having any rational reason to be, that the words would come again.

Visiting with the families would not be a quick process. We figured it would take two full days, minimum. There were ten Amish homes to visit that had children attending the school and additional homes of some of their friends. The days would start early and end late. None of them would be made to feel rushed or uncomfortable. I was visiting, not just dropping by, like I had an overnight shipment to deliver. That meant we would sit and talk, for as long or as short as they wished.

The first day of visiting had arrived. I was up before the sun. Kym and I were scheduled to meet at a cafe near her home at 7:30. It would take about thirty to forty minutes for me to get there. So I showered, had coffee, gathered my things and I was off. All the prints, now framed, were stacked carefully in the car. Each was wrapped in brown paper, marked with the name of the family it was personalized for. This way I could choose what I needed as I entered each home. The original painting was going as well. It seemed appropriate to have them see it. It would help them understand the process of making prints. And besides, as good as these or any prints are, there's nothing like seeing the original. If anyone needed to see it, they did.

I pulled away from my house feeling calm, even though I had no idea what the day had in store for me. How much grief would I be encountering? How would I react to that? Would these people be expressing anger over this atrocity? What about the children, how would they react to having an Englishman in their homes? What would their homes even look like? I tried to put all the questions aside and just take it as it came.

About 30 minutes had gone by and I was getting close. Lancaster County and the Amish community is somewhat familiar to me. I always enjoyed visiting, buying goods and interacting with the Amish. Even though this is primarily an English community, Amish stores and shops lined the streets. Hex signs and Amish goods are sold everywhere. Even though I now find myself in the rural area of this community, an occasional billboard is not uncommon here. One of them caught my eye and caused an unexpected reaction within me. It advertised horse and buggy rides. The photo portion, which took up two thirds of the board, is what struck me. It was a close up photo of a young Amish girl's face. She was standing next to her horse, smiling. At that moment, for the first time, the realization of who I was going to visit and what these people had been through hit me. Little girls, like this one in the photo, daughters of the parents I was going to visit, were brutally assaulted and killed . . . just days ago. I mean, I consciously knew that had happened. But now I was close to being in their homes and the presence of the girls who survived. The loss these families suffered was more real to me than ever. A feeling of sadness overtook me. I felt such distress for these people. These families love their children with all their hearts, and they had just watched them suffer terribly. I thought of my own son and daughter. How sad and hurt I would be if anything every happened to them. My eyes filled with tears. For a second, I doubted what I was doing. How could I do this? Others must be more qualified. Why was I chosen?

Just as fast as those feeling came, they left. These people had chosen me because I recognized and acknowledged the good in this situation. The power of positive actions was over-taking the terrible, negative actions of that day. That was key. Positive elements were going to come out of this awful act. Blessings are being looked for and recognized. That's what was happening here. As terrible as it was, that day of hurtful acts was in the past. The thing to do now was find all and any bless-ings that can come from it. I regained my composure. The calm returned. This day would be for good, no matter what I was to encounter.

Just a few minutes more and I arrived at the cafe. From the outside it looked like someone's home. It probably was at one time. Even now someone probably lived in the upstairs. Inside the cafe area was very small. There was a counter with stools, a couple of tables and a few booths. The entire place maybe seated thirty people comfortably. Memorabilia, both from a week ago and dating back as far as sixty years or more covered all the walls. This was a family-owned place that locals loved. It didn't take long to find out why. The service was good. The coffee was great. The food was home cooked and the atmosphere was easy.

Kym arrived before me and was waiting when I pulled up. The last time I had seen her was at the print signing, which was also the first time I had ever met her. But just then, seeing her again, we both felt as though we were best friends. The bond was immediate. This cause and message had built a last-ing friendship between us.

We went inside to sit, have a cup of coffee and talk about the day ahead. She knew many of the people there and friendly hellos freely came and went. We took a booth and ordered some coffee. Even though I was calm, considering the situation, I didn't feel much like breakfast. Kym was ordering and suggested I did the same. Taking her advice we both ordered your basic home cooked type of breakfast: eggs, bacon, hash browns, toast, juice. This was going to pay off later . . . we had a long day ahead.

Kym interacts with the Amish regularly, so I had a question or two for her. My main concern was not to offend them. Were there customs or etiquettes that I should know? Different ways of addressing or treating the women than the men? Things like this were what I wanted to know. I wasn't asking her to tell me what to say or not to say. Because comforting these people is something I knew would come from my heart. We were beyond that point in our conversations now. So I never bothered to bring that up. That would just come to me when the time was right. "Well," she told me, "there are really no specific ways to act." What she did reassure me of is that these are simple people, who live simple, wholesome lives separate from the pace and concerns of the English. She told me, "Don't be surprised if when you walk in, they surround you. Like in a horseshoe shape . . . and just stare. They may not say anything at first. They'll be curious. Even though this quiet observance may look judgmental, it isn't. They'll just be curious." She told me, "I've seen you talking with people. Just be yourself and you'll be fine."

When we finished breakfast and asked for the check, the owner approached us. She looked at me and said, "We know who you are and why you're here. This is a good thing you're doing. Breakfast is on us. You two have a good day." With that we left and headed out. Our first stop was at Kym's house, less than a mile away. We transferred the prints and painting into her vehicle. She would drive so I could stay focused on the visits. While at her house making this transfer, I met her husband Paul for the first time. What a great guy. He was friendly, talkative and supportive of what we were about to do. Their property was buzzing with life from all the animals in the kennel and in the fields. They had a good life here and it was obvious how much these two cared for and loved each other. With his well wishes, we were off for the day.

The families' homes and the school are all very close to Kym's home. Close enough that if you had the ambition you could walk to each of them. The total round trip would only be a few miles. This is a small, tight-knit community. As we approached each home, Kym told me the specifics: Who we were seeing; how many children they had in the school; the condition of any children who were injured and things like that. I also had a list reflecting this information.

As we got close to the first home some thoughts occurred to me. Thoughts that had crossed my mind in the previous day: What would the Amish homes look like? How different would they be from an English home? I suppose I pictured the homes in a very stereotypical fashion. No electricity meant no TV, no radio, no appliances. The floors would be hardwood, with simple handmade wooden furniture. Perhaps there would be fireplaces for both heating and cooking. Handmade blankets and quilts, draped over chairs. Things like that are what I imagined. Very Quaker-like, sparse of furnishings and adornments.

We pulled up to the first home. My questions and concerns about the Amish, their surroundings and how we would interact with each other, were about to be answered.

From this point forward, I will be very careful to maintain the anonymity of these private people. My descriptions of their homes will not give specific accounts of their individual dwellings. These places all have their own unique touches, as do all of our own homes. Those are the things that personalize them and make them the special places they are. I will not intrude on that sense of privacy. Rather, I will create for you the general look and feel of all their homes, collectively. Thereby, not infringing on the personal privacy of any one of these families. Furthermore, as I relate stories told to me by these individuals, I will not be using their real names. I will use three fictitious names: One for an Amish woman, Mary. One for an Amish man, John and anytime I refer to an injured or deceased girl, I will call her, Rebecca. All the following stories, told to me by the Amish, will have these names attached to them. These are stories that came from many different Amish individuals and couples. All are parents or relatives of the children in the Nickel Mines School. Again, all of this is being done to protect the privacy of these special friends and individuals.

After turning off from the small two-lane road, Kym and I pulled into the driveway of the first home. The house sat back from the road maybe a hundred yards. Farm fields surrounded all the homes in this area. The affected families all lived near to one another. Through those fields were the shortcuts the children would take home from school, or to visit each other. The first house we were visiting was a nice, two-story, white house, with a barn sitting off to one side. The barn in this case is much like a detached garage might be in the English world. Other homes were various colors. Some were made of brick. This looked much like any suburban home: white siding, black shutters, flower beds for landscaping, a mailbox by the road and steps leading up the front wooden porch. The lawn was neatly trimmed, the cement sidewalk and black top driveway swept clean. Bicycles and scooters lean against the barn wall. Youth and adults alike, use them to get from house to house, to the store or just about anywhere.

To pass by these homes from the street, you wouldn't even know Amish occupied them. They have very similar features to that of any other American home. But if you looked more closely, you would notice some differences. Remember I said the barn was next to the house. Well, a barn is what it is. Not a garage. Because remember there are no cars to park at these homes. The Amish don't own cars. The barn is where the drive horse and buggy are kept. Sometimes the workhorses are in that same barn also. Looking more closely, it's not so much what you will notice, but what you won't notice when looking at an Amish home. There are no electrical wires strung from the street to the house. No electricity is used here, which allowed for the view of the beautiful blue sky on this day, to be totally unobstructed.

The exterior of these homes was peaceful. Quiet. There were no blaring noises coming from inside. No TV, radio, or loud stereo sounds coming from an open door. No air conditioners cranked up and hanging from windows. The surrounding roads were lightly traveled with very little traffic. The clicking of horse's hoofs on the road was more frequent than the occasional car. It was autumn and the smell of fallen leaves was in the air. Small children were playing out front. Mostly boys. As I remember, they were playing with their dog. Almost every family I visited had a dog. Some had more than one.

Many of these households ran their own businesses: construction, home repair, blacksmithing, and woodworking. So there were buildings on the property for that as well. It's also very common on an Amish property to have several homes. Each is for various family members. As older children come of age and start their own families, a house would be raised for them and of course, there were living quarters for the grandparents. Families stay together in this community.

So, here we were, Kym and I, walking up to the first front door. I was carrying the painting, unwrapped and unframed. Kym was carrying the prints. We went up the wooden steps, across the porch and knocked.

At most every house the door was answered by a woman: the mother, grandmother or a friend. It was now about a month since the shootings and the men were back to work. They would get called in and join us, once I had arrived. Through this incident, Kym had gotten to know each of these families well. Friendly greetings, soft hugs or handshakes were passed between them. After they greeted each other, Kym would introduce me. "This is Bruce Becker. The gentleman who painted *Kindness and Compassion*, the print you've been hearing about." Smiles and a friendly handshake accompanied a warm welcome and invitation to come inside. "Hello. Thank you for coming." Or, "You're the one who made this painting. Please come in." The only other Englishmen that had crossed these thresholds, in the recent past, were state troopers and medical personnel. Each of them dealing with his portion of this tragedy in his own way and always trying to be considerate of the feelings of those inside. Now I was entering through that same doorway, also considering the feelings of those inside.

With my hand extended to gently shake theirs, I'd greet them, "Hi, it's very nice of you to have me here. Thank you so much." Or, "It's an honor to be here. Thank you for inviting me." Condolences were not to be given at the door. It didn't seem like the place or time. Introductions were first. That first instant of encountering each other was a time for me to express extreme politeness. Once inside, expressions of grief and concern were given the special attention they deserved.

Even though this was the meeting of two very different worlds, the feeling at each home was not one of tension. These were meetings of genuinely open hearts, looking for healing and shared blessings. At some homes, I found the immediate family: mother, father, children who attended school that day, siblings and grandparents. Other homes had extended family members present. Some had friends visiting, helping with anything that needed to be done, caring for children, cooking, cleaning, just as you might expect in any home that was going through such a difficult time.

"Come in and sit down. Come in and visit," they would say. From the very start, the feeling was welcoming. Smiles and curiosity were taking the place of what could have been tears and despair. There were no clenched fists in anger here. No sobbing or wailing. Sure, there was sadness. Great sadness. But

I was soon to learn firsthand, how even in a situation as hard as this, these people put their faith in God's ways. Not their own wishes.

Well, here I am inside an Amish home. Being as visually oriented as I am, I can't help but notice the surroundings. What I see surprises me. The interior looks much like any other middle-class American home. It's more modern than I expected. But why shouldn't it be. The Amish build their own homes and they build things to last. These homes are constructed with care and quality. Of course there is no TV, radio, no video games, computer or anything electronic. The kids are not busy playing with the latest hand-held, useless electronic game. They're playing with each other. There are no ipods, stereos, or CD players. The basic structure and furnishings are very similar to many other homes. There were hardwood floors, with area carpets throughout. Kitchen floors were tile or linoleum. Nice trim work. Your basic American homestyle furniture: wooden dining room sets, upholstered living room furniture, coffee table and end tables. Curtains or blinds hang on the windows. The walls have little or nothing hanging on them. No paintings, photos, or knickknacks. An occasional prayer or hand-stitched saying may be indiscriminately placed by the door or hung near the dining room table. The kitchens have refrigerators and stoves, both powered by propane. As you might expect the kitchen sink is by the window. I wondered, how many times mom watched the kids play outside that window? And now, how many times had she looked out to find quite a different scene. These are homes filled not with "stuff" but with love and respect for God and family. Everything in these homes is simple, functional, pure and humble. No excess or adornments were to be found here.

In each house, it was always the kitchen table we ended up sitting around. We talked about many things. Lots of questions were asked about the painting and the bell itself. Many stories were shared with me. Stories of how the children were doing. Stories of faith and how these strong people were coping with such hardship. They had questions about the print and its message. I was asked to tell the story of how this painting and its message developed. Kym, having heard me tell that story at every house, told me later that never was it boring to hear. She told me the story was told with feeling and made special for each family that we visited.

The bell depicted in my painting seemed to generate quite a few questions. Where did it come from? Why is it white? One parent thought I painted it white because the Amish clothe the deceased in white and perhaps I was honoring the girls. I had no idea they did that. It amazed me to hear of this coincidence. Even the Amish were reading things into this painting that were unintended. No, it was much simpler than that. I painted it white because that's the color it was and it worked for my composition. Questions came about the wrought iron hanging mechanism and the material of the bell itself. On and on they came. Questions on this topic mainly came from the men. There seemed to be a curiosity and fascination with it. As this continued I became curious about their inquiries, so I asked them to describe the bell at the schoolhouse. It quickly became clear why they had so many questions about my bell. The bells used today at schools and on homes are very different from this one. Today's bells are larger, made of black wrought iron and have a very different hanging mechanism. The bell in the painting is white because it's porcelain. The clacker inside is wooden. And its size is smaller than you'd think. The bell itself is only about seven inches tall. From all this questioning, the Amish fathers concluded that the bell I had was old. Perhaps more than a hundred years old. It was from a time when they used to hang bells by the front door. Today the school bells are much larger and hang on top of the building. This was wonderful insight to learn. To this point, I had very little knowledge of its history What I knew of its past, was learned from its previous owner, the Amish woman I bought it from.

Being strong in faith and believing that God's way, not the wishes of their own way, is what kept these families going. I was in one home, standing in the kitchen talking with a mother. Her daughter, traumatically injured, never to be her full self again, was lying in the room next to us. This loving mother said to me, "Bruce I don't understand why we (the Amish people) are getting so much attention. It's not us who deserve this attention. It's God who deserves it." I took her hand and said, "Mary, because you are so modest, I understand why you would say that. But in life there are times when we are all teachers and we are all students. Right now, you and this Amish community are teachers. You are teaching all of us how to forgive." With that she smiled at me and nodded in approval. She could accept that. She said to me, "People ask how our lives will ever get back to normal. I tell them they never will. The old normal is gone. We are creating a new normal." Given the situation this woman was facing for the rest of her life, as she stood before me with her hand in mine, I was experiencing strength and a positive attitude in action. This is a strong woman.

Remaining vigilantly positive, having faith, and looking for blessings, is how another mom told me she was coping. This is a story she told to me as she, her husband, and I sat talking in their kitchen. "On that day (the day of the shootings) John and I were asked to go inside the schoolhouse to identify our daughter. I never thought I could do it. But we went inside and were shown her body, lying on the floor. It was her. I turned to John and said, 'Where is the blessing here?' (Meaning how can we find some good in this?) Just then, the paramedic turned to us and said, 'Oh no, she's not dead. She's still alive. We need to get her out of here to a hospital. We wanted to be sure who she was.' Then they rushed her off to the helicopter. I turned to John and said, 'Blessing number one.' Everyday since then we look for another blessing. Your message of kindness is one of those blessings."

How could I respond to that? How do you react when a woman in her position, a woman who has been through what she has, places your actions on a scale of such importance? I have visited with several of the Amish families and heard tremendously moving stories. Words such as this I never expected. This emotional and positive reaction directly from one of these parents was overwhelming. All I could do was put my hand to my heart, nod my head with my eyes closed, and say, "Thank you. I'm only reflecting back the message that you and so many others are living."

The strong belief of these Amish and their trust in God was allowing them to deal with this atrocity. But they were not just dealing with it. They were even finding forgiveness through it all. Remember, these people attended the gunman's funeral. They were finding peace through forgiveness. As we English outsiders witnessed these acts in near disbelief, I was privileged to hear yet another father tell me this story: While in John and Mary's home, I found myself again at another kitchen table. Their children were with us. Some of them had been in the school that day. Others are older and now out of school. During our discussion of many topics and questions, John told me this: "The day before the school was to be torn down, I was meeting with the other parents. The questions came up: Do we want to keep anything from the school? Do we want to salvage any of it, before it's gone? Most parents shook their heads. 'No. Level it all. We don't want any of that.' 'Are we sure?' I asked them. 'It's our last chance.' A few of the fathers decided, 'Well ok, I guess we can go look.' Some of the young boys were there also and said, 'I want to go. Can we go too?' So maybe eight or so of the boys, a few of the fathers and I went to the school. The door was boarded up and the state trooper with us removed the plywood board. Before the board was barely moved away . . . John said this part while moving his open hand in a motion that mimics it being on the back of a child that is walking past you, as if you are encouraging them to move along, with a gentle forward motion." He continued . . . "It was like the hand of God pushed those young boys inside. These were the same boys who were in class that tragic day. They ran in, looking for things and shouting to us, 'Don't forget the erasers. We need the erasers. I want my pencil box. And I want my desk.'" After a brief pause so John could take a deep breath, this strong man continued . . . "We, the adults, looked at each other with tears in our eyes and said, 'We thought we knew how to forgive. Look at these children. They aren't attaching anything from that terrible day to these things. They've gotten past that.' We cried," he said. "Then we took everything we could out of that room to rebuild the temporary schoolhouse." Tears were in his eyes as he finished.

Then, as if to find some relief from that moment he continued by telling me this: "That same morning, while we were at the school, the boys knew that bells were going to be rung in the area, in memory of the girls." Now this was a moment I was familiar with. The ringing of those bells at that time is what inspired me to call WIOV. This to me was an important step along this journey. Now I was going to find out what was happening at the school at that exact time. He continued . . . "Well, the boys wanted to ring the schoolhouse bell, right at that moment along with everyone else. They wanted to be part of that. As the time grew closer to ring the bell, the state trooper was checking his watch to let us know when it was exactly time. Just as he was saying, 'Ok it's time,' we all heard bells in the distance beginning to ring." Now John is smiling, as if he can see this more pleasant image in his memory. He continued, "The boys, about seven or eight of them, jumped on the rope that rings the bell and began to pull it.

Well there were so many of them, that when they pulled so hard, the bell swung up and stuck in the upright position." Stopping a few seconds here, he chuckles along with the same boys, of whom he is speaking, now present in the room with us. Then he went on, "The boys weren't discouraged. They immediately took action. They found ways to climb up the sides of the walls and climb trees to get on the roof. When they got up there, they sat, smiling and pleased with themselves, hitting and shaking and ringing the bell, so everyone could hear it." John, along with those boys, were now all smiles. They looked around at each other and myself, nodding their heads and remembering those few moments. They all seemed very pleased with themselves that they were undaunted in finding a way to participate in that ever so small way of remembering their lost friends.

On our second day of visiting, we were in the first home before the sun came up. This was an early start to a long day. Kym and I found ourselves seated at the kitchen table with Amish parents and grandparents. Children and extended family were standing around us, filling the rest of the kitchen. There must have been fifteen or more people gathered here today. All of them were up early, had breakfast, dressed and ready to greet us before we arrived. Outside it was still dark, the sun had not yet come up. A few candles and two propane lanterns dimly lit the room. We had to be there early because this family was leaving just after our visit. They were being driven nearly two hours away (by an English driver) to visit their daughter, who was still hospitalized.

As we sat at the table they all asked questions and told stories of how the daughter was doing. The mood was friendly. Surprisingly almost jovial at times. How was that possible, I wondered? The family had gotten some good news the day before and they were now going to share it with me. To understand how good this news is, I must first tell you how badly things began. This is a bit graphic. Their daughter had been shot point blank in the head. The doctors held little hope at first that she would even live. If she did, she may never talk or be mobile again. Unbelievably, this little girl was the fortunate one. Their other daughter had been shot and didn't survive the day. She was one of the five girls who were killed. Can you imagine? Can you just imagine, having your two young daughters shot? Losing one and now trying to deal with the struggling survival of the other? How torn with emotion would that make someone? The extremes of such an emotional tug of war could be enough to rip the heart from your chest. Through the grief and horror of the moment, this family was trying to focus on any good news that came their way. They were trying to be positive and hopeful for the future. Here is the story her father told me:

With his actions a bit animated, obviously excited about something, John was seated at the kitchen table, to my left. I was seated at the end of the table balancing the painting on a stool next to me. It was facing toward Mary, the grandparents and perhaps ten additional extended family members. Everyone positioned themselves in the room so they could see it and look at me as we spoke. "Pretty early to be here, isn't it?" he said smiling at me. I told him, "The time of day doesn't matter to me. I'd be here, anytime, day or night, to visit with you and your family. Thank you for having me." "You know we lost one of our daughters that day . . . and our daughter Rebecca is one of the girls who was badly hurt. She's been in the hospital. We go to see her everyday. We have to leave early. The driver should be here soon. He wants to meet you too. Let me tell you how she's doing. She was hurt badly, shot in the head." He said this as he pointed his finger to show where the wound was inflicted, behind the ear. "The doctors didn't think she would live. They told us she would probably never walk or maybe never talk again." The rest of the family was still standing around us, quiet and still. The room still lit only by candle and lantern light.

"Thank God, she is now beginning to say a few words and even starting to act like she wants to walk. Yesterday, the doctor tested her to see if she could understand him and follow his directions. He brought one of Rebecca's friends in to be with her. He took the two of them into a room and said to them, 'I've hidden twelve Easter eggs in the room. I want you two girls to find them.' They looked at each other and just then, both of them got up and went through the room finding the eggs. Yes, Rebecca too. The doctor watched not believing his eyes. The girls laid Easter eggs up on the table in front of him. Rebecca sat down, looked at the eggs, pointed and mumbled a few words to herself (she was counting the eggs)."

"Then she said to the doctor, 'That's twelve. We got them all.' The doctor was amazed! She was talking, she was walking and she was doing math. He told us it's like a miracle. Then he gave us the good news. Rebecca will be coming home for Christmas. The day she is scheduled to come home is Christmas eve. That's the best gift we could ever get."

Well, hearing news like this, I was surprised he and the rest of the family were containing themselves as much as they were. I now understood how good this news was. As he finished, everyone else in the room shuffled a bit, nudging each other with smiles, nods of approval and speaking in Pennsylvania Dutch. As bad as their overall loss is, this was a good day in this household. None of them spoke of the daughter who was killed, except to mention briefly that they lost her. I can only assume that they are attempting to remain positive, both in their thoughts and actions.

The driver showed up with the van, to take them to the hospital. I greeted him. He shook my hand, thanked me for what I was doing and told me he was following the story on WIOV. He received his print on the day of the signing. He was one of the thousands who came out and made it such a special day. I thanked him for that.

The sun was up now. We had greeted it together through the kitchen window. The light of a new day that was full of promise for this family in distress. It was time for me to excuse myself and be on my way. This family had more important people than I to see this day. They were on their way to see their daughter.

To think of this family as lucky, or blessed, seems hard to do, since one of their daughters was tragically lost. Certainly, being aware of that fact is what tempered their joy about Rebecca doing so well. One other family I visited was not even this fortunate. The mother told me, as I sat at her kitchen table with her husband, about the loss of their two daughters. Yes, they lost two girls that day. Both shot and gone in an instant. Neither having reached their teenage years. These young girls, all of the girls that day, were taken in such a manner that was completely foreign to them. The response, of the girls in that very moment of terror to the gunman as he made his threats, with a gun in hand and sites aiming to end their lives, was to let him know they were praying for him. They were telling the man, who in no unmistaken manner, was letting them know their death was near, that they were asking God to help him. Their thoughts and prayers were for him. His actions and their response may sound unbelievable and even hard to read. But it was terribly real for those young girls. In the midst of that moment, still it was God and prayer that were present in their minds. Their faith allowed them to know that they were fine. It was the gunman's spirit, his soul that was in ruinous turmoil. These two sisters, two daughters of the woman sitting across the table from me, were included among the pure and innocent that day.

As their mother put it to me, "I lost my two helpers. The only way we are getting through this is by accepting God's way. Even though we don't understand it, we accept it. And, by the prayers of so many people." In fact this mother was so strong, the only thing that brought her near to tears, while I visited, was hearing how millions of people were praying for them. It was while I told her of people around the world feeling their pain and expressing concern for them, that she was touched to the point of having her eyes water with tears. The tears of sadness were reserved for her private time. What moved her this day was to learn of the concern and prayers out of compassion expressed for her family.

Of course, at every house I went to there were the children. Yes, I met all the children who were attending school that day. There were others I met also, including older siblings and friends. Over the course of the days I spent visiting, I interacted with all of them in their homes and at the temporary school. While I was in their homes, the children seemed fascinated with my presence. Mainly they would stare, eyes fixed on me or intently studying the painting. There was very little talk between them and myself. Perhaps this was because they were well behaved and talking to adult visitors was reserved primarily for the parents, or perhaps it was still out of shock that an Englishman was in their home. Whatever the reason, the last thing I wanted to do was have the experience of my visit upset them. Carefully, I kept my distance and directed my attention to the adults. But in every home I was certain to take some time to talk with each of the children. In some cases it was only a few seconds. In others it was two or three minutes. It felt important to me to let each of them know how people around the world were concerned for them. I made a point of letting each child know that millions of people around the world were praying for and wanting only good things for them. I knew that talking with the children could be more difficult for them than for me. So it was with a sense of ease and a gentle tone that I talked to them at all. I was always mindful to react to each one as the individual they are. Each was dealing with this differently. But I must tell you, not one of them, not one, shied away. Nor did I sense any of them experiencing intimidation or fear. My approach was always with kindness, not just in action, not a kindness that is only superficial. I believe the feeling was truly being projected from within. The parents felt it. I believe the children did too.

I also got to ride along with Kym, as she picked up the children for school. We did this after our pre-sunrise visit to the one home. She transported the children to and from school in a large van. It had just enough space for her and the kids. So, including me this day made things a bit tight. I sat in the front passenger seat and Kym drove. We picked up each child at his or her home. When each of them saw the van arrive, they came running out of the house, full of energy and smiles. Then eagerly hopped up and into the back. It was wonderful to see them joking, inquisitive and excited to be going to school. As each one got in, Kym told them, or reminded them, of who I was.

Her intent was to put them at ease with a stranger in the van. I'll never forget the simple innocence of the one boy. After getting in and taking his seat in the back, he looked up at me and said, "Oh yeah, my dad told me you were at our house yesterday. He told me about you." I turned to him, smiled and said, "Yep, I visited with your parents yesterday. So, what did your dad say about me?" With the beautiful, simplicity of a child he said, "He told me you had square glasses." Kym and I looked at each other and yes; I was wearing my somewhat square glasses. After having been through such emotional discussions and visits in those homes, we were both relieved that it was all just that simple for the children. The two of us laughed out loud. It was such a release of tension. Then I turned back to face the children and pointed to my glasses, tilted my head and smiled. Then all of us, children included, began laughing, genuine full-belly laughs. That was such a good moment.

It wasn't just boys on the bus that day. We were also transporting all the girls who survived the shootings and now able to attend class. One of them sat directly behind me. By the time she entered the bus it was quite full. So she was sitting on the very front edge of the seat just behind me, over my left shoulder. When I turned to talk to the kids, her face was only about a foot away from mine. For the entire trip she quietly stared at me. The stare was constant and all the while she had this big closed-mouth smile on her face. She spoke not a single word. No comment from her at all. Just smiles. I was not about to draw attention to her, single her out or make her feel uncomfortable in any way. If she wanted to talk she would. I made plenty of eye contact and smiled back. But was careful not to engage her in discussion if she didn't want that. I went on talking and laughing with whatever children wanted to interact with me. But all the while, there she was as close as could be smiling at me.

When the short trip to school was over and the kids were safely delivered inside, I asked Kym about her. I wondered if she noticed this girl smiling at me. So, I asked her, "Did you see that girl right next to me, smiling the whole time?" Yes, Kym had seen her and it pleased her to see that smile. Then Kym updated me on her condition. What I heard stopped me in my tracks. The fun interactions with the children over the last few minutes, was brought right back to the reality of the trauma these kids were facing. That beautiful little girl, who sat no more than a foot away from me, looking and smiling at me as we drove her to school, was most definitely a survivor of that awful day. She had been shot through the jaw. Currently, she was in the process of going through various steps of reconstructive surgery. Her silence wasn't because she was shy or had nothing to say. Talking is not something she does these days. She will again, but not yet. You see, she is very self-conscious about her mouth and jaw. This was a point in time that the healing and reconstructive processes were still in progress. Mostly, keeping her mouth closed is what she must do. Even smiling is not something she does often. Kym said just to see her smiling so much was a pleasant, unusual sight. I will never forget that beautiful little girl's face and smile.

When we arrived at the temporary school the children scrambled off the bus and scurried into the building. Kym and I were going in also. I was about to enter this place kept so secret that only a handful of people knew it even existed. I was about to be entrusted with that same secret. As we approached the door my heart beat faster with the anticipation of actually being inside this special building. My focus when encountering the children and their teacher in this special place was to be comforting toward them. I wanted to be an Englishman bringing not pain or suffering, but rather understanding and peace. I can say now, since the secret no longer needs to be kept, that even parked directly in front of this building there was no indication of what was inside. To look at this building you would think it was someone's garage . . . because it was. But after walking inside, I found something very different. This garage, a size that would fit two cars, if the Amish owned cars, had truly been transformed into a one-room schoolhouse. Desks for the students were in rows in front of the desk for the teacher. Arts and crafts projects were hanging on the walls and from the ceiling. The chalkboard was hung behind the teacher's desk and above it, in large colorful letters, was the alphabet. Coats and hats were hanging from wooden pegs on the wall near the door. There was a shelf just above the coats. On it sat a neat row of lunch pails. Once inside these walls, you were in a one-room schoolhouse. This certainly was no longer just a garage. What an honor it was to be invited into these surroundings.

Not surprisingly, as I entered all eyes were on me. Given the circumstances, I wouldn't have expected anything else. I was an Englishman entering their school. Having that happen will never be the same for them again. I met the teacher just seconds after entering. Meeting her held its own surprise. She was so young. Prior to being there, I had no idea of her age. In the English world she would still be a student herself, perhaps no more than eighteen or nineteen years old. This bright young woman was given the responsibility of educating the youth of the community. She didn't take that responsibility lightly. Now she carried with her guilt, put upon her by herself, since that tragic day. What I mean is, she feels responsible for the children and wishes she could have done more to save them from the events of that day. You see, in the early stages of that nightmare unfolding, she saw the opportunity to flee the scene and seized it. But what she is having trouble realizing is that in doing so, her quick action may have saved lives. It was her thoughtful action, once outside the building, to run to the closest farm and retrieve help. She summoned the neighbors, who in turn contacted the state police. Her quick thinking is what put an end to this tragedy before even more lives were lost. Yet she struggles with the memory of leaving the children.

When Kym introduced me to her, I expressed, as I did to all the families, that millions of people were praying for her. Then I told her how brave and wise she was to think so quickly and get help the way she did. She needed to know that she didn't cause or add to that terrible day. Rather she helped put an end to it.

Then I presented her with a framed print for herself and one for the school. She smiled with an uneasiness that clearly expressed her sadness for the children and a hurt that she must have been feeling on many levels. She spoke very few words. I don't think she quite knew what to say. As young as she was, her decision to remain silent was a mature gesture that spoke volumes.

It was early morning and school would get under way shortly. Being aware of this and of course, the potential discomfort caused by an Englishman in the classroom, I made my visit brief.

Over the course of these past two days, it was difficult at times to be sitting next to these young ones in their homes. Difficult in a way that can only be experienced by being in their presence. We would be sitting shoulder to shoulder, each of them at that youthful innocent age, maybe eight years old or so. I'd glance down and see them staring up at me. Then watch them smile and tilt their head to one side as if curious and friendly. Without them ever being aware of it, the wounds from the gunshots would become exposed for me to see: Wounds on their shoulders, legs and arms. Carrying the scars of that day, these children still smiled with the most innocent eyes. These were the physical, visual wounds that the girls endured. The boys had their own emotional scars held on the inside. The teacher told me, that it's customary when a visitor comes into the schoolroom for the children to sing for them. The children loved to do that. But there was no singing when I visited. I was told later that even this joyful act was difficult, especially for the boys. The reason being, some of the surviving girls were not back to school yet. They were still hospitalized. Others would never be back. While singing the boys were very aware that the girls were missing. These boys would try so hard to sing the girls' parts by straining to raise the pitch of their voices and sing the words those missing girls sang, just weeks before. This usually joyous act had become a sad reminder of their loss. This tragedy had touched these peoples lives, not just in the big ways we hear of on the news reports. But even in the smallest everyday things, that once were easy and full of joy.

My days spent visiting the Amish were indeed special. They were filled with many emotions: Expressions of care and concern for those who were suffering; shared sadness for their loss and heartache; a sense of honor to be welcomed into their homes and lives at such a troubled time; and an overwhelming feeling of humility to have been given such a unique opportunity of bridging the gap between our two communities.

Through it all, my intentions were that of reflecting back their initial expressions of kindness and compassion. It was those initial expressions that were now inspiring the community, the nation and the world.

The memories of these visits are something I will carry with me for the rest of my life. The feelings and emotions shared by the families and children was a unique insight to the human experience. It was made even more special, by knowing that these, already private people, opened their doors to me at an even more private time in their lives.

These past few days started by sharing the dim, soft candle-light in an Amish kitchen. Together we welcomed the warmth of the morning sunrise through their windows. Now, after our visits and exchange of hearts, we had revealed ourselves to each other as though we were standing in the brilliance of the mid-day sun. What we saw in each other was not so much the diversities and differences between us. The aspects of our lives that kept us separate in the past were unimportant. These days the focus was on what we shared in common—family, faith, life, the pain of loss, hope for the future and the realization that we cared for each other. These days were bridging gaps with the hope of building a new normal.

CHAPTER 5

Requesting Kindness

E ACH DAY I spent among the Amish ended with me coming home, back into the English community. My life was a dichotomy of two lifestyles. The differences between these two communities were astounding. My days with the Amish were filled with the emotions I previously mentioned, accompanied by a quiet calmness. The victimized families and the Amish community were allowing God's plan to unfold without holding on to the tragedies of the recent past. They were quietly living with their sadness, forgiveness and prayer. Always accepting, even when not understanding, God's ways. They were looking to the future with hope. Our days together in that serene pastoral setting moved with a solemn slowness and ease. Our discussions were of faith, the children and prayer. Time seemed to move less quickly because we focused on what matters so dearly, that of making the human connection through kindness in a time of need.

Returning home, after a day in Amish country, an entirely different life awaited me. Reporters would literally be waiting on my front porch with cameras and microphones. The phone seemed to ring continuously. People wanted to talk about my visits and wish me well. The number of e-mails I received was steadily increasing. The pace of the English world differed drastically from that of the Amish and at this time I was continually shifting in and out of both. With each shift I would transfer a bit of one into its counterpart. While I was in the Amish world, they had questions about the English. While in the English world, I fielded questions about the Amish. At times I felt like a conduit of human relations, relaying information from one group to another. There were even friends and relatives who would ask questions like, "So, are you gonna become Amish now?" They asked this like it was something someone does, with the ease of changing from cable to a satellite dish. Like you signed the paperwork and now could tune in a new station. No, I wasn't going to become Amish. Because I admired many aspects of their life, didn't mean I was going to take on that life. Just as I may admire some things about TV, I didn't have to bring it into my home. In all seriousness though, this was a role I gratefully and happily accepted.

In the process of transferring some of that information, I wrote the following letter to Casey at WIOV. This was written on the night of my final day of visiting the Amish families. Both exhausted and exhilarated by the past few days' experiences, I wanted to share these feelings with her and pass on the message I received from the families.

Casey,

> *What a moving, strengthening and heart filling experience, these past few days have been. It would take far too long to write you about all the stories shared with me, by these families. Their strength of faith and trusting in God's way is overpowering. In their own words it is that, along with all the prayers and kindness and compassion shown to them by others, that is getting them through this.*
>
> *Every one of the Amish I encountered was humble, gracious and thankful.*
>
> *They asked me to express to everyone how grateful they are, for all that has been done and is still being done for them.*
>
> *I'm exhausted. More details later . . . I promise.*

Casey was moved to the point of reading this letter live on the air the next morning. This was not something I expected she would do. But all along, Casey had been guided by her heart in this matter, as I believe she always is. She felt the people of our community needed to hear it.

Through broadcasts like this and others, news of my involvement began to reach out further into the English world. TV and radio broadcasts increased. On-air interviews began happening more frequently. Reporters for TV and newspapers were calling and coming by the house for interviews. Front-page newspaper articles were written. TV news interviews were being aired from my home and studio. I was asked to appear on multiple TV talk shows. Then these reports found their way to the Internet and the story was spreading far and wide. In every interview given, I always mentioned the important message driving my reason for involvement: That of treating others with kindness, compassion and forgiveness. This message, being spread as it was, drew more and more responses. Dealing with incoming requests and well wishes was all I found myself doing. I answered every e-mail, postal mail and phone call. Notes filled with addresses, phone numbers and e-mail addresses were piling up. Requests were coming in for copies of the print. People were expressing how they saw the importance of finding this good message in such a difficult time. They were in essence asking for more expressions of kindness and compassion. Each of these interested people was important to me. Calls and contacts came in from various states. People were in a state of emotional unrest by this tragedy and they recognized this message as a place of rest.

The day of the Bart Fire Company breakfast had arrived. This is the breakfast where I was to present prints to the state troopers and Bart crew. A Saturday I think it was. Not a Sunday, because then many of the Amish may not attend, due to church commitments. It was another beautiful day . . . now that I think of it, there seemed to be a lot of those during this time . . . anyway, with prints loaded in the truck I was off. Once again headed down the now familiar road to Nickel Mines. I was going alone. But I didn't expect it to take very long before running into someone I knew . . . or who knew me. The parking lot was very full. Cars took up most of the spaces, but there were Amish buggies also. I parked and made my way inside, leaving the prints in the truck. Greeting my new friends and having breakfast with them, was first on my list.

Through the first set of doors I went and entered the lobby area. The room was crowded as people were making their way into the main hall. Here is where you paid your money and got a meal ticket. There were a few minutes, maybe not even that long, when I was just another face in the crowd, unrecognized as "The artist who painted the bell." It felt good somehow to be just another person supporting this wonderful organization. Then almost immediately friendly familiar faces greeted me. Some of the crew were working the ticket stand and recognized me. Every time I meet any of these new friends, made through this tragedy, as soon as our eyes met the bond of friendship and camaraderie was immediate. It's a wonderfully comforting feeling. We said our brief hellos. I bought a ticket and made my way to the main hall. Along the way, I was greeted and shook hands with strangers who also recognized me. Just as in my e-mails and phone calls back home, people were wishing me well and asking if more prints would be available.

When the doors to the main hall opened, I was amazed at the sight. This large room was full of people. Any space there was left in here, was filled with the smell of bacon, sausage, eggs and coffee. Breakfast was being served in a big way. Tables were everywhere and they were all full. Hundreds of people were enjoying their meal and the friendly company. The line of people still waiting for food was a long one too. What a wonderful turnout. And who did I see in line, just ahead of me? Kym.

She was all smiles and motioning for me to come join her. We waited in line together, mainly discussing what a terrific success this was. English and Amish all together were enjoying a good meal. While in line, several of the Amish families that I had visited came up to shake my hand, say hello and simply converse in neighborly chatter. We'd talk about how everyone was doing and they would ask me what I was painting these days. If I looked close enough I could still see the sadness behind their smiling eyes. But why? Why look for that? Our time spent together was geared toward hope, the future and realizing the time we had together, here and now, was precious. It was so good to see them again.

The line was moving as we talked. It was now our turn to order. I love breakfast food. I wanted to try some of everything . . . eggs, bacon, hash browns, toast, coffee and juice. I passed on the creamed chip beef. That's never been a favorite of mine. Kym and I found a table and sat to eat. Within minutes the sergeant, who was in charge of the troopers at the schoolhouse scene, joined us. He was with his wife and young son. When the Amish families saw him, they came over to say hello and talk. He and the families had a bond unlike any other. His comforting help (and the help of all the troopers) on that terrible day will never be forgotten. These strong-hearted men and women were the ones who rushed the schoolhouse, broke in the door and confronted the grim scene within. They were the first ones inside. They were the very first line of assistance and care for the girls. Physically, they began removing the girls from the building, all of whom had been shot, some more than once.

Sheltering them with their own bodies from any unsuspected further danger, they fervently rushed them to medical assistance. Some even cradled the girls in their arms, while breathlessly awaiting the attention of already extremely overwhelmed paramedics. In one sad case, life left one of those small shattered bodies, while still in the arms of her rescuer.

These troopers did what no one should ever be asked to do. And they did it with the disciplined intensity of their profession, combined with the gentleness of caring hearts and hands. I'm certain that each one of them wishes more lives could have been saved that day. But this barrage of gunfire came so swiftly and without warning, that no one could have stopped it any sooner. Fusing together thoughts of wanting to do more, with images of the scene they discovered inside, causes me to be certain they felt a sadness second only to that of the families. Knowing the difficult role they played that day, makes it easy to understand why this bond between the families and themselves exists. So, when I tell you that these, or any of the first responders, finding a sense of peace in this image and message, humbles me I don't say that lightly.

The remainder of breakfast was so enjoyable. There was good food and good conversation between many new friends, both Amish and English. I heard the total count in attendance was over five hundred.

When everyone's meal was done and the crowd was thinning out, the fire crew began putting their attention to my presenting the prints. Many tables and chairs were folded and put away. Clean up moved along quickly. Once the main hall was well under control tables and chairs were set up in an adjacent room for troopers, the crew and myself. To this point I had no idea of how they wanted to handle this. I figured I would just be meeting quietly with each of them. Share a few comments with each and sign the prints. The crew had a different idea. The room they prepared had about ten rows of chairs, facing a long table . . . with one chair at it. Guess who they wanted at that table? Yes, they asked me to sit up there alone and talk about this message and my experiences. Then each person would be called up to me individually for his or her print. This was a surprise. I thought it would be much more casual with only a handful of people. Now I was being asked to sit before a room of fifty or so and talk. No problem. Truly. One deep breath. Settle my thoughts and let the words come. I was happy to be asked.

I took my seat and a spokesman for the crew had some very kind words of introduction. Then I spoke for about fifteen minutes, telling stories of the events that led me to be sitting in front of them all. To my surprise, just as I was beginning to hand out prints, the sergeant asked to say a few words. He stood up next to me, in front of everyone, and spoke the most respectful words about what I was doing for this community, the families and all the responders. As an expression of gratitude, he then presented me with an official Pennsylvania State Trooper hat. These he told us all, are not accessible to the general public. You must be a state trooper to wear this hat. The only way to own one of these is to go through the academy. For my actions taken in this tragedy, he was making me an honorary state trooper. That was very unexpected and rewardingly special. I graciously accepted and was quick to point out that it was everyone else in that room that deserved the honors today. I had simply been reflecting back all of their noble actions.

The next thirty minutes or so were spent signing and handing out prints to each of these first responders. One by one their names were called and they came up to the table. Many pictures were taken and there were lots of handshakes and hugs. All the prints left over from the first signing had now found their rightful owners.

Between the general public's request for prints and the support this message was receiving from those so closely involved to the tragedy, I felt almost obligated to take further action. How could I say no to continuing this expression of kindness? How could anyone say no to that? So with much thought and prayer I searched for the next move on this journey. The path was ahead of me. I simply needed to know where to step. It was time to move forward.

It felt right that more prints would have to be produced. People were asking for them specifically and for the spread of the message. If this image and its message were going to reach further and touch more people I needed to be prepared. There were questions I needed to find answers to: How would I pay for more prints? How would I handle the packaging and shipping of them? What about postage? How would I handle the incoming contributions? How could I most effectively tell people of how to acquire the prints? There was a lot to be done. My days became filled with structuring a method of how to accomplish the further spread of the message, and of course continuously deal with the incoming requests at the same time.

My days were spent working on and resolving all these issues and more. I established a fund to accept any incoming contribution: The Bruce Becker Nickel Mines School Fund. Proceeds from this fund go to the Amish families involved and to further the continuation of spreading the message of *Kindness and Compassion*. This was not a moneymaking venture for myself. All of the proceeds from the contributions would go into the fund. The printer was contacted about a second press run to produce more prints. We discussed timing and costs. Days and days were put into researching packaging and shipping. These prints, when shipped, needed to arrive safely and in tact. Postage costs were simultaneously explored with packaging. My attempt was to keep the overall costs low. These prints could not be expensive. They needed to be affordable and available to virtually anyone who wanted one. The message is for everyone, not just those who could afford an expensive print. Days of work went into these details. These prints, because they carried such a positive important message, needed to be available to whoever wanted them. As plans were being made some people were asking, "What are you going to charge for these prints?" When I responded with a number as low as possible, people were astonished. "No, that's not enough!

Your work is worth so much more. You should charge more."
Well, yes, I have been fortunate enough to have my artwork
sell for more. But this was different. These were not for sale.
They were being offered at a suggested contribution amount
and the money was not for me. It goes to the fund. "This is not
as much about the money coming in, as it is about the message
going out." That is the belief the fund was started with and still
stands.

Now and then I would stop and wonder, what am I getting
myself into? What if this really does take off and people around
the world actually began requesting these? Could I handle that?
The answer always came back the same: Yes. I can handle it. A
message of treating others with kindness is without a doubt a
positive one, worth my time and effort. Utilizing my work to
affect others in a positive manner is what I have always done
and want to continue doing. I was determined to continue.
This journey was in the hands of a greater power than my own.
But this next step was left up to me to take action and move it
forward. Getting all these ducks in a row and being prepared
was simply the next step. I would follow where it led me.

After several weeks were spent resolving the details of moving this message forward it was time to put these plans into action. I called the radio station WIOV, wondering how things
had been going there since the print signing. I told Casey and
Murph of the number of calls and letters I was receiving. To
my surprise they said they were going through the same type
of response. Calls were coming in to them everyday. People
were asking about the availability of prints. People were sending well wishes and more. They told me that the TV stations
that aired news reports of what I was doing were receiving calls
and requests also. People were asking for the continuation of
this positive message.

That was enough for me to hear. I decided we needed to
make these prints available to more people. The way to do it

was this: One more time makes them available to everyone locally . . . take care of home, so to speak. Then they would be made available worldwide. The people at WIOV and myself set up a time to meet and discuss the possibilities. We needed to do this right away.

At this point six weeks had passed since the shootings. Within days we were getting together. We met at JavaTeas once again. That's where we had been meeting to discuss the first print signing. It's a wonderful coffee shop that is centrally located to all of us. It was the perfect casual atmosphere for discussing the project. The owner allowed us to have the upstairs to ourselves that day. So there we were: Casey, Murph, the radio station production manager and myself. We shared with each other the experiences we all had been going through over the past few weeks: stories of the many phone calls, e-mails, requests for prints, well wishes and so on. I told them how I was preparing to make these prints available worldwide. Between us there was a unanimous consensus: A second print signing should be held. Well, it was almost unanimous. TJ came to the meeting that day thinking, as a business manager should, with the interest of the station in mind. Being fairly new to this area, he was not as familiar with the tight-knit aspects of our community, as the rest of us. He reminded us of all the other community efforts the station was involved in. He was skeptical about the idea of a second signing. Casey, Murph and I knew we were focused on this healing process and felt strongly about it. The typically re-served Casey was the most verbal and adamant about it. She let him know without question that we needed to do this. Murph was obviously upset as well. I on the other hand remained quiet and observant, knowing that this journey was going to unfold at its own pace and in its own way. If it were meant to happen TJ's cautiousness wouldn't stop it. By the end of the meeting, TJ agreed that if my actions received national recognition then the station would be involved in another print signing. As we all left the meeting that day Casey and Murph were not very pleased with the outcome. They even said to me on the side, quite adamantly, "This will happen one way or another." Confident as I was in the message and the spread of it and also believing that what is needed will come, I simply agreed with a smile and said, "Yes, it'll happen."

The next day I was at home taking care of a few everyday things: paying a few bills, doing laundry, maybe cleaning the house a bit. These things and much more had been put on the back burner for weeks. In fact, since the day of the shootings I hadn't even considered starting a new painting. *Kindness and Compassion* was consuming all my time. Then the phone rang. I picked it up to find out I was being contacted by ABC News. They were producing a documentary about the tragedy and asked if I would consider being involved—being featured on the program. Just like that, when it was needed, we had the national recognition that TJ was looking for.

Just as so many times before, another piece of this puzzle had fallen into place. Whenever something was needed, something that was a steppingstone into the next phase, it happened. It couldn't be second-guessed or anticipated. I simply had to be open and aware of it when it came. Time and time again this would happen. Life never fails to amaze me and I was being amazed often during these past few weeks.

After hanging up with the ABC producer, I called Casey and Murph to tell them the good news. As I told them about the documentary and being asked to be included in it, I thought they would fall off their chairs. They were incredibly excited that now the station would back the second print signing. But what stunned them even more than that was the realization that once again they were witnessing how occurrences happened just as they were needed. Seemingly spiritually interventional actions were happening in a remarkably timely fashion. Every step on this journey was propelled in this manner. They and myself were in awe of how this message of such good seemed undeterred from being squelched. As I said before, there was a power greater than myself or the rest of us at work here.

Two days later I attended an ABC interview. They were questioning the same woman coroner who had been to my house, delivering the list of print requests. She worked the scene of the schoolhouse shootings. It was held at Dr. Kirchner's home. He was the Lancaster County Coroner and a big supporter of the message behind my painting. The day started early and I was the first one to arrive. He and I didn't know each other prior to the shootings. This was my first time visiting with him. We sat, talked and had a bit to eat, while we waited for the film crew. They were driving in from New York and got lost. Dr. Kirchner's home is in the countryside of Lancaster County. Not really off the beaten path, but not on a main road either. Perhaps their GPS units were failing them. When they finally arrived and time was now tight, several of them went right to work setting up the shot location. This gave me a few minutes to meet and talk with the producer. He was flown in from Los Angles to head the project. An L.A. producer flown into New York, and then driven into the Lancaster countryside to put together a production that takes place in the middle of farmland. Hmm, I got the impression he might have rather been anywhere else. But he was very professional and went about his work trying to hold to schedule and meet deadlines. He was getting on camera what he needed by asking prying questions. Seemingly he wanted to uncover graphic details of that dreadful day. Sitting there hearing the tone of the questions and watching that coroner driven to tears with the memories she was recounting, I began to wonder if I wanted to be involved in this at all? Was this going to be a piece filled with shock value and graphic violence? That's not the message that I, or the Amish, wanted to be a part of.

At this interview I was primarily there to witness what was going on and then have a casual conversation with the producer. This was not a day for me to be on camera. When filming for the day was over, Dr. Kirchner, the producer and myself sat and talked. With the required work and filming for the day behind him, the producer was obviously more relaxed. The time now was more quiet and easy. This gave us a chance to truly share what this painting and message were about. I had the chance to convey how the painting came to be, what it now stood for and how the Amish were in favor of its message. Dr. Kirchner expressed his support of the message as a form of healing for the community. We also talked of the continuous positive response from across the country and requests for more prints. By the end of that discussion, the producer came to understand the power behind this simple image. He got it. Before long he was giving me all his business and personal contact numbers. We were discussing times and days to get me on camera and include this image and message as part of his story.

The film crew was traveling back to New York that evening. There was no time to put me on camera just then. So once again, the scheduling, deadlines and the professional production sides of the process were brought to the forefront. After checking his schedule and that of the overall production, he requested that they return that next weekend. He wanted to film and interview me in my studio. This day confirmed it. We certainly had the national recognition TJ was looking for. A second print signing was now imminent.

With all the press and media coverage surrounding the first print signing, many reporters asked that I keep them informed if anything else happened with this image. I had a pile of media-related business cards, notes and e-mail addresses. Some even gave me their personal cell phone numbers. These folks wanted to know about the message and its impact just as the general public did. Combine these with the media reps.

that had been contacting WIOV and we had a lot of people to get a hold of. So, the WIOV group and I discussed how best to handle the reporters and let them know about the second signing. But the people we really needed to inform about this were the local community. We needed to care for those in our area that were asking for and looking for a way of healing. That's when we came up with the idea to have one group assist by informing the other. We decided the most effective way to reach the community was through the media. So we decided to hold a press conference. We would inform the press. Then they in turn would inform the public. Makes sense, right?

Okay, let's pause here for a minute, take a break and do a brief recap. Ready for this? I'm an artist, a single guy working alone making a living as a painter. I have been fortunate enough to have shown and sold my work in galleries across the United States, but nothing quite like this. This serendipitous painting, of a simple Amish schoolhouse bell, has captured the attention of thousands. Its message has gotten the approval of the Amish community that is living through the most devastating of tragedies. Prints of this image are even hanging in their homes, which I had the honor of visiting. I've been thrust into the center of what's become an internationally tragic news story. Been in all the area newspapers, on TV and radio. I'm being asked to appear in an ABC documentary and now I am scheduling a press conference to announce the next move of this image, a second print signing. The best part is, all of this is being driven by the message of treating others with kindness . . . and that's an extremely simplified recap. This has been an incredible seven weeks. Where could it go from here? Well, just wait.

This all still overwhelms me as I write this. So, I wanted to make sure you're still with me. Okay, enough of that, now back to where I left off . . .

We wanted this second print signing to happen quickly so we scheduled this press conference just three days out. To announce the press conference WIOV put together a packet of info that was sent out to the various media. Actually things happened so quickly that there was no time to wait for mail delivery. They had one of their drivers hand deliver the packets to the TV stations and newspapers. We invited the media to the same hall in which the president (yes, of the United States) had just held his press conference in, only a few days before.

During the few days prior to the press conference, I was involved with many things: On-air interviews; figuring out just how to make these prints available worldwide; deciding what I would say to the media; finalizing all the shipping and handling of the prints and so much more. Those days were very full and busy. They passed quickly. Suddenly it was now the day before the conference. Let me say, I very rarely get sick. Maybe a little cold here and there through the winter, but for the most part I've been blessed with good health. The day before the conference I wasn't feeling very well and simply tried to ignore it and work through it. The next morning, the morning of the conference, I woke up with a terrible head cold, fever, body aches, and the works. I felt miserable. No way was this stopping me. What was about to happen that day was far too important. I was going to do this no matter what. I am definitely not one to take medication. I think it over two or three times before taking a Tylenol. But this day I took plenty of them along with a decongestant tablet, nasal spray and lots of hot tea. From all of this medication suddenly and uncommonly introduced into my body, I was literally buzzing. My voice kept coming and going. My head was in a fog. My fever was quite high and my entire body hurt to move. But my determination was clear. I was going to give this presentation.

I made my way to the hall with my roughed out speech and the original painting. Others that were asked to attend supporting the cause were: Dr. Kirchner, several first responders from local ambulance crews and Kym. When I arrived

WIOV personnel were already there and taking care of setting things up. This was a very large room, mainly filled with chairs for those attending. In the front of the room was a podium with several microphones on it. To the left were chairs for the guests I mentioned and myself. Media crews from several TV stations, radio personnel, newspaper reporters, folks representing the arts community and others began arriving. I positioned the original painting on an easel near the podium. A few greetings were made to all of our honored guests, and then we all took our seats to begin.

Casey made a heartfelt introductory statement about the tragedy and the message of the print. Then she introduced Dr. Kirchner. He spoke briefly, but very supportively, about my work. Then, for the first time in front of the media, he called this painting and its message "an act of healing for the community." I was honored to hear that. Upon finishing he introduced me. I hadn't told anyone how awfully sick I was feeling. I didn't want that to hamper in any way the reason we were there. With my head spinning, body aching and skin crawling with chills from fever, I stood up and walked to the podium. At this point, several additional media microphones were mounted to it. I sat my notes in front of me, gripped the podium and with blurry, hard to hold open eyes, looked out over the people who had shown up. These were our messengers, paused and ready to deliver this message and they were waiting to hear it from me. Right then I knew what I had to do. In that moment the ill feelings disappeared. No kidding, I forgot about them totally. My focus was clear and I began to speak. I kept what I had to say brief, only speaking for perhaps eight or ten minutes.

I started by thanking everyone for coming out today. Before explaining how this journey brought us to this place in time, the message of the painting was stated very clearly. Right out of the gates, before any new information was given, they needed to hear this guiding and driving message. I reminded them that it was not a commemorative piece for that tragic day. This painting had become a symbolic image of kindness. It represented the kindness shown by the Amish community, the surrounding community and now the world.

Following that, I recounted many of the incredible events that had taken place to date: Everything from where the bell came from, the serendipitous time I was painting it, the first print signing, my visits to the Amish households, meeting the children, the requests from the first responders and so on. I was conveying to them how this journey was not one that was planned or contrived. But rather how its magnificent unfolding seemed to be more of an act of grace. This was a positive force and message rising from the midst of extreme horror. I was simply a messenger who had recognized and reflected back the goodness that was being expressed by so many others.

Then I gave them the reasons for scheduling a second signing. I told them how requests were coming in from around the country and how I couldn't turn my back on those looking for further acts of kindness. The specific date, location and times for the signing were announced. Now for the first time publicly, I announced that the prints would be made available worldwide on the day of the signing. No specifics of how that would happen were made available. If the media had those specifics, they may have released them to the public. At this time I didn't want that. First we had to take care of those in our community. Locally, one more time, is where these prints needed to be available. We needed to take care of home. Yes, right here at home, the good people of this area are literally seeing, hearing and living the pain firsthand. One more time these prints had to be made available to them exclusively. To finish up, I thanked everyone again for their time.

The information I needed to convey was complete. It was done. I only hoped that through the medicated haze I was experiencing, it made sense. I left the stage and went back to my seat. Individual reporters had questions that Kym, the first responders and myself handled. There were on-camera reports from various news teams being filmed around us. Some photos were taken and then the event began to break up. As was now usually the case when any of us on this journey part ways, there were hugs accompanied by both smiles and tears.

That evening, newscasts around the area showed footage of me speaking about the painting and its message. They announced the date of the second signing. Interviews with Kym and the first responders were also shown. Now there was no turning back (not that I ever even considered that). This message was spreading and reaching perhaps hundreds of thousands of people.

December 2nd was the date chosen for the signing. This date was chosen so that we didn't interfere with Thanksgiving and still not wait too long afterward that it encroached on Christmas. The 2nd was the perfect day. It also happened to be exactly two months, to the day, since the shootings.

Now there was a bit more than a week until that day and I still had plenty to do. The printer was working on producing 2500 more prints. Everyone at the location chosen for the signing, the Christiana Ambulance Station, was putting together their plans of how to handle a potential crowd. After witnessing what happened at the first signing, they wanted to comfortably accommodate the people waiting patiently in line. WIOV was producing a few spots that would run on-air, promoting the event. I was busy seeing to all the pre-planning at my end: Ordering the shipping materials; meeting with postal representatives to discuss final postage concerns; preparing the paperwork to establish the Nickel Mines School Fund; and prayer, lots of prayer for guidance.

What took up most of my time for the next few days was deciding and acting on how I would make these prints available worldwide. The Internet seemed the best venue. I already had a website that I used for my art. So I decided to utilize it as a platform for telling the story of this journey and make it the place that prints were available. I didn't want to put the prints in any stores. They're not a commercial retail item. These prints carried a special message and had to be treated as such.

Stefan, my nephew in Boston, is my website designer. He handles the entire layout for my site. Basically he makes it all work. How grateful I have been to have him do that for me over the past few years. As you know, he was very supportive of this message and the journey it was taking me on. After a few phone conversations he was on board to assist in the site adjustments. It was decided that I would write all the text and provide it to him. He would then layout the pages and post it to the site. At specifically 2:00 p.m. on the day of the signing, he would make it go live and the prints would be available to whoever wanted them.

Creating those pages sounds easy enough, right? Well it's more work than you might think. My time was swamped as it was. Now I had to find additional time to write this story. Time to write about all these life changing, incredible events that were happening around me and to me, while I was going through them. No one else could write them. Only I knew this collection of experiences and the various individuals I encountered. Just writing them, wouldn't be good enough either. They had to make sense to whomever read them, which meant some rewriting and adjusting. Anyway, I sat down one night, after the day's work was done and began writing. That keyboard grabbed my attention for hours. I practically wrote straight through the night. By morning light I had it finished. A very rough, abridged version of the journey to date was on paper (well it was actually on the computer). After reviewing it, I sent it off to Stefan. He has a good eye for things like this, so he suggested changes. Between us both working on it, in the course of a few days it was ready.

Stefan created a private website that only he and I could view. On it he posted all the text and images. This gave us a chance to see it on screen, review the layout, test the links and make adjustments. Think about all this for a minute, from his perspective. He's three hundred and fifty miles away from me, in Boston. Taking time from his schooling, work and personal life to layout and post this information. Information about a painting with a message of kindness. An image that is increasing in its connection to the Amish schoolhouse shootings and to the dismay of some others is seemingly becoming a guiding force in my life. Now I'm asking him to do all this work for no other reason, other than because it feels like the right thing to do. Did he question it? You might think so. But not once. He understood from the beginning the importance and impact this could have. Treating others with kindness is something that he is mindful of daily.

With this information, that would soon be available on the Internet, this message would go global. Anyone wishing to have this image, one that represents the virtue of kindness could have it. Stefan would finalize the page preparations and have them ready on the day of the second signing. His foresight and openness to the importance of spreading this powerful, positive message, at a time when he could have just as easily said no to it all, provided the helping hands needed to propel its expansion. Good man Stefan.

Think back a minute, to my being asked by ABC to be part of their documentary. Do you remember that I had been contacted to be filmed? Well, as another amazing turn of events would have it, they couldn't make it to my studio the weekend we planned. They canceled and we had to reschedule. Now at first that doesn't seem too amazing. In fact it sounds a bit disappointing. But as the producer and I talked by phone, the day he called to reschedule, he was made aware of the second print signing. Well, can you guess when he wanted to be here for the filming? Of course, the same day as the signing. His intention when he called was to ask me if I would be available for the interview on that day, December 2nd. Needless to say, he was thrilled to hear of the signing. This meant he and his crew would come to town and spend the day with me at the signing.

As if my week wasn't full enough, I was asked to do something very special by Dr. Kirchner. You see, he was so impressed by several of the national reporters who covered this tragic story that he asked if I would present one of my prints to each of them. So just days before the signing I traveled to New York with one of his deputy coroners. We went from the set of the Today Show at NBC, to FOX and then ABC, presenting framed prints. My visit with Ann Curry was the most memorable of each visit. She was very gracious and took plenty of time to sit and talk about how this tragedy was an emotionally moving experience for her. The deputy and myself told her stories of how the Amish families were doing and developments in the local community. We spent more than an hour with her. Then she invited us to stay and watch the taping of a portion of the upcoming New Year's show. Not since I was in New York to present my painting to the 9-11 survivors, did I come away with such a memorable time in the city.

This entire day was memorable. Even while riding the subway I found the people to be friendly. For instance, upon entering a subway car and sitting next to a woman who was on her way to work, she noticed one of the framed prints I was holding. Inquisitively she asked about it. "Are you an artist?" "Yes," I told her. "Is this one of your pieces?" As I held it up for her to see and began explaining its story to her, she stopped me mid sentence. "Yes, I've heard about this. I've heard of you. What a tragic thing that was for those children and families. This is a wonderful thing you're doing. Do you know where you're going in the city?" I wasn't surprised that she knew of the shootings.

That was world news. What did surprise me is that she knew of the painting and myself. I was seeing firsthand that the message was reaching out. "We're finding our way as we go," I told her. She not only helped us with directions, but she rode along past her stop to be sure that we got off and headed in the right direction, up town. She even paid our fare. Now that was kindness. Those of us associated with this message were seeing it as a light found in the midst of darkness. Now here I was, on this subway, underground, in the dark, next to a stranger who saw that same light. Its glow was turning up in the least expected places.

The day after my New York trip was Thanksgiving. My family was gathering at my sister Claire's house. Each year it changes as to who will host the big dinners: Thanksgiving and Christmas. This year it was Claire hosting Thanksgiving. Being one of nine brothers and sisters, means family gatherings can be quite large. The family is dispersed up and down the east coast and some further west. Still we manage to get together often. This dinner would be a smaller gathering for us. There would be seventeen of us. Everyone always cooked and brought something to add to the dinner. For the second year in a row, I was bringing the garlic and cheese mashed potatoes. Everyone seemed to like them last year, so Claire asked me to bring them again. She called me Thanksgiving Day and surprisingly asked me to also bring along something else. She asked if I would bring the original painting of Kindness and Compassion. Having it hang in her home, for the day, she thought would show an expression of kindness in her home. To this point my involvement in this was becoming routine to family members. I heard comments spoken with indifference, such as, "Oh, Bruce is on TV again" . . . "Oh, we heard you on the radio again" . . . and so forth. I think my family was becoming numb to it all. But then this. What a nice gesture for her to ask such a thing. Of course I took it along with me. I also took a print for everyone there. We spent quite a bit of time that night talking about it all. Family members had lots of questions and I was more than happy to share my experiences with them. It was fulfilling somehow to have them recognizing the scope and impact of this message and acknowledging my role in it all. That was indeed something for me to be thankful for on Thanksgiving Day—the expression of concern by one's own family. It turned out to be a Thanksgiving I'll remember fondly.

The next few days passed quickly and now it was the day before the second print signing. Most everything was done by this time and it wasn't a particularly busy day. I tried to keep it simple, staying occupied with a few things around the house: I had my car inspected; checked in with Stefan to be sure things were in order with the website; organized the prints, pens and things I would be taking with me; personalized a few prints for people who asked for them in advance; and generally tried to keep my thoughts and energy focused on being prepared and positive about tomorrow. I knew there was some apprehension from the others involved. They wondered if we could duplicate the positive energy that manifested at the first signing. There was concern that people might not turn out again. There was excitement about the ABC crew being there. What might happen that would get captured on film? What if nothing happened? Were we reaching too far to do this again? Considerations like these had been expressed. I didn't allow thoughts like that to waste my time. By now, I was aware that this message had its own life and flowed at its own pace. Things would unfold as they were meant to. Worrying about it would only be a waste of time. It wasn't that I felt arrogant, or pretentiously self-assured about it. I simply was allowing this journey to play out in its own way and at its own pace. By now the positive force of this message and journey was strong enough and evident enough that I knew better than to second-guess it. So with some quiet reflection I ended my day and turned in to sleep. Tomorrow would be the day of the second print signing.

CHAPTER 6

A Second Time

W AKING ON THE morning of the second signing, I found we were blessed with yet another absolutely beautiful day. The morning sun was brilliant and the sky a vibrant blue. There was a cool autumn nip in the air. It was a perfect day for this event. The scheduled time for me to be there was 12:00 (noon) until 5:00 p.m. My morning moved along at a calm easy pace. I took a morning walk, as usual in the colder weather. As much as I've enjoyed a good run, I hate to run in the cold. Then it was time for a quick workout and breakfast. After a shower I double-checked my directions. The boxes of prints, pens and of course the original painting were loaded into the car and I was ready to go. As I did on the day of the first signing, once the car was loaded and the next thing to do was simply drive away . . . I sat quietly for a minute on my back deck. This was a moment to contemplate all that had brought me this far on the journey and what might lie ahead. I focused on giving my attention to each person I would en-counter today and always being conscious of their feelings and reasons for showing up. Keeping the spirit of this message of kindness in the forefront of my thoughts took all precedence.

The drive to this location, the Christiana Ambulance Sta-tion, would be about forty minutes. This station was chosen due to its close proximity to the school and its heavy involve-ment that day. Yes, there is an ambulance station even closer to the school than this one. I mentioned it before: the Bart Fire

Company. It's just a few blocks from the homes of the families and school. In deciding where to hold this second event we felt that if we did get a crowd, as before, we didn't want to bring that sort of chaotic atmosphere so close to the families. We were trying to respect their privacy. So to you, Bart Fire Company, thank you for all you did that tragic day and continue to do. Thank you also for understanding our decision of choosing a different location this day.

The drive into this area was one I was becoming quite familiar with. It seemed I was headed into the Amish country nearly every other day. This time pushing on a bit beyond the Nickel Mines area, I came to the town of Gap. This is where the Christiana Ambulance Station is located. I arrived about an hour before start time, figuring it's better to be early. Turning down the near private road to the station, things were very quiet. Traffic was light. In fact, right then I was the only vehicle on the road. This back road twisted and turned a bit until around the final bend the station was revealed. It sits surrounded by farmland and empty fields. As I cleared the crest of a small hill, I saw one of the EMT crew in the middle of the road. He was there directing traffic. Emergency vehicles were parked in the fields to the right. To the left was the station building and the parking lot, which I then saw, was already filled with cars. This gentleman was directing traffic to park in the surrounding fields. Noticing who I was, he let me pass and I was directed into the already full parking lot. They had saved a space for me right next to the building. That was thoughtful of them. Several of the EMTs greeted me. Many of these were now familiar faces. One in particular was Anita. She was very instrumental in organizing this day and had quickly become a good friend.

She and I had e-mailed each other and spoken several times. Like with many others, we were sharing our experiences since October 2nd. She worked the scene at the schoolhouse that day and had direct contact with assisting the victims. She quickly became a big supporter of this message.

I was escorted into the building where I met still more emergency personnel. They gave me a hand unloading the boxes of prints and carrying them into the building. There was one thing that seemed odd to me. Although the parking lot was full and more cars were now parking in the fields, I didn't see any people. So I asked how that could be. The workers at this station had learned their lesson well from the first signing. What they had done was taken the emergency vehicles out of the bay (that's the garage where the ambulances are kept) and in their place put tables and chairs. The room was now being used as the holding area for people waiting for prints. They also had an assortment of food and drink items available for those waiting. The people who waited out in the cold, during the first signing would now be warm, comfortable and fed while waiting. The prints and I would be positioned in a separate room, adjacent to that one. People (about 50 at a time) would be brought in to receive their prints, have them signed and give a contribution if they wished. These guys had thought the process through very well.

Then they gave me some news that set the tone for the day. Several hundred people were already waiting for me to start. They started showing up at 8:30, three and a half hours before the scheduled start time. When I heard this, I didn't want to keep them waiting any longer. I was taken in to greet them and let them know we would be starting very soon. Off I went, through the door that entered the garage bay area. It was a huge room. Large enough to hold maybe three ambulances and plenty of equipment. Just as they told me, there were the chairs along the perimeter walls. Rows of tables with food and drink stretched down the middle of the room and people were scattered throughout it all. People filled the chairs and a line was forming through the center of the room. I opened the door to smiles and waves. Everyone was very friendly. I walked around a bit, greeting some of them shaking hands and saying good morning. I thanked them for coming and let them know we would be starting soon.

As I went back into the room to be used for the signing, the WIOV crew was showing up. We all put the finishing touches on preparing the room: Positioned the prints to be handed out. Burgundy red tablecloths were put on the tables. Chairs were positioned for myself and those handing out prints. The original painting was placed on an easel behind where I would sit. Things were about ready to go and as of yet, there was no ABC crew. The city boys were probably lost again. No matter, it was time to begin. I assembled all the EMTs from the station and asked if we could take a moment for prayer and reflection on our purpose today. Gathered in a large circle, maybe twelve or fifteen of us, we held hands then Anita and myself said a few prayers. We were asking for and looking to be guided by the positive spirit of kindness that brought us together. Then I signed prints for all of the work crew and we were ready to begin.

Casey and Murph had finished wrapping up their work at the radio station and had just shown up. It was great to see them. Casey already had tears in her eyes as she hugged me and said, "This is wonderful. Here we go again." She, like all of us, was amazed how many people had shown up early. She told me she had a few doubts that we could do this again, with as much success as the first time. But she knew in her heart that we had to try . . . and now it looked like we were off to an amazing start.

About that time the ABC crew showed up, along with some other local news teams. I greeted them all and thanked them for coming. The moment was busy with preparations. So greetings, although sincere, were quick and simple as we all had things to do.

As cameras were being positioned and microphones maneuvered, the doors were opened and the people started coming in. This day of signing was under way. What it held in store for us, no one knew. But undoubtedly, positive energy and the feelings of kindness and closeness between everyone on the premises were very evident. The message of this image was once again in the air.

The procedure happened just as the paramedics had told me earlier: People entered from a door to my right; approached the table to receive a print; left a contribution if they wished and formed a line, waiting for me to sign and personalize it for them. There were large windows in front of me and to my left. The sun was shining in and that same beautiful sky I saw earlier now seemed even more radiant. The warmth and radiance of the sunlight filled the room, as that first group of people filed in.

As was the case at the first signing, I was greeted by people from the neighboring communities. These are strong, caring, hard working people who care for their neighbors. But it quickly became apparent that this message was reaching further. People were coming up to the table with stories of driving in not just from nearby towns, but also from neighboring states. People came from New Jersey and New York, even from Maine. They came in wheelchairs, with families and co-workers. The young and the elderly were showing up. All races and creeds shared the attraction to this message. They came in business suits, farming clothes and Army fatigues. Some who came out to the first signing came back a second time. People came to the table with smiles of gladness for the message of kindness and some with tears of sorrow for the children and their families. All were looking ahead hoping for better times.

Some of the people showing up I had previously spoken to by phone or corresponded with via e-mail. Remember the e-mails and phone calls I had been receiving? Well now some of those people had come out to meet me in person, make a contribution to the fund and receive a print. I had read and answered every e-mail received. But what was amazing to me is that as people reminded me of their correspondence, I remembered their letter. I remembered them all. There was no skimming over those letters. I read every word. Now faces were being put to those kindly written words. Bonds were being formed between strangers in the name of kindness.

Now, thinking back on that day, I remember that I didn't have a concept of the time as it was passing. It was hours before I even had a few seconds to glance around and divert my attention from the people in front of me. When I did, there was Casey, Murph and now Kym handing out prints with smiles. Each of them was talking to individuals about things I could only imagine. The room was noisy from the crowd. Everyone was enjoying the expressions of kindness and good fellowship to one another. The feeling in this place was very positive. We all wanted so badly to shed a light of goodness that would blanket the darkness brought on by the terrible acts at the school. It gave me such a wonderful feeling to see the warm connections being made here.

After having their print signed, people would step to the side and pause before leaving the room. That's where the original painting was presented for viewing. Thousands of people seemed awestruck as they fixed their gaze on the painted canvas. Murph was often right next to them, just inches from the painting, pointing and involved in discussions. What they talked about, I could only imagine. Later he told me of the many secondary images people were seeing in the painting. Perhaps this is the simplest way I can describe to you what a secondary image is: Do you know how sometimes you look at the clouds on a summer day and in their shape you see objects? Shapes that spur comments like: That looks like a bunny rabbit, or I see an ice cream cone in that cloud. Or even, that cloud looks like my Aunt Doris. Well, images were being seen in my painting. Images I never intended to be there. People weren't seeing images of rabbits or ice cream cones. No, these images were more poignant. Many times I was told of people seeing the face of an Amish girl, rainbows, angels, even the face of Jesus and more. None of which I had ever seen before and certainly never intended. In fact, in all my paintings I make a conscious effort not to have secondary images. Oh well, people will see what they see. I was okay with it.

About three hours now into the day, I hadn't moved from that same chair. My focus had been on each person in front of me. So focused that my thoughts rarely strayed from the task at hand. For the most part, I was only aware of the fact that people kept coming. Each of them waited for a long time to be at that table, in front of me. So when they had their turn and wanted my attention they got it. Murph came up to me, knowing I hadn't moved. He told me, "Remember how full the ambulance bay was, first thing this morning? Well, now it's at least three times that full and they keep coming." He said the line was snaking back and forth, filling the garage. That was amazing to hear. It appeared I wouldn't be getting up anytime soon.

The various news teams went about their business very politely. There were very few times that I remember them putting a mic in my face or interrupting my conversation with someone. But they were there filming it all. I remember noticing the ABC producer, just at a time when he had a very interesting look on his face. He was seated beneath one of those big windows in front of me. Somewhat relaxed, he was leaning back, legs crossed, clipboard on his lap, taking it all in. He seemed astonished by it all. I do believe he was genuinely moved by what was happening here. Again, that wonderful feeling came over me. The joy of seeing someone caught up in the kindness of this day.

So there I was greeting and signing. There was a flow, or a routine developing when something entirely unexpected happened. An elderly couple approached me. They were both nicely dressed, gray-haired and presented themselves as very mild-mannered. The woman handed me their print to sign. As I signed it, I asked them, as I asked everyone, "Would you like me to personalize this? Put your name on it?" She didn't just answer with a name as many had. Instead, she gently leaned forward to whisper in my ear. I leaned toward her and heard her speak in a very soft voice, "Yes, but I don't want to say our name too loudly or people will know who we are." I looked at her, now so close that our faces were nearly touching and she said to me, again so softly, "We're Charlie's Grandparents." I instantly knew they were referring to Charlie Roberts. He's the gunman who shot the girls at the school and then took his own life that tragic day. In the blink of an eye, I was up from my chair for the first time in hours. I moved around to the front of the table and wrapped my arms around this woman in a comforting hug. With her head on my shoulder, she melted against my chest and embraced me with a sigh of relief. Pleased to find this moment of emotional rest, we stood there for what seemed like minutes. It may have actually been fifteen or twenty seconds. Then, very quietly, our faces close enough to touch again, I looked into her tear-filled eyes and said, "Of course I'll sign this for you. I'm glad you're here. This message is for you and your family too. If you have time, I'll have someone escort you to a back room and then I'll come visit with you." A soft smile came to her face as she said, "I'd like that."

With that I took her hand in mine. With the other, I motioned to one of the EMTs to come closer. I told him very quietly, who they were. Then asked him to get them comfortably situated in a back room and let me know when they were ready to see me. I watched as he showed them the way through the door behind me.

The sudden intensity of the moment was gripping. I felt sad for them, yet so pleased they were here. The way she spoke to me will always ring in my ears—as if she was ashamed. Perhaps even frightened, wondering how people might react to them being here. But here is right where they needed to be. Here, in the midst of people believing that kindness was the answer. Since I met with the Amish families I had made several attempts to contact Charlie's family. The Amish wanted them to know this message was for them as much as it was for anyone. Those attempts all fell short. His family was talking to no one. Now this, here was his grandmother in my embrace, hopefully finding comfort.

Without missing a beat I knew I had to try and keep her wish of anonymity. For hours they must have waited in line, surrounded by hundreds of people. All the while, hoping not to be recognized. None of the people in this room was to know who they were. I turned back to the table. Looked out over the room full of people staring at me and waiting, just waiting. I smiled and nodded. Without a word I took my seat, reached my hand out to take the print of the next person and began again, "Thanks for coming. Can I put your name on this?" I said. Every person that approached me that day had my full attention, save these few. I sat talking, smiling and signing for the next few minutes. But my thoughts were of the two broken hearts in the next room. I'm not sure how many prints I signed, or people I met before they came to get me. Time was standing still. But it wasn't long before there was a gentle tap on my left shoulder and a voice in my ear said, "They're ready for you." It was one of the EMTs. I finished with the person and print I was working on and excused myself. Then stood up to leave. Someone, perhaps Murph, told the crowd I had a special family to meet with and would be back in a few minutes.

When I left the room, there was a hallway to cross, prior to entering the room I was being taken to. I stopped for just a few seconds and collected my thoughts, and asked God for guidance and words. Just let me be your messenger, I thought. I took a deep breath and reached to open yet another important door in my life. I turned the handle and opened the door. The scene inside was not at all what I expected. Word of who our guests were must have spread. This room was a good size office, maybe twenty feet by twenty feet. Standing around the outer walls was a row of EMTs from the station. The WIOV people were there also. In the middle of the room was a couch, where Kym was seated next to the older couple. It was good to see Kym there. She had been actively trying to contact this family, with the intention of offering them prints. Kym and I had been through a lot together on this journey. The ABC crew was positioned throughout the room with the cameras. There was a boom microphone hanging over the heads of this couple. The intimate, private talk I thought I would have was not going to be so intimate or private. As I stepped through the doorway all eyes shifted to me. They were waiting for me. As quickly as I took all this in, I let it all go. In order to give these two special guests my full attention, I knew the only thing I could see in that room was them. So, in my minds eye and in my heart, there was no one else in that room but these two broken hearts and me.

As I stepped inside the room, it was so crowded that the only open area for me was directly in front of Charlie's grandparents. There was no chair to sit on. They were all taken. The couch was too small, there was no room left on it. I walked over and knelt down on one knee directly in front of them. This woman, who was living with the dreadful memory of the actions of her own flesh and blood, immediately reached out and took my hand in hers. It remained there the entire time. I thanked them again for being here today and told them how welcome they were. Once again I mentioned that this extension of kindness was for them and their family. The gentleman was very quiet. In fact, he said nothing at all. Maybe he was always quiet. Or perhaps he didn't know what to say. As impossible as it may be to do, put yourself in his position. What would be the appropriate words? What would you say?

Then she spoke. She said to me, as her voice trembled, "We want to thank you for what you're doing. Thank you and thank everyone that's here for your love and kindness." Her words were simple and moving, so sincere. Here was a woman hurting in a way that God willing no one will ever again, and she found the strength and courage to be here thanking us. I asked her if there was anything I could do for them. Prints of *Kindness and Compassion*, prints that carried this message are what she wanted. We sat and made a list of her family members to receive them. As she said the names, someone from WIOV, was there with pen and paper writing them all down. "Whatever you need," I told her. "I'll take care of it."

Then she asked if we could pray together. As all the heads in the room bowed, I felt the touch of another hand now holding hers and mine. It was Anita. She was seated next to me. Anita is one of the paramedics that cared for the injured girls that day. Now here she was holding the hand of the gunman's grandmother and about to pray with her. Her eyes were filled with tears. I looked back at the Grandmother. She looked at me and said, "Lord, I thank you for who you are and how good you are and how good these people are." Then several soft exclamations of amen were heard throughout the room.

This special moment was coming to an end. People began to shuffle around a bit throughout the room. The camera crew left to go back to the signing room. Those who were crying collected themselves. I continued to hold onto the hand of this woman as I stood and helped her up from the couch. We smiled at each other, knowing this was a very good thing. Any preconceived fears or apprehensions she had were gone. Then she hugged me and with a smile from ear to ear she eagerly asked, "Can I get my picture taken with you?" We laughed and stood with arms around each other, smiling as the cameras flashed.

I walked the two of them to the door and again assured them that they would get all the prints they asked for. The feeling that this was truly a healing moment for the two of them and so many others was present in the air.

The faces of everyone in that room said it all. This was most definitely a powerful, healing moment. Every person around me stared blankly with a stunned expression. When people could bring themselves to speak, there were comments such as, "That was amazing." "I'm so glad they came." "Can you believe this power is happening again?" No one seemed to be able to speak more than one sentence at a time.

My heart and my head had been busy at work; now my physical self took charge. I turned back inside and realized how hungry I was. I had nothing to eat or drink since very early that morning, perhaps seven or eight hours ago, and I was beginning to feel it. It must have shown on my face because just then one of the EMTs approached me and said, "Here, you've been pretty busy for hours and must need this." He handed me a hot dog that he had gotten from the ambulance bay. It came from the food and drinks made available for all the people waiting in line. Oh man, that's right, I had hundreds of people waiting for me. I took two quick bites, handed the rest back to him and headed back to the signing room. It was a short walk down that hallway, but coming off the experience I just had, it was all the break I needed. You would think at this point I would be exhausted from lack of food and drained emotionally. But that experience rejuvenated me with such energy. In those few steps to the door my thoughts reflected on that amazing experience. Prior to today, this family, these two heartbroken souls, didn't open their doors to talk about this incident with anyone. Now here they were, drawn to this image by the power of its simple message. Overcoming fears, speaking through tears and seeking comfort through hugs and hands. How blessed I felt for everyone present, including myself, that we made that possible for them.

Ok, time to take those blessings and put them back to work. I re-entered the signing room. The same people I left standing were still there. I acknowledged them with a quick thank you for their patience and I took my seat. We all picked up right where we left off. I was greeting and signing prints again. The crowds, just like Murph said, kept coming. Several more hours passed with my attention focused on each of these special people. Then, unbelievably another EMT whispered to me that someone else was waiting to see me in the back room. "Sorry to interrupt, but we think you'll want to visit with them." No more information than that. As I got up to return to that same room as before, the waiting crowd was once again asked to be patient. I was led to the back room.

When I entered, there was a middle-aged couple waiting for me. From the clothes they were wearing, I determined they were English, not Amish. But to my surprise I was introduced to them as family members of one of the injured girls. Yes, one of the injured Amish girls who had been shot. We greeted each other in a friendly manner, calm hellos and handshakes. As they began to relay their story to me, my confusion over whether or not they were English or Amish was clarified. With tears streaming down her face this woman began to speak, "My husband (she touched the man next to her) was raised Amish. In his teens he decided to live an English life. I was raised English and we have been married for many years. All those years the Amish side of our family held to the tradition of having nothing to do with anyone who left the faith. For most all our lives they shunned us. We would try to visit and communicate but never could get through those centuries of tradition." She would pause periodically to wipe away tears and gently, lovingly, pull her husband close. He stood silent to this point. She continued, "But on the day of the shootings, when we heard what was happening we rushed to the scene and to their homes. This time was so difficult for them, for us all. We offered to do anything we could to help . . . drive them all to make hospital trips, help with household things, cook, whatever. His family (the husband's Amish relatives) agreed to accept our help. Since then we have been helping them nearly everyday. We see them, in their homes, take them to the hospital . . . " She paused to catch her breath and wipe more tears. This time it was the husband who reached out to hold and comfort her. "They've told us how grateful they are." She continued, "They even told us how from now on we are welcome in their home anytime. They want us all to be a family again." . . . Now a bit more animated, her hands shaking in front of me, expressing the importance of this point . . . "Do you know how long we have waited for that, to be a family again? How many years we've waited? This print of yours hangs in their home. It's become a symbol to them and to us of how kindness and compassion toward one another has brought us back together." Then she hugged me, crying and said, "We wanted to come here, meet you and thank you. And we'd like to get a few more prints for the family. One of these will definitely be hanging in our house."

What could I say to that? How do you respond to someone who tells you your actions have reunited their family? I took her hands in mine and shaking my head in approval told them both, "I'm so happy for you. That's so wonderful to hear. Thank you so much for sharing that with me." Then I reached out and shook his hand, "I wish you and your family only the best." Then for the first time he spoke. As his eyes filled with tears, still shaking my hand, he simply said, "Thank you for this . . . for all you're doing." I knew at that point that words were hard for him to find. Not to delay him in a position of feeling uncomfortable any longer, I got them the prints they wanted and we said our goodbyes.

The events of this day shed new light on how the tragedy affected so many people, so many families. In those few horrifying moments, October 2nd, families were split, broken, shattered. Now it was revealed that some families found ways of mending. They found ways to heal old wounds by assisting with the new ones.

It seemed this day was rolling on in such a fashion that just as things were calming down, another emotionally stirring episode came along. Once again, I was left to collect myself and get back to the people who had been waiting. I returned to the table and began signing and greeting. These people were wonderfully patient. They were here to show their support for the families and children. They were doing that in ways they weren't even aware of. They had no idea of what was going on through the door and in the next room. No idea how the families were reaching out and sharing their stories. Yet each time I was called away, these good people patiently waited. So as important and powerful as all my encounters with the family members were, now these people before were just as important. When at that table, they got my full attention.

Several more hours of signing and nearly an entire box of Sharpies later, I realized a change had taken place. The once sun-drenched, beautifully lit room I was sitting in, was now being lit only by the overhead lights. Accented by the rows of Christmas lights around each window. These are the windows that earlier that day presented the view of blue sky and fields. Now they were dark. More than eight hours had passed and I was still signing prints. The only breaks I had taken all day were the heartfelt encounters I described. The only food I had were the two bites of a hot dog. There simply was no time for anything else. The stream of people who came to the table was steady all day. Not one break in the line and I was focused on taking care of these amazing supporters of this message.

The end of the line did come. Casey and Murph, who had been there all day with me, told me this group was the last. Being every bit as important as the first group, I saw that each and every one of them was cared for. At this point my hands were shaky, my eyes a bit weary and my entire body was buzzing. I was exhausted, mentally and physically. I made the attempt to give of myself that day and I had. The last print of the day was now signed. As the final person left, the EMTs closed the door behind her. We were done. The few of us in the room at the time looked at each other and we knew we had done it again—the people showing up had done it again—this was a successful day. It was a great day for the power of kindness toward others.

Well, wouldn't you know it, just then the producer of the ABC documentary came into the room. He and the crew stayed there all day filming, making new friends and contacts and all throughout the day being amazed by what they were witnessing. He came over to me and said, "We'd like to interview you now. One on one, in front of the camera. Do some questions and answers." When he said that, I believe you could hear a collective gasp of disbelief from everyone who was within earshot. After such an emotionally powerful day, with virtually no food or drink, while greeting thousands of people until well after the sunset, I was beat. "Now?" I asked him. His reasoning was, "Well we're headed to New York from here and would really like to get you on film before we go." "Ok, sure," I told him. "But I need a few minutes." "Of course! Take as much time as you need." He understood.

So a few quiet minutes is what I was looking for. A bit of time to settle down and collect my thoughts. Get something to drink and just generally relax, even if only for a minute or two. Each room I went into had people still in it. They were all hustling about, cleaning up and sharing the day's stories. Even outside there were things still happening. All wonderful things. But just then I needed quiet down time, only a minute or two is what I was looking for. The only room I could find to be quiet and alone was . . . yep, the men's room. I went in, closed and locked the door behind me. I threw some water on my face and stood, leaning with both hands on the sink. Eyes closed, I thought of what a tremendous day it had been and I was thankful for every minute of it. This was powerful stuff happening. I knew it. I wanted to share these experiences with someone who would appreciate the significance of such a day while it was still happening. I grabbed my cell phone and called my nephew Stefan. Today was the day he was making the prints available online. So he was very connected to this day, even though he wasn't here. One ring, two, three and then his voice mail. You always get Stefan's voice mail. He never picks up. I left him a quick message about what was happening. I spoke very quietly. If anyone standing outside heard me, they might think I had lost it, talking to myself in the men's room. More water on my face and neck, a deep breath and I was ready. I was about to go out there, exhausted, drained mentally, emotionally and physically. I was going to give from the only tank that doesn't empty. This would all come from the heart.

As I walked into the room where I had been signing prints all day, I saw it was being changed. Some of the tables had been taken down. There were a few chairs along the wall and the camera crew was busy at work transforming it into a studio set. Large light boxes on tripod stands and reflector cards were positioned around the camera. In the middle of the room sat two solitary chairs. One was closer to the camera and one sat a few feet away, surrounded by the lights. I suspected that was the chair for me. A few feet behind my chair was the original painting of *Kindness and Compassion*. It rested on an easel in front of the cinder block wall and was lit by its own set of lights.

Little time was wasted. As I walked in, the producer asked me if I was ready. I simply smiled, glanced at the few people in the room and nodded, "Sure, I'm ready. Let's do this." I wanted to give the best account of whatever was asked of me. I wasn't nervous at all. I just wanted to be honest, accurate and sincere all the while feeling so drained from the day that I might fall out of that chair.

From where I sat, all I could see now were the bright lights pointed directly in my face. Their brilliance was intense. The rest of the room seemed to go dark. I couldn't even see the producer, sitting just a few feet in front of me. He asked if I could hear him ok and if I was comfortable. "Yep I can hear you. I just can't really see you."

"That's ok, it's you that we have on camera, not me." The soundman did a few sound level checks. The cameraman double-checked angles and lighting and all the while I heard the producer flipping the pages on his clipboard. Reviewing questions, I presumed. After all the checks were complete and the producer okayed them with his crew, we began. For the next half hour or so, it would be the producer and I talking. I thought of it as just that, talking, he and I talking.

He started by stating for the camera who I was, where we were, all the basic facts. Then he asked questions. I'm not going to try and recap for you word for word what was said. I was so tired at the time and really doubt I could remember all that. His questions were along the lines of this: So Bruce you painted this image of an Amish school bell. Can you tell us about how you came to do that? And now there's a message associated with it, tell us about that. I understand you had some surprising visitors at both the print signings, tell us more about that . . . and how about your visits to the homes of the Amish, what was that like? You met the girls who were injured, how are they doing? Do you think this incident will separate our two communities (Amish and English) further?

With each question I remained calm and focused. I sat staring into the near blinding light, unable to see much else around me and spoke from the heart. I started by explaining, as I had so many times before, how this image was in no way intended to be commemorative of that tragic day. Rather it symbolized all the kindness, compassion and forgiveness that followed. Then I gave an account of how I came to be painting this image and found a way to make beneficial use of it. Discussed the first print signing, the visits to the Amish households, my experiences of meeting the children and gave a brief update on their conditions. I spoke of how the first responders took to the image and its message, the public's reactions and requests, the need for a second signing, meeting members of the Robert's family, and told him that now these prints were available around the world.

The question that seemed to stand out to me as most interesting was this. He asked how this tragic incident might affect the relationship between the Amish and the English. That's a fair question, I thought. But somehow it seemed so "English" in its nature, if you know what I mean. Almost like, "How do we look to them now? Are we acceptable to them? Will things be ok between us? It seemed to imply concerns like that." The question seems to convey being consumed with one's own image. In comparison to what perhaps an Amish viewpoint might be, perhaps more like this, "How do I look in God's eyes now? Am I acceptable to him? Will things be ok between God and I?" Do you see the difference? I had come to realize that, as important as human relationships are to each other, one's own personal relationship with God is what all other relationships are built on.

I answered by saying something to the effect of, "There has always been a wall between us, the Amish and the English. Most of it was built by not understanding one another. This incident has actually drawn our two communities closer together. Through the expressions of kindness to these victims by millions of English around the world, that wall is coming down. We have found that we have something in common.

That being, we care for each other. It's my hope that this close-ness continues to grow. From the discussions and experiences I have had with the Amish, I believe it's their hope too."

There was a brief pause, and then from the darkness, I heard the producer say, "That should do it. I think we're finished." He leaned forward in his chair and stepped toward me, into the light. With his hand extended to shaking mine he said, "Thank you. We've got what we need." The soundman asked a favor from everyone in the room. He needed to record a moment of complete silence. Everyone was asked to sit very still, not move and say nothing. This was a technical process that would later be used to filter out background noise. But for all of us in that room, it was more than that. For that one moment, everyone within earshot of that request was motionless and silent. We were quietly present in the moment, to contemplate what we had just been through. It had been a day so powerful, healing and moving for so many people. If no one else was feeling this, for me at least, this was a moment of reflection. But I think we were all there together—present in that moment.

"Ok, I got it," was the comment from the soundman that ended the silence. With that the camera lights were turned off. My eyes adjusted for a second and then I saw something I didn't expect. During this half hour of taping, the room had been filling up with EMTs and the WIOV personnel. The walls around me were lined with people. As I rubbed my now sore neck and shoulders I looked around. All of them seemed very contemplative and quiet. Some of them were crying, men and women. What was wrong? I thought. Then Murph came over to me and putting his hand on my shoulder said, "You have no idea how many home runs you hit here today. That was amaz-ing." Then he said something to me that he said after the first signing. "This isn't over."

Those who were watching and listening began to approach me with well wishes, handshakes and thanks. The hugs came through both smiles and tears. The remainder of my time at the station that evening passed quickly. Everyone was busy cleaning up. The ABC crew was packing in a hurry to make their three-hour drive to New York. I had some help gathering up what prints were left over and loading them in the car. The final farewells were exchanged. So much had happened that day. It was difficult to find additional words as we parted ways. I walked outside into the darkness. The sun had set hours ago. The end to yet another amazing day was at hand.

I pulled out of the now empty parking lot and found my way down the back road that brought me here that morning. I had about forty minutes till I would be home. It didn't take very long before realizing my body was still buzzing from the emotionally stirring events of the day and my lack of food and drink. So, only several miles down the road, I pulled into a diner parking lot for a cup of coffee. I got my coffee and a chocolate chip cookie. Not the most nutritious thing, but treating myself with something sweet seemed just fine. As cozy and homey as this place was, sitting inside is not what I needed. Instead I went outside and leaning against my truck, in the dark, with the air chilled by the season, under the star-filled sky, in the surroundings of the quiet countryside, alone, I sipped the hot coffee and reflected on the day.

It had been a very good day.

CHAPTER 7

An Unforgettable Lunch

ANY PEOPLE HAVE asked me how this journey and how these experiences have changed (and continue to change) my life. It seems impossible for me to think that anyone could be thrust into such a diversion from ones own "normal" life and not be affected by it all. No mater how large or small, each experience we have changes and molds who we are. The following saying has always been special to me and it certainly applies to this circumstance: "The same man cannot step into the same river twice." Do you understand why? You see, it's not just about the man changing, each time he returns to the river. The river changes too. Life is in motion. Not just our individual lives but all of life is in motion. Life is always changing and you are part of life. You and I are not outsiders looking in at life as it unfolds. We are in the midst of it. We are integral players in the event. We are part of this unfolding event around us and we are continually in a state of change. And this is important—through our actions we are also effecting that change—and we are affecting those we encounter.

So yes, certainly this journey has affected me. I experienced times of extreme sadness for all those involved. There were times that surprised me, with the unusual and unexpected turns of events, perpetuating the next step. I have been amazed in the moments filled with grace, when the appropriate words were found. And of course there were the stirring times of witnessing the compassionate side of humanity, as well as the darkest possible side. All these experiences and so many more came without planning or notice. Through it all, I kept my focus and continually attempted to reflect and support the positive elements of the human spirit. I was simply reflecting back the kindness expressed by others. Many times people have told me that in doing so, I was expressing kindness myself. It is in this respect that it didn't change me. The aspect of knowing and believing that kindness and compassion are something that we are all capable of has always been a part of me. This is an aspect of humanity that I have always believed is within each of us. We are all connected in this life. Responding compassionately to one another is the most humane thing we can do. It is a choice. By making that choice we become more fully human and more connected to one another. So as this journey moved forward I was witnessing the manifestation of the compassion I believed to always be within us all. That manifestation alone was awe-inspiring.

What was ahead for this image, this message, and me was of course unknown. I was prepared to accept what came along and go where it led me. There were positive forces at work here. I knew it. I felt it and I still do. So as you read these life-changing, awesome experiences still to come, know that at this point I was settled into the center of accepting it all, unselfishly, nonjudgmentally and without regard to any personal benefit. The spiritual enrichment and personal fulfillment of seeing this message help others was reward enough. I was giving myself the permission to allow this positive force to utilize me for a greater good.

For the next week or so Stefan and I spoke or e-mailed often. He had posted all the new information regarding *Kindness and Compassion* on my website. He made it go live on the day of the signing. We were checking to make sure all the links worked and type was positioned correctly, things like that. It quickly became apparent that it was working properly. I started receiving e-mails from people who read it. Stefan's help was such a blessing. Thank God the site worked properly, because now there were TV and radio news broadcasts which were giving out the site address. They were telling people that it was the outlet for receiving the prints. People were asked, on the site, to utilize the postal mail by sending me their information and then in return I would mail them a print. E-mails thanking me for making these available came in almost immediately. Of course, the postal mail requests lagged a few days behind. But they most certainly did come. It was now mid December and many people were requesting prints to give as Christmas gifts. People loved the idea of giving a gift with such a powerful message of kindness. I had no idea that people would embrace this image and message so endearingly. So many times I was touched by the requests and comments. Many people would write or call, asking if they could stop by and pick theirs up in person, suggesting that it would save on postage. They would drop by and pick up anywhere from one to twenty prints at a time.

I can't begin to tell you how many times people, friends, loved ones or total strangers would come by the house for prints. This is the place where I live and work, alone. Having so many people in my home, so frequently, was something I wasn't use to. I always thought of myself, and where I lived and worked, as being under the radar. This was the place where the magic of painting happened, for a sometimes struggling yet somewhat successful artist. My work was shown and sold across the country. Yet very few people in this town even knew of what I did, because I didn't exhibit in this area. I liked the quiet. Now I was having person after person in my living room. We would share stories of that tragic day. They wanted to know how the children and families were doing. Most every one of them was in tears, hugging me and thanking me for this gesture before leaving me once again in the quiet of my home.

These were indeed moving times for me. The outpouring of compassion for these victims and thankfulness for this message was very touching. Never did I feel bothered, or that my privacy was being interrupted. I welcomed them all. In fact, I was empowered by the compassion expressed by these people. It was confirmation that this message had meaning.

At this point the majority of media publicity for these prints was only happening within the state. But in this world of fast-moving technology and speed of light transfer of information, the message spread quickly. Requests came in from various organizations asking if they could put a link to my site on their own. People wanted to help spread the message. They wanted to be part of the positive movement that was looking for better times coming out of this tragedy. I was more than willing to oblige. Requests came from schools, personal blogs, art communities and others. I was thrilled with all of the requests but perhaps the ones I was most proud to be linked to were those that came from first responders: ambulance, emergency rescue and fire department crews. It was an honor that they would ask to link to my site.

The requests for prints became more varied everyday. People involved in organizations and humanitarian causes were asking for donated prints. They wanted to auction them off in the hopes of raising money and awareness for their organization. Associating with this message of kindness toward others was appealing to so many. I even heard that prints were being given out as awards to individuals who expressed exemplary actions in their field. One of its most inspirational uses was hearing that the highest ranking officer in the Pennsylvania State Police force was to receive one. He was the national law enforcement spokesperson for this tragedy. He was the officer you saw on every TV news broadcast, giving the up-to-date reports on the investigation status. His reports started the day of the shooting and lasted for numerous subsequent days. The print, as an award, was given to him for his admirable handling of such a difficult situation. Can you just imagine how wonderful that made me feel? I had no idea this message and image would be reaching so many people so quickly. With every new day came a reinforcement that my course of action, in following this journey, was one to pursue.

One evening while talking on the phone with my brother Dennis, that's Stefan's father, he was recognizing the power of this message and made a suggestion. He said, "I think you should send one of the prints to the president. Who better than the leader of the free world to receive a message of responding with kindness toward others." My first response and thought were something like, "No way. Come on, the president?" Dennis was the first born in my family of nine brothers and sisters. He's quite an intelligent man. I mentioned earlier on that he and his wife of 40 years, Paula, had started and successfully ran the nation's (and perhaps the world's) most influential speech training company. It's true. They are constantly being asked to travel the world, assisting people in their communicating abilities. They work with the highest-ranking political leaders of the world and the largest and most influential heads of companies. Their list of clients reads like a who's who of the world. They even teach the Harvard professors how to teach. So, aside from listening to him because he's my older, caring brother, I have always appreciated their opinions on business matters as well. I love and respect them both. I told him I would consider his suggestion. That night as I turned in to bed I still wasn't too sure about the idea. But it was rewarding somehow for him to even suggest such a thing. For days I was fielding calls from strangers all across the country, which were all wonderful in their own way. But it was comforting somehow to talk about all this with family.

Well, if you haven't been noticing by now how my life and this journey have a way of letting me know what I should do next, this is another example. The very next morning I woke to a phone call from a woman in Washington, yes D.C. She was a government worker who heard about the print and the message. She was requesting several prints for herself and co-workers. To say the least I was a bit taken back by the "coincidence" of hearing from someone in Washington. As if that wasn't enough. That day I received a call from a congressman's office in the House of Representatives. He heard of my work and what I was doing. Because of this I was being asked to judge a Congressional Art Exhibit. Okay, those were enough connections to government, to make me put together a packet to send to the White House. I drafted a letter and together with a printout of text, that tells how the painting came to be (that goes out with all the prints) I prepared it for shipping. I didn't want there to be any mistake in shipping. So, I called the White House directly to get the proper mailing address. That day it went out as an overnight delivery. Yes, I agreed with Dennis, the leader of the free world was exactly the person who should hear a message like this.

No I won't make you wait to find out if I got a response. I most certainly did. It was less than two weeks when a package arrived for me. It was a very plain, brown, nine by twelve envelope. It was labeled very conservatively: My address was in the center and in the upper left-hand corner it simply said, The White House, Washington, D.C. I held it in my hands for a few minutes, wondering what I might find inside. From the feel of it I could tell it was being kept flat by something stiff, perhaps cardboard protecting a letter. I never expected to receive a response, but here I was about to open this package. Carefully I opened the sealed end and pulled out the contents. There were two sheets of cardboard, as I suspected. From in between I removed a letter and began to read. It was from the president. He was thanking me for the print and my actions taken to pay tribute to the victims of the shootings. He told me how he and Laura were so saddened by the event and prayed daily for all those involved. It also had the presidential seal and his signature. Now my print and the message it carried were in The White House. Who would have thought this would happen? Not me. Thanks for the suggestion Dennis.

It was about this time that I received an invitation to a Christmas party. Dr. Kirchner, the Lancaster County Coroner I spoke of earlier, invited me to his home. Every year he hosted a Christmas party and invited all of the deputy coroners and some first responders. He was asking me to attend and additionally requesting that I bring prints for those who had not yet received them. I gratefully accepted. Several deputies told me that his parties were a great time: Terrific food, friendly people and his Christmas light display was one of the best. The display was so elaborate that looking for the lights was the last step in the directions to finding his house. They were right about all of it. The lights were beautiful. The people were friendly and the food delicious. Dr. Kirchner and his wife were the perfect host and hostess. That night I saw to it that every coroner and responder present was given a print. I suppose I handed out about twenty or so that night. Of course we all shared stories about the day of the shootings and the weeks that followed. Everyone was grateful for how I recognized and expressed the positive elements in such a tragedy. Throughout the evening we appreciated each other's company and enjoyed the holiday season.

I left the party earlier than most because I had another stop to make that night. WIOV was having a party also. It was being held nearby at a local country music dance club. By the time I got there things were well under way. Two nationally popular bands were performing and the crowds were really enjoying themselves. People were everywhere, singing, dancing, and enjoying a good time. Casey and Murph had instructed me to tell the people at the door who I was and they would let me in. You see, it was a private party and you had to have tickets. They also told me, that once I was in to find my way to the VIP area and join them. I had never been to this place before. As I made my way inside I found typical club scene surroundings: Dim lighting and lots of people drinking and having a good time. The band was blasting out their popular songs and latest hits. Everyone was familiar with them from the radio. For those of you who have never been to a country-dance club, let me tell you, they do have one difference from other dance clubs. The people are actually friendly and it is not the pick up bar scene, as in other clubs. People come here to have a good time and they do. That was the atmosphere here tonight.

So I found my way to the VIP area. It was a large room off to the side of the stage. It had a private bar and tables. It was much quieter and considerably less crowded than the main area. Casey saw me as I entered. She was immediately up from her table to greet me with a smile and a hug. Kym, Paul and Kym's daughter, who had recently had a new baby, were there too. It was great to have us all together. We laughed, talked and had a few drinks. We enjoyed the music and each other's company. When the band finished playing they joined us backstage. The first band had already been hanging out with us having a good time. Now more performers surrounded us.

With the performances over, the crowd was given a chance to come backstage and have their picture taken with the bands. This was to happen in the room we had been in all night. A long line formed at the entrance to the room. People were anxiously waiting their turn to enter, have their photo taken and get an autograph. Our table was positioned in such a spot that as the people came into the room they walked right passed us. To my surprise and the surprise of everyone at the table, as these fans of the band came through many of them recognized me. They were asking me to be in the photo with them and the band. Time and time again I was up in front of the camera with the band and total strangers having my picture taken. The band members actually began to get a bit upset. They gave me looks as if to say, "Who is this guy? Why does he keep getting in the shot?" When I had a chance, after the photo sessions were over, I explained the situation about the shootings and how all these people knew me. By the time I was through explaining, all the band members were asking me for my autograph and signed prints. Some of the band members even gave me their e-mail addresses to be added to my mailing list. Now that was a turn of events I didn't expect.

Not long after that I called it a night and made my way into the cold December air to head home. I still have the pictures from that night. It was a night of fun memories with new friends.

There was an interesting topic discussed that night. Kym told me about the Bart Township Fire Company event that was going to be held this weekend. It was called The Tree of Love. They were welcoming anyone from the community to come to the firehouse and help decorate a special Christmas tree. When decorated, this tree was going to be given to The Roberts family, the family of the gunman. These caring folks wanted to be sure that his widow and her children had a merry Christmas. They were hoping that people would decorate the tree with gift cards and special ornaments. In its continuing manner of caring for each other, this community had found another way to express its kindness. They knew this family was suffering in its uniquely own way and they were reaching out yet another compassionate hand. This was a beautiful idea. Kym wanted to make sure I knew of it and attended. She said she would be there and perhaps we could go together. Thinking this was an incredible gesture by the community, I certainly wanted to go. So, we planned on meeting at the firehouse. This had been a good night in many ways.

The tree ceremony was only two days away. I wanted my ornament to have special meaning. But what would it be? No,

I didn't have to give it much thought at all. I knew right away what it would be. A bell. I wanted to hang a small white bell on that Tree of Love. From store to store I drove looking for the appropriate bell. You would think just days before Christmas that this would be an easy find. No way. There were red bells, brass bells, and leather straps filled with jingle bells, bells with flashing lights and those that played music. You name it I found it. But there were no white bells. Then I came upon this idea: If not for Christmas, when else might someone use a white bell? A wedding. That was the answer. I found small white bells among wedding decorations. They were even shaped like the ones in my painting. It seemed ironic that the bell I would give as an ornament was found among items for a wedding, considering that it would be going to a woman who just lost her husband. Now its symbolism of compassion would take on new meaning. Since it was the only store in which I found them, I bought an entire box, maybe twenty or so. Back at home I tied a simple ribbon on one, from which it would hang. Now I was ready.

Two days passed quickly and the day of the ceremony arrived. Kym and I were going to meet there about noon. That morning I got a phone call from Kym. She called me with news that hit me out of the blue. Kym knew how the message associated with my prints was meant for everyone, including the Robert's family. She and I had been trying to reach Marie (the gunman's widow) unsuccessfully for weeks. Marie still had not spoken to any media and remained very private. Kym persisted in trying to call her and this morning finally got through. When she did they discussed the tree ceremony and the prints. Marie knew of the ceremony but would not be attending because she was still not talking to anyone, especially the media. Kym told Marie how the offer of these prints was extended to her family. If she cared to have any, the day of the tree ceremony might be an appropriate time. I would be right there in the area and could bring some with me. Then Kym gave me news

I never expected to hear. She told me that Marie was interested in the prints and was inviting Kym and I to visit with her in her home. I often pace through the house when talking on the phone. But I remember just then, standing motionless in the middle of my living room and listening in near disbelief. This message of kindness had touched Marie in such a way that she was inviting Kym and I to visit with her and deliver prints. To this point Marie had spoken to virtually no one and now she was opening her doors to us.

What a unique opportunity to be able to deliver this print and its message. Sure everyone, especially in the English world, almost expected this message to reach the Amish victims and their families. But this woman was a victim also. She did not perform this horrid act. She was left with the task of picking up the pieces of her family and carrying on. She, just as much as the others involved, needed to feel this compassion.

"Kym," I said, " . . . thank you. That is incredible." Then I asked, just to be certain I heard correctly, I needed to actually say the words, "She wants to meet with us at her house?" "Yes, so bring extra prints. We're to be there at 2:00," came the response. I could hear in Kym's voice that she too knew this was special. Not much more was said. What could we say? This news came very suddenly but we both knew it was a good thing.

After hanging up the phone, I gathered some prints and packaged them for travel. Then I located a framed print I had been holding onto for weeks. This was one I had framed specifically for Marie and her family. I had it framed knowing this message was for them also. It was done in the hopes that some day it would find its way to her. Well that day had just arrived and to my complete surprise I would be delivering it to her myself. Just as I had gone to meet with the Amish families in their homes, now I was going to visit with Marie.

Having all I needed gathered together, I headed to the tree ceremony. After the thirty-minute drive I arrived at the fire company. In the parking lot were maybe a dozen cars and several Amish horse-drawn buggies. The atmosphere inside the fire hall was quite calm. The large hall had a few dozen people, English and Amish, milling around enjoying the hot chocolate and treats. The tree was positioned near the center of the otherwise mainly empty hall. On the tree hung some of the first decorations. It was still early in the day and I expected more were going to show up. It didn't take long to find Kym. She arrived before me and already placed her ornament on the tree. Within minutes of my arrival newscasters from several TV stations were on the scene. Word began to spread among us, that nearly a hundred motorcycles were on their way. The riders had banded together in support of this cause. They were making the ride from a nearby town. They were close and would be pulling up any minute. Most everyone went outside to greet them. What a scene that was. A hundred motorcycles roaring down the small roads of this always quiet, Amish community. They rolled into the parking lot and filled the normally empty space with noise and the glare of shining chrome. One by one they parked near the buggies, removed helmets, gloves and cold riding gear. Although it was a beautiful sunny day, the temperature was only in the forties. A cold day to be riding. But these men and women braved the weather to be a part of this ceremony. Once they got inside the atmosphere in that hall changed drastically. It was wonderful to see all the bikers and Amish mingling together. Between the clothes of the Amish and the leather of the bikers, there was black everywhere. Smiles and handshakes were exchanged throughout the crowd. Both Amish and English bikers encountered each other with amazement, curiosity and friendship. It was a wonderful sight.

Now the tree was beginning to fill up with gift cards and ornaments, as even more people were showing up. I made my way to the tree to hang my ornament. As I quietly did so, the gesture was seen by some of the news reporters. They approached me with cameras and microphones. Their cameras took pictures of me hanging my bell as they asked me questions: "You're Bruce Becker, the painter of the Amish school bell? Can you tell us about your ornament? What are your thoughts on this community event?" I had no problem answering their questions. This was a loving caring event. Being associated with it was a joy. But it was not my event and I wanted credit to be given were it was due. So within my answers I was certain to tell them how wonderful it was that the Bart Fire Company was doing this.

Then they asked a few very timely questions. Questions I knew I had the answers to that perhaps others didn't: "We know you met with the Amish families, have you met with the Roberts' family? Do you think Marie Roberts will show up here today?" Wanting to respect Marie's privacy, I was careful with my answers. I told them that Marie would not be showing up here today. But rather I would be meeting with her privately and if she had a statement I would be happy to pass it on. Well, this peaked their interest. They asked to get film footage of me holding my bell tree ornament, film of the *Kindness and Compassion* print and then came more questions. Off camera they asked if I would return from my meeting and talk with them again. These were some of the many reporters who tried unsuccessfully, to interview Marie for weeks. But over those weeks these reporters had been interviewing me at the print signings, in my home and in my studio. From the discussions we had, they knew I was not going to exploit Marie or anyone associated with this tragedy. So I calmly told them, "I'll come back after I meet with her. If she has a statement she wants me to share I'll let you know." I couldn't promise anymore than that.

As much as I was engulfed in the atmosphere of giving at this ceremony and enjoying the interactions between the Amish and the bikers, it was time for Kym and I to leave. There was an important meeting awaiting us. Kym knew where the Roberts' house was so she drove. It turns out that her house was so close to the fire company we easily could have walked. Pulling into the driveway, I recognized the house from the few TV news reports I had seen. There it was, the familiar Jeep parked in the driveway. That seemed to be in every TV news photo of her home. There was the front porch, which was shown in the telecasts time and time again. Marie lived on the same street used by the Amish buggies during their funeral processions. Those buggies made their way directly past the Roberts' home. This is a very small town. Smaller than you may be imagining. The number of roads that cross through the entire town is maybe six or eight. The number of streets here is very limited. So to take another route for the funeral would have put those buggies far out of their way. As we stopped the car, I was wondering how Marie handled that day, having to watch that sad procession go past her home.

When the car was parked I collected the prints, framed and unframed. Kym asked, "You ready?" I nodded my head and simply said, "Yep." With that we got out of the car and were headed for the front door. We barely had a chance to knock when Marie greeted us. I had been wondering just what state of mind this woman would be in. Would she be full of grief and sadness? Tearful and weepy? Would she be prone to anger toward her husband due to his actions and would we inadvertently receive the brunt of that? Would her actions be edgy and erratic, perhaps not sure how to act with strangers in her house? And what about the children, would they be home? All these questions and more were about to be answered.

The door opened and a woman much younger than I expected greeted us. Perhaps around 30 years old, tall, thin, long dark hair and beaming with a smile. In a very friendly voice she welcomed us, "Hi you guys. Thanks for coming." As she gestured for us to come in, Kym and I were stating our greetings, "Hi Marie. Nice of you to invite us over." We made our way inside. The house was much like that of any couple with young children. Marie was English, not Amish, so the house had all the amenities you or I might have. There were some toys scattered about the house. I saw pictures on the walls depicting family memories. Mail on the kitchen counter. Exercise equipment in one corner and all the furnishings and appliances you might expect in any home.

She asked us to sit. So we all gathered in what seemed to be the TV room. Marie and I sat on the couch across from Kym, who was in a separate chair. There was a coffee table between us. That's where I placed the prints. Marie was smiling and full of energy. The discussion between us all began as comfortably as though we had been friends for a long time. At first, we talked about the tree ceremony. Kym and I described the scene there, telling her about the bikers and Amish, the size of the tree and the many gifts that were already accumulating. She was so thankful for all the community was doing for her. She jokingly said that she hoped the tree would fit in her house. All she was asked to do was decide where she wanted her Christmas tree and make plenty of room. The fire company crew would be bringing it by later that day. She wasn't told how big it was. When we arrived, she had been moving furniture, hoping she made enough room.

When the topic of the prints came up, I presented her with one that I had framed. I was sure to tell her, how the Amish families wanted her to know this message of kindness was extended to her and her family. I offered her as many prints as she'd like. She was thankful for the offer and requested several more for family members and gratefully accepted the framed one. We also discussed how she was doing, how she was handling all this. She told us, "Had it not been for the outpouring of kindness from the community, I don't know how I would have been able to get through it all." She grew up in this area, knew the people and was so grateful for how nice they had all been to her. A tragedy of this magnitude can be enough to cause a person to pick up and move away. If for no other reason, just to escape the uncertainty of dealing with unfriendly neighbors or a potential lynch mob mentality in a community. But reactions weren't like that from this community. It was their warmth and kindness that kept her from needing to move. Actually she said she couldn't imagine how difficult this would have been if she lived somewhere else.

Then she began to share with us the specifics of that terrible day and the following weeks. I had heard from so many involved that day: the Amish, the State Troopers, EMTs, Coroners and so many others. Now I was about to hear what the gunman's widow went through. She was going to share her personal experiences. Momentarily I couldn't help but think, "How did I get here? I'm sitting in the home of the gunman, surrounded by his things, talking to his widow, with his children playing in the next room. This is incredible." But I knew it was the message that brought me here. I was here because of *Kindness and Compassion*.

All the people involved in this tragedy and now Marie were being drawn to me and I to them. Drawn together by the message of kindness. As tragic as that event was, it was this positive repercussion from it all, in which we were finding peace.

Just as she started in with her story of that day, telling us about the phone call Charlie (her husband) made to her while he was inside the schoolhouse, she realized the amount of time we had left to spend with each other would not be enough. People from the fire company would be coming by to help prepare her home for the tree. These were stories she did not want to rush through. So, she made the suggestion and requested we all meet for lunch to talk further. Kym and I were both willing. Marie checked her schedule and it was decided that we would meet two days later. There and then we would have the time to talk, without interruption.

Before leaving I talked to her about the reporters at the tree ceremony. She confirmed my belief that she was not attending because of the media. She had not spoken to them and had no intention of doing so. I asked if she had a statement she would like me to make on her behalf. She told me, "Tell them how grateful I am to the community for all the support and kindness they have shown me."

Think about that for a minute, here I am, an artist who simply painted this Amish bell and attached this message of kindness to it. Now through the power of that image, I am in the home of the gunman and after spending less than half an hour with his widow, she is asking me to make her only statement to the media. This day was another extraordinary day on the journey of this message. And considering the invitation to lunch I just received, this journey shows no sign of stopping.

Marie had not been anything like I imagined she would be. She was gracious, grateful to the neighbors and community around her, upbeat and had a positive attitude. Considering what she was going through many people would have folded into themselves. Perhaps feeling overwhelmed by self-pity, or suffering great anguish from what her loved one had done. But she was strong in her faith and already looking to the future. I was glad to have met her and I was looking forward to continuing our discussion at lunch.

Kym and I said our goodbyes. And with her smile, the one she had shown us throughout much of our visit, Marie thanked us for coming.

With the benefit of now being able to look back on it all, I am amazed at how easily I accepted this role. While those around me watched in disbelief what I was going through, none of this even fazed me. To me, the flow of kindness seemed a very natural thing. People often talk to me about the light and shadows in my paintings. The importance I gave to both of them. Light and shadow are everything to me, in my work. In fact, I have often said to my students, "When you're painting within the shadows, that's when you're truly painting. Find the hidden light within them. Bring out the hidden color. That will make your painting great." Now that seemed to be a metaphor for my life. This kindness that was not at first apparent in the shadows of such a tragedy, now shone like a light, beaming areas of new vision into the darkness. As it reached each person, it was as if, now they could see things that before were hidden within the shadows—things that gave them hope and strength.

Kym and I went back to the fire company and tree ceremony. At this point in the day most of the people were gone, including the bikers. The parking lot that was full of motorcycles when we left was now all but empty. Inside reporters were waiting for our arrival. They asked if there was a statement from Marie and would I mind being interviewed again. Of course I didn't mind. I half expected it at this point. So with cameras pointed and microphones in hand they asked how the meeting went. The specifics of my conversation with Marie I kept to myself. I told them she was holding up very well and gave them her statement. They asked a few of the questions they had earlier about the print about the tree ceremony and such. I answered them all and stood for pictures by the tree.

What Kym and I had set out to do with the day had all come to pass. In fact, more had happened than we expected. Both of us were still quite surprised at Marie's willingness to talk with us. We knew the lunch meeting would be here in what seemed like no time. So with very few words and both of us feeling good about the day we went our separate ways.

The following day was a Sunday. I decided to do very little that day. Perhaps take a day to just relax. I knew I had a speaking engagement on the coming Tuesday at a nearby high school. It was a mentoring type presentation. I would talk to the kids about what life is like as a full-time working artist. The usual talk I gave for this purpose was changing drastically due to the events of the past few months. So part of the day was set aside to prepare a few things. I decided which paintings I would show the kids as examples of my work and reviewed and adjusted what I would talk about. *Kindness and Compassion* was now high on that list.

That Sunday did come and go quite quickly. Of course there were many times when my thoughts would jump forward, wondering what the coming day would bring. But I know better than that. This journey was unfolding one day, one hour, one minute at a time. There was no way of anticipating what was to come. Only the hope that I would be courageous enough to meet any challenge presented, open enough to the guidance of navigating through it and strong enough to speak and act in a manner befitting this message.

Monday was here, the day of our lunch meeting. Just as Kym and I thought would happen, this day had arrived in the blink of an eye. We were meeting Marie at a family style restaurant in the Paradise area. Kym gave me directions because this was a restaurant I had never been to.

As I drove there my thoughts were varied. Would this be a place Marie went to often enough that people would recognize her? Would the people there recognize me? If so what kind of reaction would we get? What would I say to her? If she broke down emotionally how would I handle that? How does one begin a discussion such as we were about to have? This meeting would be different from that of meeting the Amish families. Their sadness was expected, due to the loss or injuries suffered by their children. This was different. It was her husband who was the cause of their loss. It was through his hands that this terrible incident was perpetuated. Those were the same hands that held Marie's for so many years and without warning were turned against these innocent children. How do you console someone put in that position?

Just before pulling into the parking lot of the restaurant, that sense of calm and direction that had given me guidance all throughout this journey took over again. All those questions began to fade away. I realized that allowing my mind to try and anticipate a meeting such as this, so different from anything I had ever done, was foolish. What I needed to do was approach her with compassion and kindness. The two elements of humanity that had carried me this far would lead my way again. I had to remain focused on being compassionate and the words would come. I had to remain open to truly listening to and hearing her experiences. I had to approach this situation with an open heart and open mind. Then, if needed, the words would come. Once in the parking lot, I sat quiet in the car for a minute to clear my head. Then went inside.

The look of this place was much like a large family diner. It had an easygoing atmosphere where you would be comfortable taking your kids. You could be certain to get a good meal, at a good price. Nothing auspicious, just down-to-earth home cooking and service. There was a counter and stools directly ahead as I entered. Resting on the counter were some glass-covered sweets. Menus were kept standing up wedged between salt, pepper, sugar shakers and napkin holders. Tables and booths were off to either side of the counter. There was a salad bar in the far right corner. Some waitresses were busy caring for a few customers. Others were talking and going through their tips. I felt comfortable in restaurants like this. Remember my mom was a waitress for many years. I have wonderful, warm, childhood memories of sitting with her after school, enjoying burgers, fries and chocolate milk. Seeing those waitresses took my thoughts to mom. That was comforting.

Everyone else had arrived before me and they were waiting in a booth by the window. Paul, Kym's husband, had come with her. He's such a good guy. Friendly, outspoken and loves Kym with all his being. These are two of the many people I have met along the way that enrich my life by just knowing them. They were in a booth on one side of the table. Marie was sitting alone on the other side. I approached them with apologies for being a bit late. As I took my seat, next to Marie, a few joking comments were made about my tardiness. You might say, I've been known to be late a few times.

After the fun comments and greeting each other, we realized that we were all hungry. Ordering food should be the first thing we took care of. Between the days of visiting with the Amish and the print signings, Kym had seen me go beyond hunger to the point of having my hands shake and finding it hard to hold focus, more than once. Smiling and laughing she said, "Get this man some food. I've seen him go without eating too many times and we don't need that to happen here. We're in a restaurant for God sakes." It was nice this meeting was starting off with everyone so relaxed. So we ordered and made our way to the salad bar.

My memories of this lunch are mostly of Marie talking while we listened. I won't even try to quote her. But rather give you an indication of what was said. As we ate, we began talking about how Marie was holding up and discussing the events of that awful day.

Once again, her personality was much like when I first met her, smiling, upbeat and positive. Not cheerful to the point of being forced, just sincere and genuinely personable. Discussing a topic that we all have in common can be a good icebreaker, in any group. Perhaps that's why the holidays are what we started with. Thanksgiving had recently passed and Christmas was just around the corner. The holidays can be tough enough for most families but Marie felt this one would be extremely hard on her children. To combat the difficulties for the kids, she decided to do something different for them. Something that would take their thoughts off the worries of the day, even if just for a short while. A good friend of hers, who had moved to France, had been asking them to come over for a visit. This past Thanksgiving was the holiday she chose to take her up on that offer. Marie and her three young ones, made the trip. She hoped being away in those entirely different surroundings would somehow make it easier on them. Not being around the house with all the reminders of their father being gone might be a welcome distraction. She was right. It went well. They had a very nice visit and welcomed the break from hounding media.

For Christmas they planned on taking another trip. Again feeling that a more traditional Christmas would be too hard on the children. Marie along with the kids and extended family, would head out of town. This time they decided on a Disney Cruise. This trip, like the Thanksgiving trip, would be a diversion from the difficult scene at home. It also would give the entire family time to bond and perhaps begin its healing process.

At first the idea of all this vacation type of travel seemed a bit odd to me. It wasn't the typical response to such a tragic event that I expected. I was beginning to realize just how much that sincerely positive person I perceived her to be was genuine. She was looking for positive pathways along this very difficult and rocky road. At one point I asked her about that positive attitude. I told her it was surprising and unexpected, given her situation. But refreshing to see her with such a good outlook. She said she had never been intimidated by what people thought of her, now or before the shootings. She commented that we all have a choice to be, or not to be, positive. She chooses to be positive, even in these tough times. It was sounding like her upbringing in these Amish surroundings had influenced her in a very healthy way. Her comments resonated with me. I had always felt similarly. Seeing beliefs in action, in such difficult times, was inspiring.

Marie grew up in this small town, where she now lives. She went to the school her children now attend. She knows

Bruce Becker
181

the way of life in these parts—a life of caring for one another, a life of forgiving. This was a life that inscribed on her heart the idea of trusting in God and your fellow man. A life of remaining positive even in the worst of times. She added again that it was the support of her community that was helping her get through this.

I remember telling Marie, not to feel pressured in any way to talk about anything she didn't want to. We all assured her how we understood this must be the most difficult time in her life and there would be no judgments passed here. We were here only to assist in any way we could. If talking is what she wanted to do fine. Or if she simply wanted to sit, eat and spend an afternoon with friendly quiet company that would be fine too. Paul and Kym were quick to concur with these comments and also reassured her of our sincere kindness.

Undoubtedly she felt very comfortable with us. She opened up and shared much more information. She spoke of Charlie as a father and husband, before the shootings. She told us he was a caring dad. One who was involved in his kids' activities. One activity for instance was how he and the two boys had gotten two broken-down jeeps, with the plan of disassembling them and rebuilding one good one. It seemed like forever that they worked on this project. But they did it. Even though, as Marie jokingly put it, "Charlie wasn't a mechanic. In fact, his tool box was so bare it probably consisted of a pry bar and a two by four." My thoughts went back to pulling up in her driveway and parking next to that same jeep. It suddenly took on new meaning.

She spoke of how he would play and work with the kids all day. He was so attentive to them. He was the one wanting to cut their meat at the dinner table. In many ways he was always there for them. He gave her no indication that such terrible actions were in store for that day, or that he was even capable of actions like that.

The only possible reason she could give to his actions was the comments he made in a note. A note he left behind for her (and one for each of his children) before setting out the morning of October 2nd. In it he spoke of his anger with God over the loss of their baby girl, some nine years previous. That newborn only lived for a very brief time. He harbored that anger. It festered inside him and now through his actions he was striking back at God himself. She wished he never had isolated himself in that misery and perhaps his dreadful actions would have never occurred.

When speaking of the day of the shootings, Marie mentioned how she was at home that morning and received a phone call from Charlie. He was calling from his cell phone, while inside the schoolhouse. As he spoke to her, she heard sirens in the background and simultaneously heard the same sirens in the neighborhood. She knew this meant trouble but had no idea how bad things were.

Once the police confirmed the identity of the man inside the schoolhouse, officers were sent to Marie's home. They arrived at both places, her home and the school, at about the same time. She spoke very highly of the officers, saying they were helpful and informative. With their help, within two hours of when this incident began, she had a few things packed and was heading out of town. She and the officers knew this small town was about to become a media nightmare and a horrific crime scene. Neither Marie nor her children needed to be exposed to that. She and the children headed for the home of an out-of-town relative, to seek refuge. With her car hidden in their garage, she stayed in hiding for days not wanting to be at the mercy of the media frenzy.

The kids were not permitted exposure to any radio or TV broadcasts. She wanted them to hear what happened from her. This was their father, not just a news topic. This would be devastating to them. So she fed them information in small amounts at a time. She started by telling them that a terrible thing had happened and daddy had died. I doubt you can even imagine how much more difficult it got for her to eventually tell them the rest of the tragic story. It took days of discussions through prayers and tears. I met her daughter, the day I was at her home. I'm guessing, but I would say she was about seven years old. About the same age of the girls in the school that day. "My God," I thought, as if what Charlie did wasn't bad enough, how could he have a daughter at home the same age of the girls he shot. It seems impossible to understand the internal struggle and turmoil he must have been going through that led him to commit these unspeakable acts.

Even being hidden away, at a relative's house in another town, reporters came looking for Marie. They were turned away and told they hadn't heard from her. When she did return home the pursuit by reporters continued. One reporter was so persistent Marie could no longer stand to have him continually calling the house, parking in front of her home, bothering family members and pumping them all for information. She called the police. They in turn called the reporter. They told him he would be picked up on charges of harassment if he didn't leave her alone. He finally did.

Only a very old photo of Marie had been issued to the press. So no one in the media or the general public outside of Nickel Mines really knew what she looked like. One day, while she was in the front yard, a reporter approached her. He asked if Marie Roberts was home and if he could speak with her. She looked at him squarely in the eye and said, "She has no comment," then walked inside the house. Because he didn't recognize her, that reporter had no idea that he had just received the only words she had spoken to the media. To this day she had retained that sense of privacy. How special it was that she had chosen to open up with us. I'm certain it was the kindness and compassion we offered that caused her to feel comfortable enough to share her private life.

While listening to her stories, each of us had long since finished our meals. More than two hours had passed and through it all Marie retained her positive attitude. She was not denying the horror of the actions taken that day. But in a similar way of thinking, like that of the Amish, she saw those actions were in the past. She was looking forward, to the future. Trying to find something positive to get her through it all, she saw the outpouring of compassion, kindness and forgiveness as manifestations of that goodness.

I suggested to her that she consider speaking to others. That she tell her story and convey her methods of dealing with such a tragic event. Only she would have her unique perspective on this tragedy. By speaking, she may continue to spread the attitude of looking for the positives in any negative situation. She agreed and thought perhaps she would do exactly that. She had been asked to attend some small gatherings and was considering it. Now she may view her role differently. Perhaps she could help others by telling them what she went through.

It was fascinating to sit next to Marie and hear her tell these stories. Stories that no one had heard before. This was insight to yet another person's life that was so closely and drastically touched by this terrible event. It was yet another day spent like no other in my life. The feeling at that table was truly one of kindness and concern for one another. True communication had happened here. There was perhaps a release for Marie, in allowing herself to talk about these events. Certainly she experienced acceptance, sympathy and understanding on the part of myself, Kym and Paul.

With the meal done and all of us a bit exhausted, from discussions of such emotional intensity, we had the sense that it was time for us to part ways. We exchanged some contact information, with the thought of perhaps staying in touch. Marie was hoping to hear from me in the next few days. I had told her of some writings I had been doing. They were being compiled for a future book. They are philosophical writings about life. This meeting enabled us to share many thoughts about life and approaches to it. So she was interested in reading what I had written.

After Paul picked up the check and insisted on paying—he's good that way—we all walked outside together. There were hugs, very meaningful well wishes and without much fanfare the lunch ended. These were good people and this was a lunch I would never forget.

I walked to my car realizing it was a beautiful day. The sun was shining and the temperature very warm for mid December. Heading directly home was not on my agenda. Christmas was around the corner and I was in the middle of Amish country. There was shopping to be done. For the next hour I was going from store to store and bakery to bakery. Then a thought occurred to me. I should call my brother Kevin. He's a psychologist who specializes in Post-Traumatic Stress Disorder. He might like to hear about my day. So calling on my cell phone, from inside a little store where I was surrounded by Amish treasures, I reached him in his Boston office. After being sure I wasn't interrupting anything too important, I told him how I spent the last few hours. I'm not sure but when he heard my news, I think he was jolted to the point of dropping his phone. "You met with who? You were discussing what?" Putting it mildly, he was shocked and amazed.

Most people had this reaction when hearing of my meetings with the Amish and now Marie. But for those in the business of personal therapy, psychology, trauma care, etc., the astonishment was even greater. They couldn't understand how and why I was chosen by those involved. Why I was allowed inside their world? I had no professional training, no experience at this. Perhaps that was exactly why I was chosen. I had no agenda. No expectations. I posed no threat. I was simply reaching out in kindness.

I walked among these Amish-made crafts and gave Kevin a brief rundown on how it all went. Certainly he found it intriguing. The artwork and message of his little brother, truly was reaching people in extraordinary ways—ways he knew from his profession were special. He was moved to the point of wondering if perhaps I now needed to talk to someone . . . a professional . . . a psychologist . . . him perhaps. He was concerned with my well-being. It was nice to hear the comments of another concerned family member.

After assuring him I was fine, even better than fine, we said goodbye. I went back to shopping. Everyone on my Christmas list got gifts I purchased that day, in those little towns, in those little shops, made by people with big hearts.

CHAPTER 8

Home for the Holidays

THE DAYS WERE moving faster now. Daylight hours were short. Winter was settling in and Christmas was just around the corner. Night after night I found myself on the living room floor watching "It's a Wonderful Life". I'll bet I watch that movie three or four times each season. But this year I wasn't on the floor surrounded by wrapping paper and gifts. Instead the floor was covered with prints, packaging materials, postage stamps and piles of request letters. Getting these prints to those who wanted them was a priority. Many were going to people who were giving them as Christmas gifts. They had to make their way across the country and further. Some were on their way to Canada. One group was actually being sent to Japan. Those traveling to the orient were for a group of grade school students. These Japanese school students were similar in age to those effected at Nickel Mines. When they heard of what happened in Nickel Mines their response was kind and generous. Collectively they hand folded one thousand origami cranes. The cranes were shipped here for the Amish children. In Japan the crane is a symbol of peace. It is believed that to provide someone with one thousand of them will bring peace to their life. Halfway around the world, their teacher was directing these school children in this act of kindness. What a beautiful gesture. It was Charlie's grandmother that informed me of this gift from the orient. She's the woman I met at the second signing. She suggested they get my prints in response. I was thrilled to send these just as I continue to be with each and every one that goes out.

People, who were touched by this message of responding with kindness, were requesting prints and wanting to know how the Amish were doing. One of the most surprising letters I received came from New York. It was from the producer of the ABC documentary. It arrived just before Christmas. When I saw the return address on the letter, I presumed it was to inform me of the status of the documentary. Upon opening it, I was so pleased to read what he wrote. Remember this was the gentleman who jets back and forth between L.A. and New York. When I first met him I got the impression he might want to be anywhere else, other than the countryside of Lancaster County. Well, I suppose after his stay here, filming, doing interviews, encountering the local people and the Amish, he was impressed by the outpouring of compassion. He was writing to thank me for my cooperation in the show. He told me how my actions and those of the community touched him. Additionally he enclosed a contribution check for the Nickel Mines School Fund. That I certainly didn't expect. It was another confirmation to me of how powerful this message is. He didn't have to do that. None of the people who responded had to. They all were following that tug inside of them—that pull at their heart—the one that says, yes this is a good thing. They were experiencing the compassionate feeling you get when you know your actions are not for your benefit, but for the benefit of others. Each of them, I believe, wished to continue this spread of selflessness. That itself, is an act of compassion. It's an act that perpetuates additional similar acts. Through steps like this, human compassion creates its own chain reaction to further sustain itself.

As for the documentary, he wrote about that too. He told me that it was finished and I was included in the final segment. What exactly that meant I didn't know. The final segment, what does that mean? This was a one-hour show. Did that mean some time in the last half hour or the last few minutes? He gave no indication as to what film footage was used. Was it from the signing and the crowds of people? Was it a shot of the painting, with a voice over about its message? How would that message be represented? Media representation of the message was one thing that always concerned me about my interviews. I could say all the right things in front of the camera. But once it got into editing it was out of my hands. It could be cut up however the editor chose. Well, it was out of my hands at this point too. I knew better than to second-guess the message and this journey. So I let those questions go . . . just trust in it. But this meant that the message and the painting were going to be broadcast across the country and Canada. The ABC news team recognized what I did as significant enough to include it in the telling of their story. I never would have thought such a thing would happen. This was amazing to me. The show was scheduled to air at the end of January.

Christmas was just a few days away now. Christmas is a big event in my family. I mentioned earlier that I have eight brothers and sisters. Yep, I know, big family. One my parents did a great job with, by instilling in us the importance of togetherness. With all my siblings grown and having children and grandchildren of their own, it's not uncommon for about forty of us to gather for the holidays. We are all close. My family members are my best friends. Some other families may dread the holidays. Not mine. We plan months ahead, figuring out ways to traverse the country and spend time with each other. So at Christmas, even though we exchange names for gift giving, I like to give a little something to everyone. The young kids get fun toy gifts and something maybe a bit more meaningful for the adults. This year I knew what I would give. Remember I bought an entire box of white bells, when I hung one on The Tree of Love? Each of those remaining bells would now become a Christmas gift. I spent at least two or more of those winter evenings tying bows on each bell, then individually gift wrapped them all. I wanted to be sure that every household got at least one. Perhaps each would become part of that family's traditional tree ornaments. Every year it might be taken down from the attic, out of the box from among the tinsel, decorations and garland. Maybe it would be displayed on a Christmas tree covered with other family loved ornaments and lights. Lights are everywhere at Christmas. Lights that shine as an expression of hope and goodwill toward others. Perhaps this would be a small reminder, that living those virtues throughout every season can truly make a difference. A reminder of the year when this small bell rang out with a message of kindness that was larger than us all.

When Christmas happens in the Becker households it's so much more than just a one-day event. It can last for a week or more. After we all spend time with our immediate families and children, we'll travel across the country to meet and share with each other. Presents are still being opened on and after the first of the New Year. During Christmas week this year, my sister Linda had a dinner at her home. Many of us, some from out-of-town, gathered to share each other's company, exchange gifts and catch up on the happenings of our lives. This gathering drew about twenty people. Among the relatives attending was my brother Kevin. He had made the trip from New England with his family. Not knowing who had my name in the secret Santa exchange this year, I was handed a gift by Kevin. He told me it was from Stefan. This year Stefan had drawn my name. Kevin was delivering the gift for him. Stefan couldn't make it to PA, as he had work and school commitments in Boston. It seemed so appropriate that Stefan had my name, since he and I had worked so closely with Kindness and Compassion. His gift found its way to me nearly a week after Christmas day, making it one of the final gifts I'd receive this year. I was soon to discover how his gift reflected his thoughtfulness regarding our interactions.

It was a small package, about the size of half a loaf of bread. This was not your typical brightly colored wrapping paper, full of Santas or snowmen and topped with a big shiny bow. No, this was wrapped in plain brown paper held together by string. There was a little bit of weight to it, maybe a pound or two. It felt very solid. Putting aside the chatter and excitement of the many people in the room exchanging presents with abundant laughter, I sat quietly a bit transfixed on this unique package. I began to open it by untying the string and peeling back the paper. Unveiled was a small, seemingly very old, antique, tin box. There was writing on it that was difficult to read, having been worn away by time. It was rich in colors of burgundy, gold and black, all of which had faded over the years into a patina full of history. From its weight I could tell it wasn't empty. This box, that could have been the gift itself, turned out to be the special container for more treasures inside. Lifting the lid revealed additional uniquely wrapped items.

There appeared to be two separate items inside. One was wrapped in white tissue paper and the other in black cloth. Again there was string tied around them, where normally a traditional ribbon might have been used. There wasn't much normal or traditional about this gift. The white one was on top, so I removed and untied it first. Inside I found two very old, metal, tin-like, bells: one silver and one gold. They were tarnished, worn with age and strung together with a white cloth ribbon. This off-white piece of old cloth looked like something you might find in a box being saved with old jewelry, in a drawer of your grandmothers' house. Something that had fond memories attached to it. This medley of metal and cloth was unique and old. Stefan knew the importance of a bell in my life these past few months and his gift reflected that. This was very thoughtful. Already these were more than enough and yet there was more. I set the bells aside and from the tin container, removed the black cloth wrapped gift. This is where the weight was coming from. This was heavier than the bells. I placed it on top of the now closed tin box then tugged on the end of the string to undo its gently tied bow. The black cloth fell open. As the soft cloth slid away from the gift within, it revealed something quite unexpected. There, on top of the black cloth, sat two wrought iron figures. Figures of Amish children, one boy and one girl. These little metal figures only stood about two inches tall. They were seated side by side on a plain flat bench, also made of iron. All three parts: the boy, the girl and the bench were separate individual items. As I picked them up to examine them, they appeared to be handmade. Most of the surface was unpainted. The black of the metal made up the coloring for the bench and some of the Amish clothing. Only the faces, hands and shirts were very simply covered in paint: blue for the shirts and flesh color for the face and hands. These little figures made a very big impact on me. This was such an appropriate and thoughtful gift. It was certain to find a special place in my home.

By this time I had already given out, mailed off, or sent across the country with traveling relatives, all the white bells I was giving out. Now through Stefan's thoughtfulness here I was receiving these Amish figures and the gift of bells myself. I reached for my cell phone and gave him a call. But as is often the case with Stefan, I ended up leaving him a message. That message was to thank him for his generous gift.

When my family gets together like this it's very common for us to do things in small groups. Occasionally we'll do things as one large group. Sometimes the women would want to shop, or the kids get together and play video games or go to a movie. Maybe the guys would go to the outdoors store, or watch a game. But the point is we would do things with each other. Flea markets and antique shops were high on the list of things to do.

There are plenty of them in this area. Many of the out-of-town folks like to take full advantage of that. We have our favorites and there was talk of going to one tomorrow, Green Dragon. Now don't ask me why it's called Green Dragon. I've been going to this place for years and the name doesn't associate with anything there. The name, Green Dragon, implies something oriental. That couldn't be further from the reality of this place. It's a market where farmers, craftsman and many Amish sell their produce, baked goods and wares of all kinds. You can find furniture, clothing and antiques. There's even a livestock auction. And of course there's food. Food of all kinds. Much of it straight from the farm. Anyway, we all enjoyed going there. In fact, in the summer I'm usually there once a month. The other weeks I can be found at other markets in the area. I love going to the markets—anything to stay out of the grocery store and away from factory-made foods. This local produce is wonderful.

After the usual family debate, about what to do the next day and how everyone would spend their time, a decision was reached. Everyone wanted to visit Green Dragon. I knew this market was on the way to the Nickel Mines area. So I offered an idea. If anyone had an interest in going to Nickel Mines or drive through Amish country, I would be glad to show them around. Up till this point in the family gatherings, there was little or no talk about the painting, the message or my involvement with the Amish. My family can be a tough crowd and I don't think they realized the hundreds of thousands of people this message had reached. I knew there was the possibility, that the harshness of the tragedy could make it hard for some of them to visit that area. My family enjoyed visiting the Amish country. But that might be difficult to do right now, given the extreme circumstances there. It could be hard for them, to be in the vicinity where such a devastating event took place. So, I didn't force the issue, just put it on the table for consideration.

In an unusually quiet fashion for my family, the decision was made by the end of that night. To my surprise, tomorrow's day would be Green Dragon first and then on to the Amish country. Those who could make it, were taking me up on my offer.

The next morning we gathered at my sister Claire's house about 8:30. That was the starting out point for our day. Coffee in hand, everyone showed up just about on time. Fifteen of us would be spending this day together. We determined how many cars were needed and who would drive. I was a passenger on this trip, riding in my sister Linda's car. I have been making the trip to this area a lot these days. For numerous reasons I was driving down there three, four times a week, or more. But this would be the first time in months that I would be going down there and not driving myself.

So off we went. The family caravan set out. I believe we used four very full cars. We started a day trip that would perhaps change everyone's view of what I had been involved in. I had some ideas of where I would take them and what they might see. But what this day held in store for them was more than any of them could imagine.

As planned the market was our first stop. The parking lot was very full. But we all found a place to park and began our search for bargains. There are hundreds of stands here, both inside and out. The vendors were all open on this exceptionally warm late December day. The place was true to form in that there were people everywhere. This is a place where you will find all ages and nationalities, people bustling around with arms full of bags containing the days special finds, and food. Food is everywhere here. Food is one of the major elements at Green Dragon. All kinds of food, healthy and not so healthy. But it's not everyday that we were all here together, so we were going to enjoy it all.

With fifteen of us it was tough to hold the group together and still enjoy what all the stands have to offer. There are so many things to see and so many people wanting to see them, that staying together as a large group wasn't going to work. Through the process of stopping and starting at various stands, we began to break up into smaller groups. So we decided to meet up in a few hours. So off we went in separate directions seeing what there was to see, buying what there was to buy, and eating what there was to eat.

Time passes quickly with so much to enjoy. Several hours of laughter and shopping had passed in what seemed like minutes. Slowly we all made our way back to the designated meeting spot. One by one family members arrived carrying bags filled with plenty of goodies: produce, baked goods, and a variety of household and craft items. Everyone enjoyed showing the others their finds. Many of the tempting desserts and food items would be for sharing back at the house.

With very little discussion, we agreed that our time here was done. The next destination would be the Nickel Mines area. I was leading the way for the rest of the day. So they all looked to me for our next step. I thought to call Kym. Why not get her involved in this day and have her meet my family? So in the midst of the vendors and shoppers, both Amish and English, I reached her on my cell phone. She was thrilled with the idea of meeting everyone. She was in the midst of a few errands and would be back home shortly. The idea of including her in our day would later turn out to be a good one. Everyone in the family has a cell phone so I suggested that we go to our cars and stay in touch by using them. The car I was in would lead the way. We had all been to the Amish country plenty of times: shopping, antiquing and such. And of course by now, you have an idea how often I've been there. But never had the rest of my family gone as far down the back roads as I was about to take them.

For most of the drive we headed down the main street, passing lots of shops, stores, restaurants and such. Much of this area was familiar to some of the family. The further we went the less familiar it was to all of them. We kept going, passing all the stores. The road narrowed from highway, to four lanes, then to two. Now only small houses lined the side of the road. Traffic slowed. Horse and buggies are common in this area and caution is always best. As we passed various landmarks I would point them out to the people in the car with me: "That's were Kym and I had breakfast before visiting the Amish families . . . or . . . That's where I pulled off to collect my thoughts late at night after the second print signing." Things like that. I wished I could have shared all these comments with those in the other cars. My sister Linda and myself used our cell phones to take care of some of that. But without a doubt, those in the car with me got the most information.

After several miles of driving on this two-lane main street, I directed Linda to turn. All four cars in sequence turned onto an even smaller road. There were no lines down the middle of this road and no shoulder on either side. The small homes that lined the road we left behind, were replaced by wide-open fields and farmhouses. Up and down, curving right and left the caravan made its way through the countryside. There was so much I could show them, but we only had this one day. I was wondering as we made our way, just where to begin.

I decided we would start at Kym and Paul's house. I knew Kym might not be home just yet. But Paul may be. Kym and Paul own both a buffalo ranch and a dog kennel. There would be plenty for everyone to enjoy. It's not everyday you get to see a herd of buffalo up this close. In the kennel they had several rooms full of puppies. There were dogs of all kinds and my family are all dog lovers. I thought they would like this. Besides it was close to where we were, making it a natural first stop as we headed into Nickel Mines.

A mile or so down the road we were there. I instructed Linda to pull into their parking lot. All the other cars followed. They may have all been wondering, "Where are we and why are we here?" I was quick to give everyone an extremely brief version of who Kym and Paul were and told them that this was their property, ranch and kennel. Updates such as this would put our stops into perspective. It would give them a clearer understanding of the people I encountered over the past few months.

As we stood in the parking lot, it quickly became clear that the atmosphere of the day was changing. Everyone had suddenly found themselves in the midst of new and strange surroundings. No one knew yet how close he or she was to the schoolhouse. But I could feel in the air that their thoughts were of the tragic incident, which happened just down the road from where we were standing. Everyone seemed more attentive as I talked to them. The boisterous laughter of Green Dragon now seemed distant. The stories of my involvement with this community, learned by reading the newspapers, watching the TV news and such, was suddenly all around them. They were standing in the cool mid afternoon air, sensing the reality of it all. Just how deeply into this Amish community I would take them, they didn't know.

We made our way inside the kennel. I figured we would find Paul there. We did. He was hard at work as usual. By his big smile, handshake and hug I knew he was glad to see me, as I was him. After a quick introduction to everyone, fifteen of us, I told him this was part of my family. Once his initial shock wore off, he showed everyone around. They loved seeing all the puppies. We spent a good half hour playing with them. Then it was time to head out across the road to have a look at the buffalo. Perhaps Kym would be back soon and they would meet her as well. It had gotten colder so several people went to their cars and got jackets. Then off we went, heading for the fields across the road. As we started up and across the road a large van pulled into the parking lot. It was Kym. This was the vehicle she used to pick up the children at the Nickel Mines

School. She was the bus driver for the kids since the day of the tragedy and this was their school bus. As I previously told you, normally the kids would walk to and from school. But these days the parents felt better about them being driven by someone they felt comfortable with. Being driven made it less likely that they would encounter media and curious onlookers. This was a Friday and Kym was just returning from delivering them all home from school.

Seeing me as she pulled in, Kym stopped the van, rolled down the window and gave a yell, "Hey Bruce! It's good to see you. How are ya my friend?" Recognizing her I yelled back a comment that referred to a running joke we had with each other. She and I would jokingly compare our two SUVs . . . whose was bigger and better, all in good fun. "Kym, hey girl. What did you do, trade in the old one? Driving this big vehicle now are ya?"

We laughed a bit as I walked to the van. Everyone else had stopped to look, hearing someone call my name (here in the middle of nowhere, where they knew no one). But the draw of the buffalo had a grip on them. A few could be seen across the road and they continued on. Kym told me where she was returning from and I updated her on our having been inside to see Paul. Then she made a generous offer, which would bring the reality of this place even closer to everyone. So I called them all back and told them the new plan: With the family huddled around the open window of the van I made a very quick and humorous introduction, "Family this is Kym. Kym, this part of my family. We'll do the name thing later. There's just too many of us for that right now." I wanted to get on with telling them our plan. "Kym has offered to have us all climb in the van, where it's nice and warm. Then she'll show us around the ranch, take us to see the buffalo. Then take us around the Nickel Mines area. This way we all get to travel together instead of walking and using several cars. Good idea?" Everyone really liked the idea and expressed their thanks. At this point they didn't know this was the school bus for the children of Nickel Mines.

So scurrying around to the other side, the sliding door was opened and we all piled in. That was an interesting sight for me, watching my family jumping into the same school bus that I had watched the Amish children get into. It was a tight fit, but hey we're a close group. No one complained. We all thought this was a treat. I sat in the front. That way Kym and I could describe what they were about to see and where we would be going. As everyone was squeezing in I told them the news about the van itself, "You guys, since the schoolhouse tragedy, Kym drives the children of Nickel Mines to and from home and school. The van you are in right now is their school bus." Immediately I could feel their focus on my words and the surroundings intensify. "Kym is just getting back from picking the kids up at school and taking them home. Not more than five minutes ago the seats you're sitting in right now were filled with those children. They were sitting where you are now." The expressions on their faces told me that the reality of being in this van was a bit heavy for some of them. So to help ease the intensity of the moment, I made some kind of joking comment, like, "So you might want to be careful not to sit in any gum stuck on your seat." Then I went directly into the lighthearted topic of more lengthy introductions, rattling off all their names for Kym. She of course picked right up on lightening the atmosphere and made some funny remark like, "Stop right there. There's no way I'm going to remember all those names and I don't want to hear anything about there being a test later." We all chuckled a bit and in traditional Becker fashion there were a few quick comebacks. But it was as evident as the warmth in that van that every one of them was beginning to realize the closeness I had with this incident and this community and now they found themselves literally surrounded by it.

The entrance taking us to the buffalo herd was only about a minute away and we had already pulled in. Kym suggested we all get out and have a closer look. Not too close mind you. There was a fence between the herd and us. A fence that in reality was a false security, because if those animals were smart enough they would realize they could easily break through it. Still it was an amazing sight to be so close to such powerful animals. Every time I visited Kym I enjoyed watching these majestic beasts.

After walking the grounds and Kym fielding all kinds of questions, it was time to move on. So back to the van we went. As everyone was jockeying for a position to sit, Kym and I discussed driving them past the grounds of the old schoolhouse. Also we would go to the spot where people from all around the world had placed countless flowers and gifts. Then drive past the new schoolhouse. So we set out to do just that. I told everyone where we were headed and this time being cautious about it, asked, "Is this okay with you guys? Will this be too upsetting for any of you? Maybe you don't want to go?" With very calm nods of approval and quiet murmurs of, "That's okay. Yep, that's fine," we made our way there. All along the way Kym and I pointed out places we thought might be of interest to them. Comments like, "That farm is where the teacher lives . . . some of the children live there . . . these are the roads that were packed with media vans." They all listened intently as they looked across the landscape of farmland. It was as though I could read on their faces the pictures that were being painted in their minds: Amish children at play . . . what the teacher might look like . . . or the madness of the media blitz.

For a brief moment we stopped in a parking lot that overlooks the grounds where the schoolhouse stood. Directly in front of us was a pasture that blended seamlessly into the fields around it. Having not been told that this is where the school once stood you would unknowingly drive right past it. That's how the Amish wanted it. All around us was quiet and calm. In every direction all you could see was farmland and farmhouses. While parked there we described how different this scene was not so long ago. How for the first time, like never before, these peaceful surroundings had been thrown into turmoil. Then for just a few seconds, what seemed like minutes, there were no questions, no talking at all. All of us, Kym and I included, quietly sat in humble observance.

Eventually the questions did come. My family was piecing it all together. They were remembering the scenes they saw on the news and placing these surroundings into perspective. So as we began to drive away Kym and I answered what we could. Questions about how many children were in the school, the teacher, the police, the media and so on. As we talked we showed them the grounds where hundreds, perhaps thousands, of gifts, candles, stuffed animals, prayers, cards and such had been placed for the children and their families. Kym was the person who cared for these things. She would light the candles and tend to them and keep the grounds in order. She was the one who gathered those heartfelt gifts together day after day then deliver them to the families.

The atmosphere in the van was taking on a more somber, almost solemn air. It was apparent how meaningful this was to everyone.

From there we drove to the area where the new school was to be built. The plan was to build it on land owned by one of the families with children in the school. With no building yet erected, there wasn't much to see. The actual site sits back a bit from the road. But we drove past anyway. Somehow knowing that a new school would be built was a thought that brought hope.

Then I made a suggestion to Kym, "How about we take everyone by and drop in on John and Mary." (Here again, as before in these writings, I am using fictitious names.) This

Amish couple and their children had become good friends of mine. They are one of the families I have become comfortable enough with to just drop in on from time to time. They have several children, some of who attend the Nickel Mines School. Kym also knows them quite well. "Sure that's a good idea," she said. So I turned to face everyone seated in the back rows of the van and said to them, "How would you like to visit with some of our Amish friends? We could drop in on them now." Heads turned to look at me, then at each other. They didn't expect to hear that. The tone of their responses was definitely one of surprise. Responses were something like this, "You mean go to their house? Now? All of us?" "Sure," I said. "They're really good people. I drop in on them pretty often. They live just down the road." Their response was positive but with a bit of uneasiness. That was understandable. They were now treading in territory that none of them was familiar with. If you think about it, in the English world, fifteen people don't generally just drop in. They call first. But that couldn't be done here—this couple had no phone. To them friends were friends and having me drop by was always a welcome thing. In fact, that invitation was extended to all of my Amish friends in return. I wish they could have the opportunity to visit with me at my house. But it was my car that allowed me the convenience of traveling to see them. A means of transportation they opted not to use. It was much too long a ride for their horses and buggies to venture to my home. So dropping in for a quick visit this day seemed a very good idea to me. If for a minute, I thought our stopping by would bother John and Mary, I would have never suggested it. As we made our way there I fielded questions about the special household we were headed toward: "Do they have children? Did they attend the school? Were they injured? How often do you visit them?"

The curiosity of everyone sitting in those back seats was peaked. Think about it: This group set out earlier in the day with the intent of visiting a familiar flea market and perhaps a drive through Amish country. Now they had met Kym and Paul, dear new friends of mine who took them up close and personal with a herd of buffalo. Then suddenly found themselves riding in the van that transports the Amish school children who lived through this tragedy. Everyone then visited the grounds of the schoolhouse, both old and new, saw the spot that was chosen by thousands to drop off gifts honoring the girls, and now I was taking them to the home of an Amish family whom I regarded as friends. A family with children attending school the day of the shootings. Not your everyday occurrences for family members who now lived in cities quite a distance from here. But for me, over these past few months, this is where I had spent most of my time. It was hitting home with them just how involved I had gotten.

It was only minutes until we arrived. As we pulled into the driveway we made our way past a few buggies parked in front of the barn, which was to the left. To the right was their home. It's a comfortable place where this young couple is raising three boys and recently added a newborn baby girl. I thought perhaps I should go to the door first, leaving everyone to wait in the van until I said my hellos. It might be best to let them know they had this much company. As I got out of the van, the two family dogs were first to greet me, pretty much as usual. These were dogs that presented the look of intimidation simply by their size. These are big dogs. If they didn't know you and you them, you probably wouldn't step foot on this property. Thankfully they had good memories and approached me with friendly tails wagging, brushing up against my leg wanting to be petted.

The barn door was open so I was pretty sure that John was working inside. You see John is a blacksmith. That's why there were several buggies in the driveway. They belonged to customers and were here to be repaired. So rather than head for the house I went to the barn. Many times prior to this I

found only Mary and the kids home. John would be off doing a job. They are all so sweet. I love visiting with them all.
But engrained into Amish society, is a comfort level that exists
only when the husband is home when someone (an Englishman especially) is visiting. So I was glad to see that he was
home this day. As I turned the corner, yep there he was, just as
I had seen him many times before. Horse and tools in hand, he
was shoeing a horse. When he heard me come in he looked up,
"Hello Bruce!" he exclaimed. "Hi John, hard at work I see," I
responded. With smiles and excitement, he left the horse and
headed for the door toward me. There was that hardworking
hand, black from the tools, fire and animals, extended in kindness to me once again. What a welcome sight that always is.
While shaking his hand, I didn't waste any time in telling him,
"I have some family members with me. We were shopping in
the area and stopped in for a minute so I could introduce them
to you. They'd like to say hello if that's okay." "Sure, sure, have
them come in," he said. As I turned around toward the door, I
saw they were already out of the van, past the dogs and made
their way to the barn. They had been standing in the doorway
behind me watching as John and I greeted each other. So with
an arm wave gesture, I welcomed them in and delightfully said,
"Come on in guys."

I didn't have to ask them twice. They came in and curiosity took over. They were looking over everything: his tools, the
anvil, and the horses. No one was shy about asking him questions. Nor was he about answering them. I was so glad to see
that. He put aside his work for the next few minutes and visited
with us, just as I suspected he would. He showed them around
and talked about whatever they asked. It was during this time
that he generously offered his personal thoughts on my actions
for the community. He spoke of the healing benefit that my
reflection of *Kindness and Compassion* had on so many. To hear
him speak so positively about me was humbling. For him to

say it to my family made it even more so. They were getting an unsolicited testimonial on my prints and its message from a source that could not have been more involved on that tragic day. We were in the home of a father who had children in the school that very day. And those children were now standing right there with us.

It didn't take long for the kids to realize they had visitors. While we were talking, they scampered into the barn with those big curious eyes and cheerful smiles, "Hello Bruce. Hello," they said. "Sure, you remember Bruce. Well this is his family," John told them. My family was amazed at where they were and how welcoming an environment this was. As they all encountered the children and explored the barn, John and I had a few minutes to stand by the windows and talk alone quietly. "So how are you guys doing?" I asked. "We're good. The baby is good. Getting ready for winter." For the most part we kept the conversation light and brief. But we also touched on how the children were doing emotionally, in the temporary school. You see, as more time passed since the shootings, some of the children's internal struggles with that day began to surface in various ways. We often talked about the challenges of being a parent that is dealing with such hard times. But right now, with so many new visitors around us, we both knew this was not a time to discuss that in depth. So our talk turned to more simple things like the new windows he would be installing.

About fifteen or twenty minutes had passed. It was time for us to be moving on and let John get back to his work. As we all made our way out of the barn, I noticed Mary had come out to greet us. From the porch steps I heard her say, "Hello Bruce." "Hi Mary. I have some family in town for the holidays. We were in the area and dropped in to say hi." "You have a big family," she said smiling. "This isn't even half of them," I told her. Putting her hand to her cheek in surprise, she simply said, "Oh my!"

As I walked past a large barrel by the barn door, I saw it was full of old horseshoes. I asked John what that was about. He said they were used ones he would be getting rid of. Reaching into it he pulled one out, handed it to me and said, "Here, have one." I looked at everyone now beginning to get in the van. Then back at the barrel. Before I could say anything, he knew what I was thinking. "Sure, take one for everybody." "Thanks John. As simple as it seems, they will really like these." I called to everyone to come back for a minute. As they got close I explained about the barrel. Each of them expressed, as I knew they would, that they would like to have one. "Thanks John . . . oh this is nice, thank you," came the comments. To John these were just items from his work to be discarded. To my family they would become treasured mementos of a visit long remembered. Then I think it was my brother Perry who asked about the tradition of good luck and the proper way to hang it on the wall. "Does it hang with the opening facing upward or down?" he asked. Well, John being a blacksmith knew a great story about why the horseshoe symbolizes good luck and was eager to share it. Everyone stood attentively watching and listening to him go on about God and the devil and horseshoes. It's hard to explain to you the warm and uplifting feeling it gave me to stand there watching my family, in this environment, listening to John talk, while his children were playing around us and everyone grasping the cherished memento of the day.

The story John told is one I heard for the first time that day. It was new to me, so I'll tell you as best I can remember. As John told this story, it was obvious how much he enjoyed sharing it. This was a fun, folklore, sort of tale and he was going to enjoy this as much as we would. Right from the start, he became more animated, his arms motioning around in broad gestures, with lots of smiles and expressions on his face and in his voice. I could see this was the lighter, fun side, of John. It was almost as though he was telling this story to his children. Which is a bit odd, because John is probably younger than any one of us visiting and listening to this story. He told it something like this:

> *The devil, as you may know, is sometimes portrayed as half man half beast. From the waist up he resembles a man. From the waist down he has the legs and back end of a horse. (There's a name for this creature, at the time of telling the story John couldn't remember it. I can't remember it right now either. Anyway . . . the devil, pretty much always, liked to wear horseshoes on his feet, especially while on Earth for some reason. Maybe it was a vanity thing. This one day he needed a new pair. So, he found a blacksmith. In his mean devilish way, he insisted that the blacksmith make a new pair of shoes for him and put them on him right away. What the devil didn't realize just then, is that God sends His angels, His messengers, or even Himself, to earth in many forms at different times. This blacksmith was one of those disciples . . . and even though the devil didn't recognize him, he recognized the devil. So, the blacksmith agreed to make the shoes and put them on him. Into the workshop they went. The blacksmith forged and shaped a beautiful new pair. He sat them on the anvil and asked the devil to come closer. Then he asked him to turn around and raise his foot, to have the old shoes taken off. As the devil did so, and he was removing the old shoes, the blacksmith pushed the new shoes back into the fire. With the old shoes now off and the bottom of the devil's feet exposed, the blacksmith quickly nailed the burning red-hot shoes onto the devil's feet. Well you can imagine how terrible that felt. The devil pulled away, kicking and stomping and yelling in pain. He was doing anything to try and get those off. The pain was absolutely terrible. He threw his body around in that barn doing whatever he could to throw those shoes. Eventually*

> *he did. Then he ran, as fast as he could, to get as far away as possible. Never wanting anything to do with horseshoes again, especially on Earth. So, it doesn't matter if the shoe is pointed up or down when you hang it. Anytime the devil comes around, just seeing a horseshoe will scare him away. It's a good thing to have a horseshoe in your house.*

I was so glad Perry thought to ask how to hang these gifts. That question lead to the telling of a story, which enhanced that moment further. Even today, more than a year and a half later, when we get together this story comes up in conversation. Now, having a story to go with the shoes makes the day even more memorable.

By the time he was finished the sun was beginning to set and we all knew it was time to leave. Plenty of smiles and handshakes accompanied the many thanks and goodbyes. We all headed back to the van, saying goodbyes to the kids and Mary as well. Everyone squeezed in, finding a seat for the ride back to Kym's house. The mood in the van was unmistakably positive. All of us had just experienced the kindness of this loving family. The conversation consisted of how pleasant the visit had been. They were all glad to have had this opportunity. Even the simplicity of these old horseshoes was seen as a genuinely unique keepsake, inspiring smiles and friendly comparisons of one to the other.

The closer we got to Kym's house the more our conversation changed once again to the topic of buffalo. As we pulled into her driveway Kym asked, in her always friendly manner, if any of them had ever eaten buffalo. That's why she and Paul raised them, for the sale of the meat. Since I met them, my freezer hasn't seen red meat other than buffalo. They kept it well stocked for me. A few of the family with us hadn't tried it. So Kym invited everyone inside for a taste. All fifteen of us went from the van into her house. Being that there were so many of us, we filled her kitchen and the rest were spilling into the dining room. As we were getting warm sitting and standing around her kitchen table, Kym went right to work. She pulled a tenderloin from the refrigerator. One she had cooked earlier. She heated it on the stove and then sliced it up for everyone to sample. About this time Paul came in from the kennel to find he had a house full of people. He joined right in with the light-hearted conversation and the sharing of his favorite food. We sat and stood around for quite some time sharing family stories, details about the buffalo, talking about living in the country and life in the Amish community. The hospitality shown by Kym and Paul to my family was such a shining example of the spirit of this community. We all felt so welcomed.

The print of my painting was hanging on Kym's wall in her dining room. At several points during our visit various family members noticed it. Those seeing it from across the room would look at me, point to it and make a motion of positive approval. With a smile and nod of the head it was as if they were saying, "There it is, just like we heard, hanging in homes that dealt with this tragedy directly. Good job." Furthermore, it was while we were in Kym's home that she expressed to everyone her own heartfelt thoughts about my actions, using words like generous and compassionate. I of course told them of the many ways and things she was doing to help the families. Kym's big heart was finding ways to express kindness to them every day.

Feeling warmed and having a bit of food in us it was time to end our stay and return home. On our way out Kym continued to discuss life on the ranch. She showed everyone the building that housed the frozen meat ready for sale. This ranch was both a love and way of life for Kym and Paul. They enjoyed sharing it with us and everyone enjoyed its uniqueness.

One more time the caravan of cars was on the move. We rolled out of the driveway and into the darkness of the countryside. I was in the first car leading the way home. I don't know what the conversations were like in the other cars, on that ride home. But I do know that the discussion in Linda's car, the one I was in, was predominately one of astonishment. Linda even said to me, "My God Bruce, that was all so amazing. With you spending so much time in that area, I'm surprised you haven't decided to move there. These few months must have been incredible for you." It felt good to know that now my family was beginning to share in these experiences and understand firsthand the impact this image and message had on these people. People I now call friends.

We all gathered that night at my sister Claire's house, where we started the day. By the time we got there it had been a long and eventful day. About twelve hours had passed since we left that morning. One by one everyone came into the warmth of yet another family get-together around her kitchen table. This is the same kitchen in which we had all grown up. This had been my parents' home. The home where they raised us. When they passed away we all so badly wanted to keep this house in the family. It was decided that it would go to Claire and Jerry. They had proven to be tremendous caretakers. The place was now in better shape than ever. Mom and Dad would be so proud of them.

As is customary after a day at the market, packages containing the day's purchases were put on the table and the surrounding counters. From them began the emergence of delicious baked goods, produce, candles and all sorts of unique finds. With the introduction of a few drinks, both cold and warm, this group had just found its next location to enjoy each others company. We shared stories of what life had presented to us from the various parts of the country in which we now lived. Work, family, friends, sports, fun, religion, politics, science, love and hate were all fair game in our discussions. No topic is off-limits with us. Hours passed before we called it a night.

Throughout those hours each one of my family that was along that day approached me individually. I was thanked time and time again for sharing this part of my life with them. Each of them had experienced a day that created memories for a lifetime. Each of them was changed by the experiences of this day. They expressed to me that now they understood how and why I seemed so consumed by following the journey of this image and its message. They only had a few hours to experience a handful of people who were new in my life. Yet it moved them so deeply. If you multiply those experiences by perhaps thousands, it gives you an idea of how much I was moved by all this. Now my family had seen, felt and experienced, the power and impact of this message firsthand.

My brother Kevin, the psychologist, put it to me this way: He talked about how physically being in the location of where a tragic event occurred can change one's outlook and emotional response to that event. That's what happened today. They had not only been in that location. But they met and interacted with some of those involved. Having done that along with me, it gave them the opportunity to view me not just as brother, uncle or nephew Bruce. But now they began to understand and view my involvement more objectively.

That's the colder, more clinical description of the day. To me it meant that those closest to me, my family, were beginning to understand my actions. They were given the chance to experience, firsthand, the community and some of the people directly affected. The family I wanted to receive support from for the past few months now understood what I was involved in. But more than that, they were also seeing how this entire community had been touched and was responding. Today wasn't the same as watching it on the evening news or reading about it in the paper. To actually stand with your feet in the dirt where things happened, have the sun shine on your face while you smell the cool air coming off those fields and talk to the people effected by it all, that's what it took for them to feel it at the most human level and they felt it.

They say there's no place like home for the holidays. Well, coming home this holiday took my family to places they never expected. This day, we were more at home with each other than ever before.

CHAPTER 9

English Encounters

T HE HOLIDAY SEASON had come to a close. Another year had passed. This New Year was beginning for me like no other before. My dealings with the Amish community, the media, distributing prints and everything to do with *Kindness and Compassion* had kept me so busy that I hadn't painted anything in months. I have never gone this long without painting before. It had now been three months. If I would have simply decided to take three months off for any other reason I probably would have lost my house, or gotten so far behind on bills that I would be terribly in debt. But somehow, things were still in order. I was doing just what I was meant to be doing. It's amazing how much order there is to life when you relinquish the control you only think you have, to a power higher than your own.

For the first time in months I was seeing enough of a break in those activities that I had time to paint. Now mind you, during those months I never stopped seeing images I wished to paint. I just didn't have the time to paint them. So once again I took up the brush.

I decided to paint an image of an empty bowl. I know that sounds very simple and even juvenile. But through the treatment and attention I gave this bowl, it is far from empty. This bowl is full of life. My depiction of this plain, white, porcelain bowl captures not just the image of the bowl, but if possible, also its history. It may sound silly, but I look at this image and get a sense of family. A sense for its use in preparing everyday meals and special treats. A sense that it's been held by caring hands. In my painting, the bowl sits in front of a windowsill, on top of a blue and white-checkered cloth. The light through the window is backlighting it. It is an image full of extreme lights and darks. As for color, well, I find color in places you would never dream of it being. In painting this bowl, I mixed up and used twenty-six colors on the inside of the "white" bowl itself. Beautiful hues of lavender, blues, greens and sienna, blending one into the other, creating a rich depth and smooth curve to the polished surface of the porcelain. Contrast that against the dark shadowed areas and texture of the cloth below and you can only imagine the enchantment this image creates.

It took less than two days to paint. That's pretty much the usual amount of time for me to complete one canvas, beginning to end. When it was done I noticed it had an elegant yet simple feel to it. The colors are all earth toned. There is a wonderful quality to the three-dimensional depth. The sunlight pulls it all together in a very humble natural way. As I looked at the finished piece, I couldn't help but see the influence of the Amish surroundings I found myself in over the past few months. This could have been a scene in the kitchen of any of the homes I visited. Yet this was my bowl, sitting on my windowsill, in my kitchen.

I've always said that everything happening in my life comes to the easel with me. Sometimes consciously, sometimes not. Perhaps my experiences and feelings of the calm quiet lifestyle of my new friends were expressing themselves in my work.

Whether those experiences were showing up in my work or not, was difficult to tell at this point. This was only my first painting since the tragedy and its aftermath. But what was becoming clear to me, is that this journey, these experiences and my involvement in this tragedy, were creating unexpected changes in my life. This message was still spreading and I was still hearing about it.

Knowledge of my involvement after the shootings was widening like ripples in a pond. The message was reaching more people everyday. First my days were mainly filled by encountering those directly involved with the shootings: local media, the Amish families, the first responders, state troopers, EMTs, the gunman's family, local community and so on. Then came a second wave of effects: my friends, my family, my relationships all were being affected in one way or another. People were hearing about what I was doing and I was hearing feedback from them. As you've now learned, that feedback was both positive and not so positive. Now this message had spread further. As I write this, looking back on the timeline, I can see how the effect of this message and my actions took time to generate a sense of participation (if you will) from those hearing it. As I've said many times along this journey: Things were happening at their own pace, in their own time. Not my time, God's time, and times were changing.

Now, things were taking a turn in a new direction. More frequently individuals from a more widespread English community were contacting me. The individuals and groups I heard from became more diverse. But what stayed constant was the reason they contacted me. All were drawn by the message of kindness. As I look back and recognize the acts of kindness I was reflecting through this image and its message, I realize how that in turn helped others recognize them as well. People were seeing acts of kindness being lived and being lived in the most difficult circumstances. They saw them being lived by the Amish, the first responders, the local community and now to my surprise, my actions were considered in that group.

My contact with the Amish community and others I had met along the way continued. Many of those people I now

considered friends, perhaps friends for life. But the base of individuals I was encountering was broadening.

More frequently I was being asked to speak publicly about
the tragedy and the power of this message that stemmed from
it. People were touched by the remarkable resilience of those
affected. They wanted to hear firsthand how kindness, compassion and forgiveness played such a positive role in such a
devastating event. I found myself speaking at church groups,
business luncheons, school assemblies and breakfast meetings.
These events were all scheduled, structured gatherings. Additionally, as I was going about my daily routine, individuals
wanting to hear about what I was experiencing approached me.
I found myself discussing this journey and message with total
strangers at cafes, galleries and parties. I was even stopped in
the aisles of stores, while shopping. As before, I gave my attention to each and every one of them. None were about to be
turned away when reaching out for acts of kindness. I was more
than happy to take some time with whoever approached me.

Even more surprising than this, was when I began to be
recognized for my actions by the presentation of awards. These
were awards presented to individuals who act thoughtfully for
the community, or are seen as outstanding in their field. One I
received is given to individuals who take a stand against hatred.
Another actually has the words on it " . . . in appreciation of
tangible and significant assistance given for the furtherance of
better understanding and friendly relations among peoples of
the world." Now that's stating something worthwhile of recognition. I was shocked that people were seeing me that way.

The Art Institute, where I teach, actually set aside an entire
evening, held a rather gala event, invited hundreds of people to
a lavish dinner and presented me with their own special award.
They were recognizing me for the achievement of utilizing my
art for the betterment of the community. That was a special
night. Many friends turned out, as well as many people I had

never met. But most of all, I was thrilled to have my kids, Tim and Molly, by my side that night. Rewards for recognition of kindness, now there's something that is uplifting and the world could use more of. I was very grateful.

So are you beginning to understand what I mean when I tell you that the message and my actions were now finding their way into the English community? No longer were my days solely filled with the quiet emotion of the Amish families. Now the English community was responding more directly in its own way. Each was just as unique as the other, just as meaningful, just as sincere—just different. I humbly appreciated being recognized and accepted by both communities. Through it all, my constant observance of myself being simply a messenger held true. It was the message of *Kindness and Compassion* that touched people's hearts.

Now it was time for that message to go from reaching hundreds of thousands, to millions. The day of the nationally televised documentary was fast approaching. Everyone involved in the tragedy knew the time and date it was to air. Many of these people (coroners, EMTs and such) were interviewed and filmed. So word spread among us all. The date, time and my appearance in the show were primarily made public by WIOV.

During the week prior to it airing, Casey and Murph talked about it several times during their morning show. The day it was scheduled to be shown, they invited me to the studio for an interview. I had no prior knowledge of what my role in the documentary would be. All I knew was like everyone else: the date and time it would air and that I was to be included. Remember the letter from the producer? In it he told me my portion would be in the final segment. Well by now I was a bit nervous about that.

Since I still had no TV in my own home, the plan was to watch it at my sister Claire's house. My daughter Molly was going to be there as well. It was scheduled for 10:00. I showed up about

9:45. Knowing there were still a few minutes before it started, I stood outside, alone, in the cold night air wondering what was about to happen. Only a minute or two passed when Molly pulled up. She asked if I was nervous. I guess it showed. A quick hug and brief answer of, "Maybe a little," then we went inside.

It was Claire, Molly and myself that would watch together. Tim had to work. Jerry had to work and as for other family members, I suppose they were watching at their own homes or perhaps not watching at all. The only one that let me know ahead of time that he would be watching was Stefan.

For those of you reading this that saw the show, you know how it went. For the rest of you, here's how I experienced it: The three of us sat in the TV room of Claire's house. The lights were very dim and the big screen TV was in front of us. In general, the show consisted of reenactments, interviews, a narrator and lots of footage from the Nickel Mines area. As the show starts the story is being told beginning with early morning October 2 (the day of the shootings). Reenactment footage of that morning and shots of the Nickel Mines area fill the screen, as a narrator talks about Amish country, the children and the school. Comments and comparisons are made about school violence around the country. Such as what happened in Arkansas, Colorado, Minnesota and others. It's pointed out how the Amish view the outside world, the world of the English, as evil. Remarks like that won't win you points in my book, or perhaps those of the Amish either. Differences in lifestyles between the Amish and English are made clear. Then comes the introduction of Charlie, the gunman. His background, childhood and family are discussed. The narrator seems now to have intensity in his voice. It was an aggressiveness that to me had the tone and quality of a TV commercial for a horror movie. Phrases such as: horrifying a nation, mass shootings, hatred toward God and exploding anger were used. There is talk of how Charlie's past is building to explode on the morning of

October 2. This continued for the first fifteen minutes or so. Then came the first series of commercials.

At that break my cell phone rang. It was Stefan. He was calling to express the same concern I had. This appeared as though it was going to be a shock value program, emphasizing the terror of that day. We kept the discussion short because the program was coming back on. The commercial ended and the program picked up where it left off telling the story of that day: There was talk about the Roberts family and how they were an everyday part of that Amish community. It's mentioned what a wonderful mother Marie is and the caring father Charlie was. Charlie's background was again brought up, with references to their daughter, the one who unfortunately passed away just after birth. More comparisons were made to other acts of school violence. All the while, step by step, the narrator was leading the viewer through the actions of the community that morning where and what Marie was doing, the children preparing for a day of school, and Charlie making his last minute preparations before entering that classroom.

The reenactments became more graphic. Never were acts of violence actually carried out on screen. But rather implied by combinations of narration, subject content shown, camera angles and special effects. Through these reenactments and voice-overs the viewers learned of Charlie's gruesome actions that morning. There was staged film footage pretending to be Charlie in his truck, as he drove to the scene. Actors performed roles of what may have been happening inside the schoolroom, all filmed in very soft focus and primarily in black and white. These shots included close-ups of boards barricading doors, plastic strap ties to be used on young hands and feet, Charlie on his cell phone, the frightened scampering of young feet, school desks and guns, definitely guns.

The program was only an hour long and this went on for nearly forty minutes. Programs that emphasized such violence were a primary reason I didn't have TV in my home. Granted, what was being depicted was for the most part based on fact. I suppose, for those not as closely involved as myself, it may have answered some questions about the details of the day. But as for me, it was hard to watch so much attention given to such violence. The loss of life and terror those children endured was indeed tragic. But there was so much more that was positive to this story. I knew it. I saw it. I had discussed it with the Amish and I was living it. I am certain that it's the positive elements of this story, that the Amish would want promoted.

This was being aired to people all across the northern continent. Were they going to receive the message of kindness, compassion and forgiveness? Were they going to be given a glimpse of what special people the Amish are, or how uniquely this community responded? Or were they simply sitting through another made-for television docu-drama, where violence is what sells?

Once the representations of what happened inside the schoolhouse were over, news footage of the scene was used. Lot's of it. Overhead shots of the school grounds and hand-held camera shots of the chaos of that day were shown. This was interspersed with interviews of neighbors, various authorities on violence and members of the Nickel Mines community. Still there was little or no talk of forgiveness or kindness.

With about fifteen minutes remaining in the show, finally the tone of the program changed. The topic turned more toward discussing how the Amish and the surrounding area dealt with such tragedy.

The narrator's comments shifted. He told how nothing like this had ever happened before in the Amish community. Shock was spreading through the local area and around the world. Now the Amish and the English were mourning together. The direction of the program was turning toward forgiveness, acceptance and God.

It was stated that with no memorial, or site of pilgrimage for the families or curious tourists, comfort was sought elsewhere. The Amish, who normally don't accept assistance from the English community, recognized the extreme circumstances they were in and welcomed the extended hands of kindness. This is where the painting and myself were introduced.

There it was, my painting. It filled the screen as the camera zoomed in even tighter showing its color and detail. The narrator spoke of how this image and its message became a sensation. Not a word I would have chosen to use, but I didn't write this script. How glad I was to hear the first words out of my mouth, while on screen, were my explanation of what this image stands for: Not the tragedy of that day, but rather the kindness and compassion being expressed by so many. Then, there I was on screen. It was the footage shot after that emotionally powerful day at the second signing. I thought I looked a bit rough. I had good cause to be. But no matter, the message is what was important and it was being stated.

Footage from the day of the print signing was used: Brief images of Casey and Murph greeting people and shots of myself signing prints and embracing people. All of this seen while the narrator told of how the Amish themselves had shown up for prints. Then he spoke of my meeting with Charlie's grandparents. Film was shown of when I was talking and praying with them. His grandmother was shown thanking me for all that the community and I were doing. They showed clips from my interview, telling how we prayed for healing for all the families involved. From that same interview, I gave a quick update on how the surviving girls were miraculously recovering.

Now the narrator commented on how the community was caring for each other and how acceptance and forgiveness were trumping the violence of that day. Finally the positive side of this story was being revealed.

But others interviewed were not in agreement with what I said and saw. Some gave their comments on how they thought this incident would drive the Amish even further from the outside world. How they would see the English as evil and corrupt. I remember sitting forward in my chair, in front of that TV screen, with my hand waving at the screen saying how wrong I thought that was. How wrong I thought those statements were. I knew the Amish weren't thinking that. I met with them and I knew differently. I was disappointed that the show would end that way. Then as the credits began to roll on the screen the narrator said, "But Bruce Becker is among those who sees things differently." Now shots of me speaking interjected with images of the quiet Amish countryside were shown. My voice was heard saying, "I sense exactly the opposite. I don't see them (the Amish) distancing themselves from us at all. We've never been this close before. So whether or not it continues or it changes . . . it already has been a turning point. My hope is that it does continue and I believe it's theirs too." With that the show ended.

The credits rolled on in front a complacent image of Amish life. It showed a young Amish girl riding in a buggy, while the sound of a bell was ringing in the background. They had given me the last word. Mine were positive words of togetherness between our two communities. But while reviewing the program again, to write this portion of the story, I discovered that the true last word wasn't given to me. It was given to that ringing bell—the one ringing in the background. I don't think that was a coincidence. It was meant to be there. The message of this bell continually seems to find new ways of delivering itself. Here it is a year later, as I am writing this, and it's revealing itself to me in yet another new way.

The very first comment I heard as the screen went black was Molly saying, "Dad, that was great, they gave you the last word." To make that comment she had to take her cell phone from her ear. For the last fifteen minutes she had been receiving calls from her friends—"Your dad's on TV" . . . "Put on the TV, your dad's on." My phone also began ringing just as the show ended. Calls were coming in from family members that watched. They were telling me what a wonderful message I delivered and how I saw things so positively in the midst of such a terrible tragedy. The comments were nice to hear and I appreciated them all. But at that very moment I wasn't feeling as positive about the show as others. Don't get me wrong, I was thrilled that ABC saw my involvement as important enough to include. I thank them for that. But I just sat through a one-hour documentary about this event that dedicated only about twelve minutes to a truly power-ful and positive element in this story. Considering the headline type of treatment that tragedies are given by most of the media, I suppose I wasn't surprised, just disappointed. Perhaps my being so immersed in the kindness of the aftermath made me one of the few who was viewing it this way.

Well, there it was. The documentary had aired. What would come of it only time would tell. I didn't hang around Claire's very long, just a few minutes. By now it was after 11:00 p.m. and Claire had work tomorrow. So I headed home. Molly left too. She was meeting some friends. A few minutes later I was home. As I walked inside all the lights in the house were turned off, except for one or two. The darkness made it easy to see the light on my answering machine was blinking. There were phone messages waiting for me. Now mind you the show had only finished about twenty minutes ago. Pressing play the messages came one after the other. There were familiar voices of friends and some were total strangers. All were thanking me for my involvement with the Amish and praising my appearance on the show. First of all, I was shocked that anyone called at all and secondly that they called so quickly.

I took off my coat, turned on some lights and got a drink from the fridge. Then I went to my computer to check my mail, as I do every night. As surprised as I was by the phone messages, what I now found was even more surprising. There were pages and pages of e-mails waiting for me. I couldn't believe my eyes. I scrolled through them with amazement, wondering which to read first.

It was now about 11:30, and the end of a long day that started early with a live on-the-air interview, with Murph and Casey. The rest of the day was pretty much filled with anticipation about the documentary. Then of course there was the rush of watching the show itself. It had already been a full day. Should I even dig into reading these now? This could take hours. Curiosity got the best of me. I opened a few. Mail was coming in from all across the country. The words I read were so moving. One person wrote of having a terrible tragedy in her own life and how she had given up on humanity. But hearing what I said revitalized her belief in mankind. Hearing me speak gave her hope again. Someone else said, "Yours was the voice of reason on that program." I was shocked. Stories like this I wasn't prepared for right then. I stood up, and backed away from the computer and wondered for a moment what to do next. My appearance on the show had only lasted for a few minutes. Apparently what I said had an impact. The message had been heard.

I reached for my cell phone and called Molly. I told her what I came home to find. She must have heard a sense of excitement or apprehension in my voice because her immediate response was, "You have to get out of the house. Get away from it for now. Take a break and come have a drink with us." It didn't take much to convince me. In minutes I found myself grabbing my coat and heading for the door.

I walked into the bar where Molly and her friends were waiting. The place was crowded and noisy. But all I could hear were the words from those letters repeating in my head. It was obvious that Molly was glad to see me as she greeted me with smiles and a hug. We sat down and I ordered a drink for each of us. My drink would sit in front of me for the entire night, untouched. A drink wasn't what I needed. Apparently all I needed was to talk this through with someone. Molly was wise beyond her years that night, because she knew that's what I needed before I even did. So that's what we did for the next few hours, we talked. We talked about what I had been going through for the last few months, about the Amish families, about the girls, about all the people I met. We talked about the media time I had been getting, about the documentary and about the exposure it had to so many people and the positive message I sent. We also talked about what kind of response it might continue to get. A response like I was already seeing happen so quickly.

Around 2:00 we left the bar. Molly continued on with her friends, going to one of their homes. She was still hitting her stride at that time of night, like twenty-one year olds do. I, on the other hand, was finishing a long day. One I thought was over hours ago. I made my way home. I stood out back on the deck before going inside. Looking up at the stars I thought about how far this message was spreading and once again reassured myself that I was ready for this. Inside the house was dark and a bit chilly. There was no intention of looking at my mail or even checking the answering machine again. I went straight to bed. Tomorrow would be a new day. I would deal with it then.

The dawn did come and before I could even get out of bed the phone was ringing. I didn't answer it. The machine would get it. I stayed in bed listening as a message was left. It was someone calling from Alabama, or Florida, or Georgia. Honestly I don't remember where the first call came from. But they came from all across the country and Canada. That day and for days to follow it seemed the phone didn't stop ringing. No I didn't just let the machine take the calls. I would answer it when I was home and when I wasn't the machine would take a message. When I did pick up the voice on the other end was always surprised. There seemed to be an awestruck hesitation in their voice and they'd say something like, "Mr. Becker. Is that really you? Thank you for taking my call." Perhaps they didn't know they were calling my home. I live here. I answer the phone; it's something I do.

These people were a joy to talk to. Calling in response to the show, they were letting me know how thrilled they were with the things I said and how I used my art for such a good cause. I was beginning to wonder just what it was I said. It went by so fast I might have missed something. No, I knew what they were hearing. Even though it was brief, they heard and felt the powerful message that had driven this image from the beginning. This message of kindness didn't have to be loud or boisterous. Perhaps whispered, or spoken softly, was more appropriate.

People called to tell me how they visited Lancaster County and how much they loved the Amish country. How encounters with the Amish were always memorable and how sad they were for these families. Every caller was very pleasant. So many commented, "What a wonderful place it must be where you live." Of course I agreed with that. Calls like this went on for days, until days became weeks. I spoke to so many people, answering their questions and giving them my time.

As for the e-mails, well it's the same story as the phone calls. Beginning the morning after the show I spent the entire day reading and answering them all. Well, almost all of them. You see, as fast as I would answer a few, new ones would show up. My next few days were spent both in front of the computer and answering the phone. This tragedy and the message of kindness toward others were touching people's hearts. Talking directly to individuals and reading their letters was very moving. But a few of the letters in particular were emotionally stirring. These people were telling me such personal stories. I read about troubles that families were having, inspiring stories of overcoming hardship. I even received stories from parents telling me of their own sons and daughters who died. Time and time again the words of how inspiring this message was to them came up on my screen. I read every one of those letters and everyone got a response. Just as the phone calls did, this went on for weeks.

Eventually the postal mail caught up with the e-mails. Letters came in piles: more stories, more well wishes, prayers and requests for prints.

One of the letters I received was from a church pastor in South Carolina. In addition to requesting a print, he told me he had spoken to his congregation about the tragedy and the painting. He asked if I could ship a print to him right away. He wanted to address this topic further with his congregation and would like to have it available to show them. Wanting to oblige a request as special as that, the print was sent out immediately. Neither he nor I knew at this time how this message was about to bring our lives together.

The very same day I received this request, someone locally put me in touch with a young woman in South Carolina. I was told she was a person with a strong sense of spirituality and would have an interest in my actions and the message.

We contacted each other through e-mail a few times and then spoke by phone. It turned out that Julie had grown up here, in the Lancaster County area, near Nickel Mines. She moved to South Carolina just days before the shootings. Furthermore she had just started attending the same church as the pastor who requested the print. Here I go again, I thought. This was sounding to me like another incredible connection and coincidence on the journey.

Many evenings we talked by phone. I would tell her stories of the journey I was on and share philosophical ideas. She would tell me stories of her spiritual awareness. You see, Julie is a person who seems to be as connected to the spiritual aspects of being human, in the way that most people are connected to the physical aspect of being human. Does that make sense? What I mean is she is more spiritually guided than most. It was through these shared philosophical ideas and spiritual ways of approaching life that we quickly became long-distance friends. As weeks of discussions passed, she planned a trip back to visit her family in PA. That was the first time we met in person. During that visit I took her to the Nickel Mines area. That was a very moving experience for her.

Since Julie was a young girl she knew she had this gift of feeling, seeing and connecting with spirits. Both those within each of us and those that had passed on. While getting to know her, through our long-distance phone calls, she shared with me a vision she had. This was a vision that came to her before she and I ever met. It happened the day of the shootings in Nickel Mines. That day Julie had no knowledge of the tragedy. She had just moved into her new place in SC. There was no TV hook-up, no newspaper delivery had been set up and she hadn't started her new job. Those first days were spent unpacking and setting up a new home.

This is the story she shared with me: The night of the shootings, while in her new home, she had a vision of five young Amish girls. (Visions like this, she sees with her heart as much as her eyes.) The girls were standing somewhat in a row. The one that seemed to be in the front and center was communicating with her. The young girl told Julie that they were fine. That their purpose had been fulfilled and that the world was about to experience forgiveness and kindness in a way it had never before seen. This would be happening soon and she should watch for the sign. At the time Julie had no idea what this could be referring to. She had visions before and their meaning would eventually become known. So, as strong as this vision was, she didn't fully understand it and just let it be.

Okay, now I admit, I'm a pretty open-minded guy. But hearing this gave me reason to pause. At first I wondered if I should maybe hang up the phone and change my number. But I didn't. This journey had taken plenty of unusual turns and I would see this one through as well. Through the course of our many discussions, I came to know that Julie was not one to falsely manufacture a story like this. She was genuine. Neither of us made a big issue of it or got heavy handed about it any way. This journey would lead me where it was suppose to. We shared the story and let it go.

The other thing I came to find out from her, was that the pastor at her church, Ed, was working on producing a short film. It was going to highlight the power and importance of forgiveness in our lives. As an example of this, he intended to express how important forgiveness is in the Amish way of life. This film was planned and in production before the shootings at Nickel Mines and before Julie moved there. When the shootings occurred Ed was devastated. But through that tragedy he saw forgiveness like he never had seen before.

Now let's look at how these elements of three different people's lives have brought them together. I receive a print request from this pastor, at a time when I know neither he nor Julie. Then a friend introduces me to Julie, who has this vision of five Amish girls telling her to watch for signs of forgiveness like never before seen. Then she happens to join the congregation of this same pastor who contacted me who happened to be working on a film about forgiveness and the Amish. Now she and I become friends and she is telling me of his film. Many unrelated circumstances were connecting us.

She and Ed talked about my inclusion in the film. He loved the idea of having me be a part of it. He wanted me to speak to the congregation, tell stories of this journey and have it filmed. We discussed the idea of him flying me down to film my portion. These discussions went on for several weeks. My indecision about whether or not to be a part of this film was something I grappled with. I simply wasn't sure if this was something I should be involved in.

Talking to Ed and Julie got to be something I was doing several times a week. During one of those discussions I told Julie of a conversation I had with one of the Amish fathers, just that day. Our discussion dealt with forgiveness and I thought she and Ed would like to hear it.

John (the Amish father) and I were sitting in his shop and he told me this: He said there is a Bible passage where someone asks Jesus how many times I must forgive someone. Jesus says to him, forgive him 70 x 7 times. "Well," John said, "I always figured that meant if someone kicks me I forgive him. If he kicks me again, I forgive him again. If he does it again I forgive him again. Now the English media keep saying that we have forgiven Charlie. They say it like it's something we as a community got together and decided to do as a group. No, it doesn't work that way. All individuals must forgive from within themselves. It's an individual process. I have forgiven Charlie," he said. "But because I'm human I may wake up tomorrow and the hatred for what he did may rise up again. So, I have to forgive him again . . . and again the next day . . . and the next. So, now I've learned that I may have to forgive someone for the same thing 70 x 7 times."

I thought this was tremendously insightful. When I completed telling this story to Julie, there was a long pause from the other end of the phone. Then she said to me, "Do you know what the name of our movie is?" I told her, "No you guys told me what it's about but not a name." She paused again then said, "It's called 70 x 7 . . . we need to get you down here."

Stunned as I was by this connection . . . I agreed. Arrangements were made and I would soon be flying to Charleston.

CHAPTER 10

New Hope

THE DATE FOR another speaking engagement was approaching. This appearance, like every other one, would have its own interesting encounters. It came about through a phone call I received from a woman named Louise. She and I had previously never met, yet she, her pastor and her church congregation, had heard of my involvement with the Amish, the painting and its message. She called asking if I would be willing to speak to the congregation. One of the factors that would make this interesting was that I would be speaking during two of their Sunday morning services. That in and of itself isn't what was interesting. People speak during church services all the time. But by now you can see how complex and detailed this journey has been. This is a story I could spend hours telling. What made this interesting is that they were only allowing me five minutes during each service to speak. I had the task of condensing my story and the message into just five minutes. To do this I put together an outline of the key points and read over it several times, while carefully watching the clock. The last thing I wanted to do was run long and have my appearance become an interference with the service. The other reasons that made this appearance so interesting were factors I wouldn't learn until that day.

On the Sunday of the services I drove half an hour to the church. The last mile or so took me across winding, snow-covered, back roads. Approaching the church I reached a slight hill and made my way safely to the top. As I crested the hill I saw the church on the other side. It was a large stone building that sat majestically in a valley of snow-covered fields. This building was a dignified looking structure. I arrived early. Parked right next to the door and made my way inside with an arm full of prints. Louise greeted me just inside the door with smiles and a hug. Then she introduced me to her husband Bill and the church pastor. Prior to this we had only spoken several times by phone. What a cheerful, inspiring woman she turned out to be. They took me to see the sanctuary where I would be speaking and helped me set up an area to make prints available in a separate back room.

The interior of this church was beautiful. It was full of the traditional elements thought of when envisioning a large old stone church: dark wooden pews, stained glass, and an ornately carved wooden pulpit on the altar. Among all the traditional decor there were elements that indicated the contemporary flair of the day: There was an area dedicated to a three or four piece band. Including a full drum set, keyboard and several guitar stands and amplifiers. In the back of the room video equipment was being set up. Off to the right of the altar was a large retractable projection screen. Amidst all this blending of old and new there was an overriding sense of humility, respect and concern for one another.

Just before the service was about to begin, I was hooked up with a wireless microphone and told that my presentation was going to be filmed and recorded. The option of speaking twice (once at each service) or showing the film of me speaking at the second service was offered. I decided that trying to fit all I had to say into five minutes would be difficult enough to do once, so showing the film at the second service sounded good to me. That would also make it easier for me to be available to those wanting prints after each service.

As the service began I took my seat with Louise and her family in the second pew. It was an inspiring service. The band and the singers were wonderful. Words to the songs and calming inspirational images were projected onto the large screen. The congregation was engaged right from the start. The atmosphere in the room and attitude of the pastor were both inviting and invigorating. About halfway through the service, just before he introduced me, the pastor spoke about the Amish tragedy and the importance of forgiveness. I walked up front to the altar, thanked them for inviting me and began. I started by telling them of my time limitation and how they were about to hear the most abbreviated version of this journey ever told. The next five minutes went by in a flash. But I believe I hit all my key points and left them with a closing message of how to incorporate kindness and forgiveness into their lives. As I sat down the smile on Louise's face told me that it went well.

Afterward she and I went to a room in the back where people were directed to go, if they wanted prints. It was only a few minutes before people started streaming in. Families, elderly, teens, they all came requesting and contributing. This is when things began to get more interesting. A gentleman came up to the table requesting a print. He was dressed in a suit jacket, button-up shirt and nice pants—much like anyone else attending church. But he was also wearing multicolored sneakers, which I thought was kind of interesting, or odd. I was seated behind a long table and he was standing on the other side. At first he seemed a bit nervous, but the longer he talked the more at ease he became. He was soft spoken, with gentle mannerisms, as he told me how moved he was to hear about my journey. At one point he was down on one knee with his arms leaning on the table telling me that he had been a youth minister for the past seven years. A youth minister, perhaps that explained the sneakers. Anyway, his life was dedicated to helping others discover the power of God in their lives. This may have been his calling, but it wasn't his only profession. He also was a screenplay writer for a major motion picture company. He said he was in the middle of developing a story that dealt with Jacob Ammon, the founder of the Amish community. My interactions with the Amish community and my direct involvement with their actions of forgiveness were of great interest to him. It wasn't long before he asked me if I would consider being interviewed and included in his screenplay. I thought, "Are you kidding me? You want to include what I've been doing in a movie?" I may have even said that out loud. Our conversation only lasted a few minutes. Mostly it was him talking. Then he gave me his card and it was left that we would get in touch with each other.

When he was gone, I asked Louise about him. I wanted to know if this guy was for real. She spoke very highly of Vince and told me how much everyone in the church loved him. She told me how he had recently spearheaded the construction of a new cafe, developed specifically for the youth of the community. It was a place they could gather with the confidence of finding companionship, spiritual growth and fun. It was called The Journey Cafe. The "journey" cafe I thought. Now there was a name that got my attention. This place was sounding wonderful already. While all this was happening the second service was in progress and already coming to an end. The second wave of people wanting prints was on their way. I met with and saw to it that everyone was taken care of. In between the people approaching me at the table Louise and I were having a deep conversation about God, life, my beliefs, her beliefs and so on. One of the things she shared with me was how she saw her life's role as being an inspiration to people doing God's work. She saw herself playing a supportive role to those spreading a message of love, togetherness and fellowship. Her role, as she viewed it, was to assist those spreading God's messages. Then Louise offered her help to me, however I might need it, in spreading this message of kindness.

I had gotten many offers of assistance from people before. But somehow this one was different. There was a sense of genuine divinity attached to this one. It's hard to explain it even now. Her offer rang of such sincerity and depth of source. It appeared that we were laying the groundwork for a lasting friendship. Ever since that day Louise, her family and I have become friends. It would be hard to recount the number of times I was searching for guidance or looking for an answer and out of the blue an e-mail or phone call from Louise would show up . . . right on cue.

When I was all packed up and driving away from the church, I realized how this, oh so short, speaking appearance had brought me to meet someone who could become a very good friend and be very supportive along this journey. I also was astonished that I had been asked to have my story included in a screenplay being written for a major motion picture. Not something that happens everyday or ever. I tried to keep my focus on the drive home as it all sank in. I'll just have to see what comes of this. I mean, the idea of being involved with a movie has the sound of immediate appeal. But the last thing I wanted to do was have my experiences with the Amish manipulated for the screen, or made into something it wasn't. I knew the Amish were in favor of this good message continuing to spread. But I had no idea in what ways that would happen. Confused about it, I gave it some thought over the next few days and decided to simply stay open to what might come. Trying to guess the future would be a waste of time. This journey has been filled with unexpected twists and turns. If this journey and message were to be delivered over a medium such as that, so be it. But I wasn't going to be pushing for anything. It will find its way.

Later that week, I received a phone call from Kym. She told me that she was just visiting with John, one of the Amish father's who had children attending the Nickel Mines School. I knew John and had visited with him and his family several times. He was the man given the task of restoring the original schoolhouse bell. It was taken down just before the building was demolished. Kym had good news. The work on the bell was finished. It had been newly powder-coated, looked beautiful and was ready for hanging in the new school. But her even better news was that the offer was being extended to me to come visit, see the bell and take photo reference of it for a second bell painting. Did you hear that? Yes, I said a second bell painting. This man, father to children at the school that awful day, an upstanding member of the Amish community, was suggesting to me to do a second bell painting. Well, this was an invitation that doesn't come along everyday and one I wasn't going to miss. My schedule that day included teaching and other appointments. That just wouldn't do. I canceled the classes and cleared all my appointments. Within less than an hour I was making my way to John's house.

As I drove, I began to think about John's suggestion of a second painting. The Amish had already expressed their approval of the first painting. Then they told me of their approval to make my speaking appearances and now this. The idea of a second painting was okay with them. Should I be reading this as a sign that continuing to find new ways of spreading the message was the thing to do? Living with the principal of treating others with kindness and compassion is something that has always been prevalent in my life. Conscious attempts are made to express it through my actions, daily. Why should I shy away from methods of sharing those aspects of life with others? Even if that method was foreign to me, like including it in a film. Just as I had been doing all along, I would stay open to all possibilities, even that one.

It wasn't long before I arrived at John's house. Kym and I had made arrangements to meet there. She had already arrived. The two of them were outside talking. As I pulled up their attention was directed toward my truck. Hearing me pull up, John's wife Mary came out to greet me also.

It was nearing the end of February and winter was beginning to fade. This was a shirt-sleeve day. The sun was shining bright and warm. So we stood outside greeting each other and talking about how everyone was doing. Then John, knowing why I was there, said, "Well, do ya want to see it?" Without hesitation I responded, "You bet I do." We walked toward his garage. He went inside and wheeled a child's old style wooden wagon out to the driveway. On it sat the bell. It was just like the one that had been hanging outside the temporary schoolhouse: jet black, about twenty inches tall and fourteen inches across at its widest point. It was thick wrought iron, solid and heavy—hence the wagon to move it around. Upon seeing it, this bell brought forth the feeling within me of studious nobility. It generated a presence similar to what you might feel if viewing the bells from much more scholarly halls. Say for instance an Ivy League school, or some private institution of higher learning. I remember feeling similarly when walking the grounds of Harvard University, while on one of my many trips to the Boston area. I know that sounds silly to make such a comparison, but that's how I felt. This humble bell from a one-room Amish schoolhouse was carrying with it the presence of honorable, majestic, moral principals. This was the bell from the original schoolhouse. The bell that called the children to school each day and told them when the day was done. This was the bell that called them to school even on that most tragic day. This bell is the one the boys from that classroom persisted to reach, by climbing walls and trees so that it could be rung, in honor of their friends, the girls who didn't survive that awful day. Now here I was, being given the opportunity and privilege of photographing it and painting it.

In a genuinely grateful tone I thanked John, "Thank you for this opportunity. This is indeed special of you to allow me to do this because I know how special this bell is to you." Then after a pause to once again visually take in its presence, I looked at John and asked, "So it's okay with you if I photograph it?" "Sure, do what you need to," he replied.

As it sat there, now on the driveway where John placed it, the brilliant mid morning sunshine was blanketing the bell in intense warmth and light. The blackness of the shadowed areas was deep and rich, while the sunlit areas seemed to ring with reflections of light. It appeared to have such strength. It actually seemed to exude a sense of anticipation to be ringing. Its function was to ring and it seemed to be speaking to me of longing for just that . . . calling out to the children once again. I took my time photographing it from many angles, always being careful not to mistakenly point my lens toward my Amish friends. I would never want to offend them or cause them to feel any mistrust with me holding a camera, while standing outside their home. They trusted me and knew better than to think I would photograph any of them, without permission. But I was very conscious of where I was, what I was doing and moved about carefully.

When I had all the images needed, I told them, "Okay, that should do it. I'm done." Kym, John and Mary were all curious about how I would paint it. They wanted to know what kind of setting it would be in, things like that. Suggestions were made and questions were asked. It was great to see them enthusiastic about another painting. "How will you paint it? In its new bell tower? Because when it's installed in the new school it will be enclosed and not be viewable. Maybe you could show it with an open bell tower or none at all. Will it be in a school setting? With a blue sky?"

The questions came one after the other. I didn't know yet how I would depict it. What I did know is what I would title it. I must admit the idea of doing a second painting had crossed my mind before today and I had already chosen a title or rather it chose me. As you now know, I almost never title my work. But this name came to me in a moment of inspiration, days perhaps even weeks ago. It would be called *New Hope*. I don't know why exactly. It just felt right. It had a positive sound to it. Just as the sound of the school bell ringing again would be positive as well. So at this point a name is all I had. So I shared it with them. I looked at them and said, "I'm not sure how I'll depict it. But it already has a name. I will call it *New Hope*."

We visited for a bit longer. Standing around talking about this and that, as friends do. John asked if I had been to the construction site of the new school. As close as I was with this community, I would not think to impose on going to the new site. The Amish, on Amish private property, were building it. It was no place for an Englishman to wander in without being invited. So I told him, "No. I heard about the construction, but haven't seen it." He immediately invited me out to see the progress right then. I was thrilled. "Great, I'd love to go, thanks."

John was about to be heading there himself. He is very involved in this building project. Construction is his business. His driver would be along shortly to take him. Kym and I rode together in her car and started out first. I knew where the school was being built and whose land it was on. But I hadn't been there since before construction started. It was just a short drive to get there. Once this school is finished, the walk for the children would be even shorter. They could cut across the fields we had to drive around. Arriving at the property, we proceeded down the long drive. There it was, the new school. Very few people were permitted on this property. It was private land, owned by parents with children of school age. From the outside, the building looked nearly ready. The only work left to complete was topping off the now muddy driveway and some finishing work on the inside.

We parked next to the building and went inside. Two workers (young Amish men) were busy going about their jobs. They took the time to talk with us about the flooring they were installing and pointed out a few features: the hat and coat rack area, the updated, less drafty windows, they even pointed out the outhouse (a separate building not far off through the windows). This one-room schoolhouse would be similar in many ways to other Amish schoolhouses, it was modern only in the elements that were going into its construction. The principals and teachings held within these walls would remain constant. I took notice of the new chalkboard. First what struck me was that it wasn't black. It wasn't the classic, black slate panel with a wooden chalk and eraser holder below. You know the kind I mean: The style that used to be in all schools. This was made of what most new "chalkboards" are these days. It's some white, solid vinyl-like material. No more chalk here; it would be erasable markers instead. Something was already written on the board. As I walked closer to read it, I couldn't believe my eyes. In black marker, right there in the center of the board were the words, "New Hope Amish School." A warm chill (if that's possible) ran through my body. I was stunned. I had to shake my head and refocus my eyes to read it again, New Hope Amish School. New Hope, that's the title that came to me for the second painting. How could that be? What did that mean? After overcoming the chill and the sense of wonder, I read the words out loud, "New Hope Amish School." I turned to Kym and asked her to look at this. "Kym, do you see that?" I asked as I pointed to the board. "That's the name I just told you I was going to use for the new painting." "Oh my God," she said. "You're right." I hurriedly and anxiously asked the workers who wrote that and why. They told me they thought it was written by one of the parents. It's the name chosen for the new school. Kym and I looked at each other in amazement, not knowing what to say. Both of us were overcome by a sense of awe. We again had the experience of feeling there were powers greater than ours at work here.

Just then John and his driver pulled up. He went right to work discussing the project with the workers. Kym and I wandered around, further examining the building. Once I got the okay to take pictures I did, both inside and out. Being sure to get a few shots of the "writing on the wall." That's how it felt. As though this was a message written on the wall for me to find. An instruction to continue the spread of this message and follow the path of this journey. Kym and I didn't stay very long. We left the men to their work. Even as we drove away, Kym and I never spoke of it again. It didn't need to be spoken of. Simply accepted.

One of the things I talked to John about earlier in the day, had to do with a friend of mine coming to visit him. Darrin is a journalist who covered the story of my journey since its beginning. He's a young man with a wife and new baby. Making his living by writing for the paper and selling stories to various magazines, he wrote one of the front-page articles about me in a local newspaper. We talked often, he and I. He would call and curiously ask how things were going or I would call him and fill him in on the latest happenings. The ease of our friendship was comfortable enough that I could call him at work or home. He was fascinated by this journey. I grew to know his character to be honest and trustworthy. I wouldn't take just anyone to visit with the Amish, especially if they were from the press. But Darrin is a good and decent man. He was the only media-related person I felt comfortable taking there.

John was open to the idea of meeting him and we decided I would bring him by in a few days. When that day came we were fortunate again to have beautiful weather. Darrin showed up at my house about mid morning and we were off. He was excited and a bit nervous about the day ahead. More than once he asked if there were appropriate or inappropriate ways of handling himself around the Amish, just as I questioned Kym. He didn't want to mistakenly offend anyone. I told you he was a good man. I gave him a few simple pointers, nothing too cumbersome or extreme. I assured him that he would be meeting genuinely nice people. They may not understand all of our English ways, but they knew good character when they saw it. So be yourself and you'll be fine.

I planned on having him visit several households. Our first stop was with John, who I had just been out to visit with and see the bell. As we pulled up Darrin was a bit quiet, with the anticipation of the moment. I got out of the truck and went to the door. Darrin waited by the truck. Mary told me that John was in his workshop, next to the house. So in we went. I introduced them to each other and in his normal fashion John was quiet. Both of these men were soft-spoken . . . perhaps I would have to get a conversation going. I reminded John that Darrin was the reporter who wrote the front-page article about me. Remembering that Darrin was a reporter John was taken back and said perhaps he shouldn't be talking to him. Most Amish shy away from any media. I assured him of Darrin's good character and John knew I wouldn't bring anyone to his home under false pretenses or with intent to pry. Darrin also told him his visit was of a personal nature. If it were John's wishes none of this would be printed.

It wasn't long before tensions eased and friendly talk was abundant. In fact, John was so comfortable that he did something I never thought would happen . . . ever. Now, I knew that the temporary school was right there next to us as we spoke. It was the building just feet away from where we stood. This was a Saturday and it was empty. But nevertheless, there it was. John knew I had been inside visiting the children and teacher, during one of their school days. But others would never recognize it as such. From the outside it looked like John's garage, which it was until a few months ago. Remember, this place was kept secret from all outsiders. To my surprise, John wanted to invite Darrin inside. John nodded to me and said, as he looked toward the garage. "How about we show him something?" I was shocked. "That's up to you. You know I would never tell anyone about that." John walked away and came back in a few seconds with a set of keys. We were actually going inside. As we approached the door John said to Darrin, "Here's something for you to remember." Then he opened the door. As we stepped in I told Darrin what this place was. His jaw dropped in amazement. I told him of the secret nature of this place. How he was among only a handful of people that knew of its existence. "I'm honored that you would show me this," he said. "If you want, nothing will get written about this. I will tell no one."

The room was much like I remembered it: Full of life and color. Wooden student desks faced the teacher's desk in the front of the room. Alphabet letters and drawings were hung on the walls. Pegs for the coats and hats to be hung and shelves for lunch boxes were in the back of the room. Everywhere was evidence of youthful learning. Darrin walked slowly around in shear amazement to find himself in these surroundings. He asked a few questions about what he saw and John offered a few stories and insight. John shared with us his interpretation of what happened that dreadful day. To use his words, he said, "The devil's plan to play a card of evil backfired, because of all the good that is now coming from such tragedy." In saying this I knew he was referring to the kindness that was spreading and the closeness of bringing people together.

We didn't stay inside very long, maybe ten minutes. Once outside, Darrin thanked John several times. Now he knew something very few people did. As we prepared to leave, we said our goodbyes and headed back to the car. While walking away, I watched Darrin as he looked again at that building. Where moments ago, when glancing in that direction, he saw only a garage, now stood a building of great importance to this community. Behind his eyes, as he gazed, I could see his mind wheeling with visions of the children. Pulling away I said to him, "Well I didn't expect that. That certainly doesn't happen everyday." Darrin simply responded shaking his head,

"Wow. I'm shocked. What an honor." We talked briefly about the importance of keeping this place a secret. He understood and agreed. To this day he has kept his word.

Before leaving the Nickel Mines area we stopped and visited at two more Amish homes. The topics of our discussions varied. But of course there was talk about the day of the shootings and how the children and families were doing. Family members offered stories of their personal involvement on that tragic day. We even discussed forgiveness. Darrin was also hearing firsthand comments about the impact of my painting and its message. It made me feel good that this friend and reporter was having the story I told him substantiated by the actual people involved.

In addition to visiting the temporary schoolhouse, Darrin was gaining insight to these families that few people had. But the schoolhouse visit of course put his day trip over the top. By the time our day was done, we had been in Nickel Mines for several hours. The entire drive back was spent talking and recapping what we had been through. He had learned more, done more, visited with more families and of course seen more than he had possibly imagined.

Prior to this day he had commented that the story of this journey had to be told. Now he was convinced of it. Being a writer himself, he would love to be the one who writes it. But if that was not to be the case, he offered any assistance in helping me write it. Either way he felt strongly that this story had to be told.

Darrin wasn't the first to express how this story had to be written. That it had to be told for the world to hear. Practically right from the start all sorts of people were suggesting it. Or perhaps better stated, they insisted it be done. They and I both knew that the media would not cover this story of kindness. It didn't have the flash, or violence, or the drama that's required to make the evening news. The only way people would learn about this small community rejecting violence and meeting it head on with kindness and forgiveness, is if someone told it. The people I encountered along the way, were letting me know that someone must be me.

I heard them. But this wasn't the time. There was more to happen. There were further steps to take. It didn't feel as though this was the time to write.

Darrin's encouragement and the happenings of the past few days could not have come at a better time. My first meeting with Vince, the screenplay writer with the multi-colored sneakers, was just a few days away. I would be telling him my story. I didn't know what to expect from that meeting. How would it go? Would he ask a lot of questions? Tell me about the story he was writing? Or when he heard some of the things I've been through maybe he'd think I was crazy. Well, it didn't matter. The day had come for the meeting and I was going.

The Journey Cafe, where we were meeting, was about twenty minutes away. I arrived on time and Vince was waiting to greet me. The cafe was closed at this time so the door was locked. He let me in, locking the door behind us. Yep, he was still wearing the multi-colored sneakers this time with shorts and a t-shirt. This was a pretty laid- back guy. He offered me some coffee or something to drink. Being a cafe there was plenty of it around. The place was beautiful: hard wood floors. It was very spacious with upholstered chairs everywhere to accommodate plenty of the community's youth. There's an area where live bands can perform, a separate room with a pool table, foosball and pinball machine. A large screen projection TV for the kids to watch movies could be lowered from the ceiling. And of course the coffee and soft drink bar. This place was an amazing asset to the community.

We took our seats, in those comfortable upholstered chairs, facing each other in the middle of this large room. Vince reminded me of the screenplay he was working on, the story about Jacob Ammon, the Amish and how kindness and forgiveness were so integrated into their lives. He wanted to see if my story could be worked into his. He thought perhaps it could be used as an example of how the Amish of today live a life of kindness and forgiveness. So as he sat across from me, with his pad of paper and pen, he said, "Why don't you start at the beginning?" Well that left it pretty wide open. What actually was the beginning of this story? I gave him some background on myself, my art and then picked up with the day I found the bell. . . .

Three hours later I stopped talking. He hardly ever said a word. Not that he had to. The story came flowing out of me. He sat writing, nodding, chuckling and at times showing outright signs of amazement. The intricacies of this story were so great that over the course of three hours I had only gotten to the point just after the first signing. To say the least, Vince was blown away. He was awestruck by the series of coincidences, acts of divine intervention, call them whatever you will. But he found the way things unfolded on this journey to be captivating. "You can't write stuff like this," he said. "Truly amazing."

Both of us had the will and desire to continue. But we had to end that first meeting because of prior commitments. It was decided that we would meet again and pick up with the story where it left off. As we both left the cafe that day, I found that now there was another person in my life that felt this story had to be told. Vince was saying, just as Darrin did, "You have to write this story. Even if I incorporate it into my film . . . you still need to write it." If he was that impressed, I thought, just wait. Being such a short distance into conveying these encounters, he hadn't heard the half of it. So much more lay ahead to tell him. As for me, well, this journey was continuing. I was in the midst of it and neither of us knew what was to come next.

The next day I was going to an event called a Mud Sale. I guess I could best describe it as an Amish flea market or Amish yard sale: a very big one. It was being held on the grounds of the Bart Fire Company, just outside of Nickel Mines. This was an all-day event. But the word was to get there in the morning. The Amish start their days very early.

When I got there it didn't take long to find out why it was called a mud sale. This was March and the ground was beginning to thaw. The event was mainly outdoors in a field and with so many people attending there was mud everywhere. I arrived about mid morning to find thousands of people roaming the grounds. I would say the crowd was ninety-five percent Amish and five percent English. It was a sea of black topped off with straw hats. Visually this was an amazing sight for an artist. Some English came with cameras and were using them. But I didn't dare take pictures. I knew better than to insult or cause these people to be uncomfortable at their own event.

At this sale you could buy everything from homemade crafts, tools, farm equipment, baked goods, furniture, clothes, quilts, buggies and more. There was even a horse auction. I had no idea it would be as big as it was. Yes this was an all-day event indeed.

A repeatedly, unexpected situation I found myself in throughout the day, was to be walking among the Amish and hear my name called out by someone who knew or recognized me. There were also the times when I saw some of my Amish friends, walked up to them, call them by name and chatted about the day. In the middle of thousands of people from a completely different culture than my own I was right at home and it felt wonderful.

While wandering the grounds, minding my own business and exploring the enormous amount of goods being sold, my cell phone rang. Being surrounded by thousands of Amish when that happens it turns a few heads. It was Kym. She was calling to tell me about the mud sale and asking me to come out and join her. She was already here and quite surprised to find out I was too. With a little maneuvering through the crowd and with the help of utilizing specific stands as landmarks we found each other. It was good to see her and her new grandchild. Paul was back at the ranch and tending to the kennel. We talked and walked together for a while, then went our separate ways to perhaps meet up again later. What a good friend she had become. I was glad to see her there.

One of my Amish friends, that I saw that day, invited me to have breakfast with he and his family the next morning. You see, the next day held a wondrous possibility for me. Kym and Paul were going away and a temporary school bus driver had to be found to replace Kym while she was gone. There was a possibility that I would be that driver. I was being considered for the job, temporary as it was. I would pick up the children at home and take them to school. Then back home again in the afternoon. What an honor. After making the morning school run, since I was going to be in the area, I was being asked to have breakfast with John, his wife and family.

When I ran into him at the sale, we talked about a very unfortunate event that occurred at the temporary school the previous day. This accidental and yet unfortunate occurrence would be a major setback for the children and the families.

The temporary school, as you now know, was on the property of one of the parents. As you also know, the location of this school was a secret from all but a handful of people. On that same property lived an adult who had a tool sharpening business . . . hand tools, farm tools, blades of all kinds. Let me remind you here that on the day of the shootings the gunman entered the schoolhouse carrying an armful of two by fours, tools and weapons. Well, this day (yesterday) an Englishman, knowing that this sharpening service was offered, pulled up to see the gentleman and have some tools sharpened. He knocked on the house door but no one answered. After looking around the property and finding no one, he headed for the garage (the now temporary school that was currently in session and full of children). The Englishman thought perhaps the gentleman he was looking for was working inside. Having no idea of who he was about to walk in on, he opened the garage door and stepped inside carrying an arm full of saws, blades and tools. Well you can just imagine the shock and fear that jolted through those children when that door was flung open. This gentleman found himself face to face with a room full of horrified children who were experiencing their nightmare all over again.

Can you just imagine how those children felt? How that teacher felt? The several seconds of terrifying silence that followed must have lingered like a lifetime for everyone in that room. Then one of the girls thought she recognized him as one of their drivers. She asked, "Aren't you Mister A, our driver?" Realizing the severity of his mistaken actions the man responded, "No, I'm just looking for John to have some tools sharpened." Within seconds, he was apologizing for the interruption and quickly left.

Those few moments were a major setback in the progress being made by the children. They were only in the beginning stages of dealing with the terror they lived through on the tragic day of the shootings. They were only just beginning to cope with the reality of their nightmare and now this. An event so similar to what happened that tragic day, it nearly paralleled in appearance. Experiencing just those few seconds of possibly going through this nightmare a second time, was enough to push the children back into the shadows of that dark day, that still existed so freshly in their minds.

Having heard of this event, the parents agreed that no one from outside their community should interact with the children in the near future. The idea of someone else driving the school bus could be too much for the children to handle. So I was informed that driving was something I would not be doing.

I had heard this same story from Kym, just yesterday, right after it happened. Hearing it from John was every bit as riveting. Was I disappointed about not driving? Sure. But of course I completely understood the parents' wishes. My feelings of disappointment were totally inconsequential when compared to my sense of heartache for those children. What a shame for them to have such a resurfacing of terror in this new safe environment. My concerned feelings and best wishes were with the children and the teacher. I only wanted, as always, what was best for them.

Knowing how much I was looking forward to the possibility of driving, my friend did not want to worsen the news by rescinding his offer of breakfast. I had visited with his family several times and had become very close with them. He told me breakfast was still on. "We want to have you over for breakfast anyway," he said. "If you're willing to drive out tomorrow, we'll be ready for you whenever you want. How's eight o'clock? That work for you? Maybe nine? What works for you?" Grateful to hear his offer, I accepted and told him, "Thank you. I'm looking forward to it. I'll see you, Mary and the kids at eight. Can I bring anything?" "Nope. We'll take care of everything. You just show up."

I spent the rest of the day walking the grounds, sampling traditional Amish food, buying a few items and enjoying the crowd. Quite unexpectedly in the early afternoon we got a sudden downpour of rain. Space inside the fire hall was limited but thousands tried to cram in and escape the weather. I was sitting along the wall, with Kym and her granddaughter. Kym took advantage of the opportunity to feed her as the crowds swarmed in. I stood up, giving my seat to an elderly Native American Indian woman. She, Kym and I began to chat with some friendly conversation. Kym, as she energetically has the habit of doing, introduced me as, "The artist who painted the Amish school bell." The woman knew of the painting and said, "Oh, *Kindness and Compassion* (calling it by name) well that makes perfect sense that you would give me your seat. A perfect gentleman." Then she said, "You know all things happen for a reason. It's rare that I hurt myself. But this morning I fell and my leg is still bothering me. Giving me your seat is exactly what I needed right now." She continued, "I was suppose to meet you." "Oh really? Why is that?" I asked curiously, thinking here we go again. Then she told me about the chief of an Indian tribe and the holy man of the same tribe who heard of what I had done. Both wanted to meet me. They wanted to discuss my journey . . . this journey of compassion.

Okay now just picture this. Put yourself in my place for that minute. Here I am, an Englishman surrounded by thousands of Amish. Standing with my back to the wall of this fire hall due to a sudden, out of the blue, downpour of rain. In front of me the room is packed full of black clothing, bonnets and straw hats. Shoulder to shoulder Amish. Next to me sits an Indian woman, who I don't know, and she's telling me of a chief and a holy man who want to meet with me. It's not as if hundreds of strange occurrences haven't been happening to me thus far. But every now and then one stops me in my tracks and I have to ask myself, is this really happening? This was one of those times.

She went on to tell me of her Indian heritage and how moved she was by the expression of kindness through my painting. I gave her one of my cards and she told me she would be in touch. Just as suddenly as it began, right then the rain stopped, as did our fateful meeting. It was as passing as the rain. The sun was shining as bright as could be and the crowd made its way back outside into the even muddier fields. What could I make of this brief encounter other than to take it in stride? As is the case with my life, I would stay open, be positive and right now walk back into the sunlight.

Shortly after that I left the sale and headed to the field where I had parked my truck, earlier that morning. I found it completely covered in mud. The other vehicles driving by, coming and going from the field, had totally encased it in mud. I mean it was everywhere. Once inside I could not see out of a single window. Ah well, somehow it seemed a fitting, humbling end to my first mud sale.

The next morning was one I greeted with great anticipation. I was up early, showered, dressed and hit the road toward John and Mary's house. Breakfast was waiting. I arrived to smiles and a warm welcome. Upon entering the house I saw the table had already been set and Mary was cooking. "Hello Bruce," she said with her bright smile as I entered. "Just finishing up a few last things." My timing was perfect. The kids, four of them, were playing in the living room and came running to greet me. Longing to be friendly, but shy, they stood silently around me. Their smiling eyes said all the hellos I needed to hear. "You know Bruce. Say hello to him," John instructed them. So with their soft voices the children of the house welcomed me. What a beautiful sight. Everyone was dressed in matching colors. Of course the boys and John had black pants and the girls and Mary had black dresses. But all their shirts were a matching color, a soft peach. I mean everyone's shirt, even John and Mary's. It was like they dressed up for company. I felt so honored.

After a few minutes of friendly talk, mainly about the mud sale, John gestured to the table saying, "Have a seat." I carefully chose a chair in the middle of the table. Leaving both heads, or ends, of the table for Mary and John. Mary continued to prepare and lay food out for the meal. Coffee was poured for John and myself. Mary asked if I wanted anything else to drink. John suggested some milk. (I happen to be a big milk drinker.) "No, he doesn't want that milk," Mary insisted. That made me curious. "What milk?" I asked. That's when John stepped outside to the back porch and returned with "that milk." It was a one-gallon, wide mouth jar, with a screw-on lid. It was nearly filled to the top with, what else, milk. Mary laughed and said,

"Bruce you don't want that. I don't think you'll like it." "Why? What is it? Why won't I like it?" I asked. She explained, "It's not like what you are used to from the store. It's straight from the cow this morning. That's the milk we drink." I exclaimed, "Are you kidding? Of course I want some." John poured a glass and set it at my place for breakfast.

Before we started eating we all held hands, Mary, John, the kids and myself. John prayed, thanking God for the meal and friends, then asked for God's blessings upon us all. We sat and ate and talked for nearly an hour: eggs, toast, apple butter, bacon, sausage gravy, and grape juice. There was even dessert. Dessert with breakfast I wasn't used to. It was a slice of pineapple, topped with a slice of caramel, and then topped again with homemade whipped cream. That's one sweet dessert for any time of day, let alone breakfast. The meal was wonderful. Filling both to the body and soul.

After breakfast we all visited together for several hours. It was fun to watch the kids play. Mary and I particularly got a good laugh from watching the girls play church. Yes, they were pretending like they were in church. She said they like to do that a lot. They set up their little chairs in the living room. Each one got a Bible and holding it open on their laps, pretended to read out loud. None of them was old enough to read and everything they said was in Pennsylvania Dutch. So I couldn't understand a word of it. But it was cute as could be. Later, I ran a few errands in the area and John rode along with me. That gave he and I a chance to talk.

A lot of wonderful memories were made that day . . .

. . . As for that glass of milk, well perhaps there is something to be said for freshness, or maybe it was the company, or the surroundings, but that was the best glass of milk I may have ever had. Days like that bring us all new hope.

CHAPTER 11

Then There Were Two

I T TURNS OUT, the TV documentary that included myself
and the painting received a positive viewer response. So
much so that the station decided to air it again. The first
time it was on they showed it twice on the same night. Now it
was going to air two more times. The difference being that this
time it would air on a Sunday night (rather than a Wednesday
as was the case the first time) and now it would show during
prime time. Well if you think my surprise to being in this
documentary at all was overwhelming, imagine my surprise to
hear that it would be showing again.

Every few months, for the past several years, I had been
staying in contact with supporters of my work through my
e-mail newsletter. These past few months I had accumulat-
ed many new names and contacts for that mailing. People
were asking to be kept informed of what I was working
on and doing next. So as requested I was sending out my
regular newsletter, only now it included information about
my experiences on this journey. The most recent newsletter
addressed the upcoming second showing of the documentary.

As awareness of the show was spreading, more requests
came in for me to make appearances: radio broadcasts and TV
talk shows were calling. Newspapers were contacting me and I
was being asked to make more speaking engagements. Time to
myself for painting was hard to find.

On the day of the show, since I had no TV, I planned on watching it at my sister Claire's house again, just as I did the first time. This time there was no word from any family members, regarding it airing or them watching. At this point, I had made many different media appearances: TV, radio, and newspapers. Now perhaps it was old hat for them. Whatever the reason all was silent on that front. I did however hear from all those directly involved with me from the beginning: Casey, Murph, Kym, and various supporters of my work, Louise, Vince, Julie and others. All of us were excited that this message and image were going to be delivered again and to so many people. A day or two before the show, Casey called with a request that had a special purpose. She asked me for the names of all the girls who lost their lives in the tragedy. She planned on dedicating her cookbook this year, to the memory of the girls. Remember I mentioned to you earlier that her cookbook reaches thousands of people every year. This year she included a memorial dedication to each of the girls and everyone affected by the tragedy. Additionally she included a picture of her and I standing by the painting, on the day of the first print signing. She was doing this, now five months after the tragedy itself. In the minds and hearts of those involved like Casey, the first responders, so many others, and myself the passage of five-months time seemed like the blink of an eye. Dealing with the families, the concerned general public and the media, kept it very present in our day-to-day lives.

So the day of the show arrived and I found myself at Claire and Jerry's house. This time Jerry wasn't working and we got to watch it together. Remember Jerry was the one who called me to tell me of the shootings, as they were occurring and I was painting the bell. It was just the three of us sitting in the darkened TV room waiting for it to start. Jerry was his talkative self. He was full of energy and had plenty of joking remarks about how my face was about to be plastered on the big screen. His humor and wit has a way of lightening any atmosphere. But he never has quite given himself enough credit for his spiritual insight and intellect. Both are sharper than he realizes. I have grown to appreciate our friendship a great deal. Claire, the mainly quiet, mild-mannered woman that she is, welcomed me once again into her home to watch this with her, for yet a second time.

Right on time the show began. I won't go through it in the detail as I did earlier. But I will tell you that as the show progressed Jerry's joking remarks quickly dissipated. The atmosphere in the room became much more somber. The severity of the scenes being shown and the detail of the gunman's action that day seemed to even change the temperature in the room itself. Jerry was seeing this program for the first time and I of course was watching for the second. So I could view it differently this time. What I watched, as much as the show itself, was the response it was stirring in him. It seemed to me that his reactions may be a gauge for how others were viewing it as well and it was touching him. The sense of drama, horror, tragedy and loss was apparent in his tone of voice as he made comments. Few as those comments now were, they had a sense of heaviness about them. A serious, perhaps even concerned tone was prevailing. Of course his ever-inquisitive mind was pondering the reasons for Charlie's actions and just what it is that drives a person to do such terrible things. But nevertheless, he was also feeling the angst of pain and trauma for those involved. He and Claire have two daughters themselves and now four grandchildren, each of which they love dearly. By viewing these acts of contemplated violence, his protective bubble of parental instincts was perhaps momentarily pierced. Is that how this was affecting other viewers? I wondered. Is that how it affected people when it actually happened? I know it certainly made me think of my children when it happened. And what of the youthful viewers? How were they processing such violence?

How would they handle seeing and hearing of it being inflicted on those of such innocence?

When the program showed me speaking and conveying the impact and importance of the message of kindness, there were no smiles or laughs about my face on the big screen. Rather, having the message follow such sad images and the tears of those parents, the words rang with clarity. Declaring an unfathomable response to the violence we had just watched. It was the response of the Amish that seemed unheard of, by the English. Nevertheless it was the Amish response.

The program did eventually end, but the heaviness in the room lingered. Jerry and Claire commented on the detail given to the gunman's actions and planning. They talked about violence in schools in general and the interaction between the Amish and English. Jerry appreciatively commented on the fact they gave me the final and positive word on the matter.

So watching it for a second time, I came away with a slightly different attitude about it. I didn't have the initial shock of seeing the people I knew, the print signing, myself or any of that. Instead, I could focus more on the overall impact of the event and the importance of forgiveness and kindness. Witnessing Jerry's reaction was surprisingly helpful. It helped me to understand more clearly how this was being viewed by those not as closely involved as myself.

When it was over I headed home. Just as had happened the first time, my answering machine and e-mail box were filling up fast. Once again people watched and were responding. Letters were coming in from all across the country and Canada. And just as the first time, I would read and answer them all. One of the letters came from a fellow artist and teacher, named Sandra. I met her at the opening of an art center located here in town. It's where she has one of her studios. We were both teachers there. I suppose I added her to my e-mail list when she gave me her card. She received my newsletter informing her of the show. She told me in the letter, that she and her son had just watched the documentary and were very moved by the Amish ability to forgive in the face of such tragedy. She wrote, "I'm sure there are others who are yet to see this and should . . . surely it makes your heart and soul happy to be able to touch others through your work . . . keep up the good work."

Only a few other artists had contacted me about this experience. Previous to this letter, Sandra and I had only spoken at any length, perhaps twice. Occasionally we passed each other in the halls and exchanged a quick hello. Yet every time I encountered her I got this strong feeling that she was preoccupied with something. She was always busy, but I had no idea with what. Brief as those meeting were, each was powerful somehow. I couldn't explain it. But I knew this was a person of good character. I was also very impressed by her work. So it was a pleasure hearing from her.

The mail in general was much like before, people telling me of tragedies they had been through and requesting prints. These are a few excerpts from the mail I received:

> *"What a fabulous symbol of forgiveness . . . I have great interest in acquiring a copy of the print Kindness and Compassion. With the hope that this will influence my rush to judgment . . . You unknowingly inspired so many people . . . Thank you for the beautiful work and beautiful healing sentiment . . . your painting touched my soul . . . I have witnessed a great many things in my military days, but nothing that has bothered me as much as this tragedy . . . I have learned so much from the Amish people and their gentle way of dealing with grief and forgiveness from this tragedy. What wonderful people and how lucky you are to have them as neighbors. They are lucky to have you as their friend as well."*

The mail went on and on like this. As was the case after the first airing, I was very moved by it. In response to the e-mails and postal mail, the house once again became like a shipping warehouse. At least every other day I would set aside time to read the letters and ship out prints.

One of the more interesting responses I got to this second airing of the program happened like this: It was morning a few days after the show aired. I was finishing up a workout and I heard a knock at the door. When I answered it I found a woman and a young girl there to greet me. "Hello," she said. "I'm sorry to bother you. But are you Bruce Becker? The painter of the Amish schoolhouse bell?" "Yes, that's me. Can I help you?" I responded. With a nervous excitement in her actions, she unrolled the paper she was clinching in her hand and showed it to me. It was a printout from my website. She said, "I would like to get a print of *Kindness and Compassion*. But simply ordering one by mail wasn't going to do it for me. I had to meet you. So my daughter and I just drove here from Baltimore, MD. I hope that's okay." This woman had just driven over two hours to find me. I must admit, I was caught off guard and surprised. What else could I do but invite her in. So I did. We sat and talked for a short while. I offered her something to drink, but she declined. Then I showed her the original painting and the bell itself. With tears in her eyes, she sat in my living room and told me of her friends that wanted to come with her but couldn't get off from work. As we parted, she thanked me for all I was doing with hugs and smiles. Can you imagine how good that made me feel? What a wonderful gesture on her part. To this day I'm not sure of her name. But if you're reading this, thank you.

To further give you an idea of how diverse the group of people was that I was hearing from: In one week I had been invited to share meals with an Amish family, a Jewish couple, an Italian Catholic family and an Evangelical Christian family . . . and that was just in one week. Since then people of almost every race and religion have favorably contacted me. This message was cutting across religious boundaries. It's simply about treating others, all people, with compassion and kindness. No matter what their ethnic heritage or religious preference.

Between the print signings, website, TV and radio appearances, newspaper articles, the ABC documentary and word of mouth, this message was spreading. But I realized there was one group (one very important group) that may not be hearing about this. Nor could they get prints for themselves. The Amish. Think about it. They didn't have TV or radio, they may not be reading the paper and they weren't using the Internet because of not using computers. I wish I could say that I came to this realization on my own, but no. It was one of the Amish that contacted me. An Amish gentleman that owns a framing business in the Nickel Mines area reached me by phone (which is unusual in itself). He told me that Amish customers looking for the print were approaching him. How could I have made that oversight? Prints were only available over the Internet and they don't use computers.

We set up a time for me to visit him at his shop. I showed up with prints in hand. We talked. We laughed. We had a wonderful visit and he took his first batch of prints. Since then I have been back to see him several times. He has reordered prints and continues to be the only outlet for them, other than my website. I'm glad I got that cleared up.

The trip to Charleston, South Carolina, was fast approaching. That's the trip I was making at the invitation of Julie and Ed, the pastor of her church. They asked to include me in their short film about forgiveness. I was going there to be filmed while speaking about my involvement with the Amish. Two things about this trip were concerning me. Not what I would speak about. Not the flying or traveling. Not even speaking before the crowd and camera. What concerned me was that the Amish would be okay with this story being told on film and the safety of the painting while in transit. So I addressed these issues before leaving.

About a week before the trip I made a special visit to a few of the Amish households. We talked about how everyone was doing and chatted about things in general, as friends do. While there I made a point of letting them know where I was about to go and why. I wanted to know how they felt about it. I guess I was looking for their blessing. Pleasantly they responded very positively. They were in favor of spreading this message of kindness, compassion and forgiveness. In fact, unexpectedly, one of the most touching points of view on the shootings was told to me that day. One of the mothers who lost her daughter said, "If my girl would have died by being hit by a car, while riding her scooter, I would have more trouble dealing with her death than I do now." A bit baffled by that comment, I asked, "Why? What do you mean by that? She died so tragically. How could being hit by a car be worse than what happened?" In a very insightful manner she said, "If she died by being hit by a car there would be no sense in that. I would have trouble understanding it. But now her death has brought forth such goodness, such compassion and kindness in others. That gives her death meaning and I can accept it easier. Good has come from this tragedy." Wow, remember this was coming from a mom who had her young daughter slain in cold blood. Now that is understanding, insight, forgiveness and compassion at work. That is an example of seeing the good within the negative. That is an example of accepting God's way even though at first we don't understand it. That is an example of how the Amish live. So having been given their blessing on my journey, I left feeling even better about making this trip.

Next I had to tackle caring for the safety of the painting while it was in transit. Up to this point all the appearances I made were relatively close to my home and studio. The painting would get wrapped up in a sheet or blanket and put in a box. Then it went in the back of my car and I was off. It was always in my direct care. With this trip, it would be checked on a plane as luggage. That was a scary thought to me. You know how poorly luggage can be handled and it's much too big to be a carry-on piece. So with the help of a good friend and talented student of mine, we laid out plans and constructed a specially-built carrying case. Eric, my friend, has an extensive array of woodworking equipment. His wood shop (which is his hobby) is filled with virtually every conceivable wood tool. This guy doesn't cut any corners (so to speak) when it comes to his woodworking. It took us two or three evenings at his house to complete the project. It looked beautiful, much like a handmade oversized wooden briefcase. We worked in the shop as Marissa (his wife and also a wonderful student of mine) made us dinner. They were such a big help: great food and this beautiful, sturdy case. I couldn't have been happier.

So now my major concerns were cared for and it was time to travel. The church where I would be speaking purchased my flight ticket. They also offered me the option of staying in a hotel (that they would pay for) or since I had become friendly with Julie I might want to consider staying with her. Staying in someone's home, while traveling, can be much more comforting somehow: friendly talk, more sociable meals, someone to show you around, etc. So I planned on staying at Julie's place with her two boys.

I'm going to preface the tales of this trip by telling you that this trip is filled with amazing events. As I describe these occurrences they may seem beyond belief. To use Vince, the screenplay writer's words: "You can't write stuff like this." At times, reality on this journey has been stranger than fiction. This trip was no exception.

My niece Katie gave me a ride to the airport. She left me out at the terminal and with bags in hand I said goodbye. I was carrying one soft-sided suitcase, my backpack (which pretty much goes everywhere with me) and the wooden case containing the painting. At the check-in counter, I had my ticket reviewed and without saying what was in the wooden case, asked if it could be handled in a way that would protect its contents. I simply said that what was inside was fragile and that I had concerns about checking it with other luggage. No one was told that there was a painting inside. I didn't want anyone to know. The check-in attendant suggested I gate check the case. That means I get to carry it to the gate and just before boarding the plane, hand it to someone who personally loads it on board. Then when I arrive at the next airport, it will be taken off and handed back to me. It wouldn't have to move with the other bags. That sounded acceptable. Still there was no mention of its contents. To look at it, this case could contain anything from documents, to fine china, to computer equipment. For all anyone knows, I could be a traveling salesman and this case held the hopeful profits of that dying breed.

After leaving the counter, my next stop was the first security check, where I would turn over my suitcase to be loaded on the plane. Here also they would scan my backpack and wooden case. Approaching the gate, yet still at least twenty feet away, the guard (a big man maybe six feet tall and two hundred and fifty pounds) was standing with his back to me. He had no earpiece, or headset and microphone, to communicate with other security. Even if he had, no one could have told him what was in that case. No one knew except myself. He turned, looked right into my eyes and without hesitation said, "You're the one traveling with the painting." I couldn't believe my ears. No one knew what I was carrying. I told no one. My body was blanketed with warmth and my knees went weak. I simply replied, "I am." Then he said, "I know about the painting." Then he quoted me its exact size to within half an inch. I was stunned as he said, "I'll take that bag," and pointed to my suitcase. Then looking at the wooden case said, "You can take the other one and go on through."

What was that? I thought. How did he know all that? That case never left my hands since I walked inside the terminal. It was never x-rayed. He didn't even x-ray it. No one was told of its contents. Strange. This trip was off to quite an unusual start.

I had a plane to catch so I continued on. A short distance further I had to go through another security check. The guard was at his position, seated at the entrance of the checkpoint. Without standing or moving at all, he looked at me and stated, not questioned, "You have the painting in there." Again, I'm stunned. "You have no tubes of paint, just the finished painting, correct?" Too shocked to say much I simply said, "Yes, that's right." "Okay go on through," he said as he motioned me forward. Slowly I made my way to the next guard. The guard who examines your bags. He x-rayed my backpack and boots. Then opened the case to examine it. After passing over and around it with a detection wand of some kind, he closed the case and allowed me to pass. It was almost like the security guards were protectors of the painting . . . custodians and gate-keepers watching over it and myself.

If I hadn't lived through the seemingly miraculous circumstances of the past seven months, I would have never been able to believe what just happened. I'll bet it sounds a bit farfetched to you reading this, but I had come to realize that nothing was out of reach when it came to this journey and this message.

I arrived at the gate, turned the wooden case over to the attendant and carefully watched him put it on the plane. Then I took a seat and waited to board. An announcement came over the speaker saying that the plane was overweight and over booked. We were asked to store things as compactly as possible. Like I needed to know that. This trip was unusual enough already and I hadn't even left the airport. While boarding, I noticed that this little plane was a propeller plane. Not even a jet engine. Now I'm getting nervous. Then I saw duct tape, yes duct tape wrapped around a portion of the fuselage. Can you believe that? As I sat down, I saw there was more duct tape holding parts of the overhead compartment in place. Now I was completely nervous. But I stayed put in my seat and prepared for takeoff. During the flight, that plane vibrated more than any other I've been on. My body was practically numb from the vibrations by the time we landed. Through it all, somehow I knew things were going to be all right. Perhaps it had something to do with the incredibly unusual send-off I got from the security guards. I was where I was supposed to be and there was a sense of safety in that.

This was the first of two flights it would take me to reach my final destination. Thankfully the second flight was uneventful and wonderfully smooth. I even got a free drink from the flight attendant. I think I needed that.

The three-hour layover in the Washington-Dulles Airport held its own interest. As I walked through the terminal, carrying my backpack and case, there was a couple seated at a table watching me. When I got close to them the gentleman said to me, "Architectural drawings or a painting?" Immediately following, the woman said, "It's a painting." "Excuse me?" I replied. "You're an artist and that's a painting." Now how would she know that? I look pretty much like anyone else and this case gives no indication of what's inside. We got to talking and I explained to them just what painting was in the case. Even with such a brief recounting of my experiences with the Amish they were enthralled. Out of the blue, the man pulled out a twenty-dollar bill and said, "Here, this is for the kids and your fund."

I certainly didn't expect that, nor was I soliciting for it. Wanting him to get something in return, I opened the case and offered him a print. Yes, the case was built to hold prints as well as the painting. Once it was open and the print was being pulled out, this couple got their first look at the image. Upon seeing it, the woman got out another twenty dollars and asked for one as well. So here I am in the middle of Washington-Dulles Airport. My case is open on a tabletop. I'm handing out prints and taking money for them. Other people around us are starting to take notice. They are curiously watching and coming towards me. Now I'm getting a bit concerned. Don't people have to have licenses to do things like this? Am I gonna get arrested or fined or something? Before things got out of hand or security showed up, I thanked everyone, closed up the case and moved on. With an eventful start like this what else could this trip hold in store?

By the end of a long and head-spinning day, my travels finally got me to my destination, Charleston. Julie and her two sons were there to meet me. Together we discovered that my suitcase (the one I checked as luggage) had been lost. I had a speaking and filming appearance the next day and now no clothes. Julie asked one of the customer service people at the baggage claim about it. She got the response, "Bruce Becker? That name sounds familiar. Wait here." The woman returned a few minutes later with my bag saying, "It came in on an earlier flight." Somehow I wish I had too.

The next morning greeted us with an approaching Noreastern Storm system. This was a major spring storm, with cold from the north and moisture from the south. Those of us living in the east know that's a bad combination. Although the brunt of the storm was well north of us, the wind was beginning to blow hard. After a shower and breakfast, Julie, her boys and myself headed to the church where the filming was to be done. We arrived early. I met Ed (the pastor) and several other church members. We set up the painting where I would be speaking, then organized a back room for the distribution of prints. As the time to begin drew closer, Julie and I were with Ed in his office. We were talking about the Amish, forgiveness, the film and my airport experiences. Then just as Ed asked that we all pray together that things go well through the day, suddenly all the electricity went off. We had a church full of people waiting for the service and for me to speak, not to mention the cameramen working on the film and the TV news reporters who showed up. Now the church was dark. The only light is what was streaming in through the windows and that was sporadic because of the passing clouds. We lit all the candles and decided to hold the service in candlelight. This was not going to stop us.

Ed began the service in his usual manner with greetings and prayers. When the time came for me to speak he introduced me. I walked to the front of the church and stood before the congregation. It was now more than seven months since the shootings and I was given twenty minutes to talk about it all. How I was going to do that I wasn't sure. I did have an outline to guide me if I needed it. It was rolled up and clinched in my hand. Standing there and about to begin I realized that simply following the course of events chronologically was not what I wanted to do. I turned to Ed and said, "I was going to talk about the events that brought me here. But inside me it feels as though I should do otherwise. If it's okay with you, I want to share a few stories of my encounters with the Amish and then answer questions." With his nod of approval he said, "Yes, of course, please."

Several stories were told to the crowd. Stories that I've already shared with you. Then there were comments and questions. A gentleman stood and asked me, "Is it true that the Amish don't use computers or electricity? And if so isn't it ironic that we have no electricity here today." Pretty observant I thought. The crowd thought so as well, as was evident by their response of deep sighs and smiles. Then I responded, "That is true and our electricity may be out, but here in this building today we definitely still have power."

My appearance, including the questions, actually lasted forty minutes. No one seemed to mind it running over. Ed shortened the remainder of the service, so as not to keep everyone there too long. There were tears, some laughs and prayers. Then it was over. The camera crew got what they needed for the film by running off their power packs and the TV reporters interviewed me for their local news. Then I moved on to sign and distribute prints. It was only then that someone came into the room and announced that every other building in the area had electricity. They all had lights and power. The church was the only building in the area without electricity. Interesting I thought, as I remembered Louise telling me that as one attempts to spread the word of good, sometimes it's met head-on with obstacles trying to halt it.

This group of people: Ed, his family, Julie, the congregation, everyone involved in the making of the film, all of them had a genuine interest and concern for what happened in Nickel Mines. They had a true appreciation for how the Amish made such positive choices in their lives. They sincerely expressed to me the importance they placed on forgiveness and treating others with kindness. It was an honor, being asked to participate in their project and given the chance to speak to them.

Later that night a few of us had dinner together: Julie and her boys, Ed and his family and myself. While in the restaurant the news came on the big TV screen and showed its coverage of my appearance. They used footage of me speaking, as well as answering the reporters' questions. I suppose they aired the right footage because even the waiters came over to me asking how to get a copy of the print.

The following morning began a day of sightseeing and getting ideas for paintings. I was headed into old town Charleston. It was a beautiful city with lots of heritage and great architecture. There were plenty of photo opportunities for paintings: interesting window structures, old cemeteries, cobblestone streets and so much more. I must have taken a hundred photos. Tomorrow I was scheduled to fly home. So after some time spent downtown and the day coming to an end so was my trip . . . or was it?

The next morning Julie took me to the airport to catch my flight. The storm was still blanketing the northeast. Every flight listed on the board was on time and leaving as scheduled . . . but mine wasn't listed. Julie checked at the counter and found out that my flight had been canceled. It was the only one that airline canceled all morning and there were no other flights home. So I had to book one for the following day. I guess it wasn't time for me to end this trip just yet.

When we got back to her home there was a message waiting. It was a talk show host from a local TV show. He was asking that if I was still in town could I give him a call to make an appearance. Was this why I was supposed to still be here? We tried to call him, but he couldn't be reached. So perhaps not.

With time now to spare we headed downtown to see more of the sites. Again the images for paintings seemed to be everywhere. I took lots more photos. There were also many beautiful galleries. I visited as many as I could. While walking from one gallery to the next I got a phone call. That's how and when I learned of the tragic University of Virginia school shootings. The school was under lockdown right then. One of the students had stormed a building and in a violent rampage shot, killed and wounded many of his classmates. When would it end? More killing in a place set aside for learning. More senseless acts of violence. Those poor students and families. My heart immediately went out to them. After the experiences I had been through with the Amish I knew how devastating this would be to all of those involved. After hearing the news I could think of nothing else. The day of sightseeing ended right then. I felt as though I wanted to do something to help. How could this message of kindness be utilized? What could I do? I was in South Carolina and the shootings occurred in Virginia.

That night after dinner I put on the TV and caught the local news. Of course there was plenty of coverage from Virginia. It was followed by a story of how the local community was reacting. The newscaster reported that the same church where I spoke, while being filmed, planned a prayer vigil for the next evening. They were inviting people from the area to gather for the purpose of consoling each other and praying for peace for all those involved. The instant I saw this I felt compelled to find a pen and paper. Words of prayer and comfort came flowing out of me. The page in front of me filled with a message for all those who gathered. I wrote so fast that I didn't even know what the words would be until they were on the page. In minutes it was finished.

The thought crossed my mind of staying an extra day and attending the gathering. But no, that didn't feel right. It wasn't necessary. My speaking appearance to the congregation and now these written words were all I needed to do here. It was time for me to leave. The next day I left as planned. Julie took what I wrote with her to the prayer vigil. Ed, while leading the meeting, read it as the lead prayer for the gathering. It turns out that one of the victims in Virginia had a family member in attendance at the vigil. He was moved to speak to the crowd. He told them that everyone he knew from back home was dealing better with this terrible circumstance because of the lessons learned from the Amish . . . the lessons of forgiveness and kindness. He was very grateful for the prayer I wrote, the prayers of everyone there and the church's concern.

Hearing that the congregation was moved by the message of forgiveness and kindness to the point of holding that vigil and then to have this gentleman express how his family and town were being helped by the same lessons of the Amish, confirmed for me that I was right where I needed to be and why. Perhaps I wasn't in South Carolina to be in the film.

By the way, the film I'm referring to, the reason the church group had me there in the first place, well it turns out that everything else they filmed was just fine . . . except for my portion. For some unknown reason, all of and only the footage of me, every time I was on camera, there was no sound. None of that film was usable. That film was eventually completed and I was never in it. Maybe all I had to say while there, was heard by the people who needed to hear it. Perhaps the reason I was there wasn't to be in a film after all. Interesting how things work out, isn't it?

I returned home to find more letters and requests for prints to be sent out. Included in my messages was a request from a writer. He wanted to send a photographer to my home. He needed pictures of me to include with an article he was writing about my journey. Additionally, I had another appointment with Vince to continue telling him of my journey and there was a call from Louise to return.

All of this got taken care of: The prints were sent out. The photographer took her shots and I had my meeting with Vince. The meeting was another three-hour session. Three more hours of me talking and him writing. Once again he was astonished at what I had to tell him. He shared with me that he was considering changing the entire story line of the screenplay. Now he was thinking of dropping his original plan, which focused more on the history of the Amish. He was interested in writing the story of my journey, this message and the impact it could have on the lives of individuals hearing it. I couldn't believe what I was hearing. So many people told me how what I was going through fascinated them and how it should be written. But now this screenplay writer is telling me that it should be a film. Unbelievable. One day I'm filmed for a movie that I mysteriously never end up in. Then a few days later it's being considered that an entire movie is made about this journey. What does a person say to something like that? I was never in this for any kind of recognition. I had to put all of these notions of films and books behind me and stay focused on what was truly guiding me. So forward I went, a day at a time.

Louise was contacting me with a request for another speaking engagement. She asked if I would teach a master's class to some advanced students, at the high school where she teaches. Then speak in a forum open to the general public. The speaking would be held at The Journey Cafe. If I wanted, I could exhibit my work there also. Additionally I still had my teaching schedule to keep up and paintings that I wanted to start. So much was happening as soon as I returned. But it was painting that was at the top of my list. I had come back with some images I badly wanted to paint. In the past seven months I had completed only one painting. All my time was committed to the message of *Kindness and Compassion*. Not a single regret mind you, but painting is how I make my living and the living was getting tight.

It's not that I didn't want to be on this journey anymore. It wasn't that at all. The painting of *Kindness and Compassion*, as well as my personal expressions of kindness toward others, will always be a part of me. But I needed to find a way of integrating this journey into my painting, my work and my life. As much as I honor all that this journey has taught me and exposed me to, I needed to find a way to make it part of my life. Not my entire life. Honestly, I was on the brink of losing just about everything. All my time, money, and energy went into the spreading of this message and assisting those devastated. Any money coming in for prints went directly to the fund, not to me. I was basically broke. No one knew this No one needed to. Things were getting very tight. I mean, come on, it's been seven months now since I did much else. The bills keep coming. It sounds attractive to have CNN at my door wanting an interview. But when they leave I'm alone in the kitchen making a peanut butter and jelly sandwich for dinner. I hadn't really worked in almost eight months. I needed to paint.

Eventually, what began to happen was all the elements in my life (my painting, my family, things I enjoy and all the day-to-day chores, as well as all the new elements that were outcroppings from *Kindness and Compassion*) began to find a way to coexist and work together. Even better than that, they began complimenting and enriching each other.

Let me be clear here, the importance of the painting and the message it carries was not diminishing. Not at all. It was finding a way to be incorporated into my life. A life in some ways not unlike many of yours. Well, okay, maybe different than most. But it's one that is filled with many facets and varying intricacies. The varieties of elements in my life were being enriched by this journey. But did this mean that *Kindness and Compassion* was going to play a lesser role, or take a back seat? Not a chance. This message and my experiences were finding ways to stimulate everything I did.

Just as planned, I started painting again. Canvas after canvas was being completed. Each one better than the last. I was painting with the veracity of a man possessed. It felt better than wonderful. It was exhilarating to a point that I can only describe as catching your breath after resurfacing from being underwater for too long. That first breath. That rush of air that fills your lungs reassuring you that the life you knew was still yours to grasp. That first breath that gets sucked in as deep as possible. That's the one that surges life itself back into your being. I breathed it in with great welcome. The rush of painting was coursing through my body. It was the invigoration of the creative process.

This high comes to me only through my painting. This is what I love to do. This is what I know. Day after day I would get up, put on my paint clothes, head to the studio and create.

Sometimes eat, sometimes not. Just paint. This is the life I have wanted since being a child. The life I made for myself. The one that was put on hold for the past seven months. The feel, smell and color of the paint were energizing me like it always had. I knew this feeling and I liked it. I was back. The work, if I do say so myself was very strong. New aspects of imagery were being developed. I was seeing and creating images that were groundbreaking. Compositions filled with light, color, realism and abstraction all simultaneously flooded over the canvas surface. These images were like nothing ever done before. This was evident to me from the first brushstrokes on the first canvas. These were my best works to date. No one was seeing these paintings until I felt it was time. I had a show coming up in a few months and this new body of work would be kept under wraps until then. I was painting again and that's when I'm at my best.

It occurred to me that one of the images I painted could be used as a beneficial learning tool for my students. So carefully I took it along with me to one of my classes. As I was heading into the building I ran into Sandra, one of the artists I knew casually, who wrote me such a nice letter about the documentary. Seeing that I had a painting with me, she stopped and we talked a bit. Only twice before, in the years I had known her, did we ever really speak. Otherwise it was always just a quick hello in the hallway. Today she made it very clear to me how much she admired my work. She was very complimentary. She said, "I rarely, if ever, ask anyone for a favor. But I know about the public speaking you've been doing. I may be doing some myself. Would you consider helping me out with a few pointers?" Here is a woman I had only known in passing for years and now Kindness and Compassion was acting as the bridge that brought us together. I liked that. "Sure. I'd love to help however I can. We could get together. You could tell me what you're working on and take it from there." We left it that we would get in touch through e-mail, then went our separate ways. That night's class went very well, and I could not have been happier with my paintings.

During all this time I continued to fill requests for prints, stayed in touch with the Amish, and remained open to any new developments on the journey. I remember a day while reading print request letters that I needed to order more shipping materials. But I couldn't find the materials catalog anywhere. All of my contact information for the company was in it. I couldn't even remember the name of the company. I was at a loss. Feeling a bit frustrated, I literally was sitting at the dining room table, facing the front door, with a request letter in my hand and more stacked up beside me. Just as I was asking for an answer to this dilemma the postman dropped a brand new catalog for that company through the mail slot, right in front of me . . . I mean right then, as I was asking for an answer it was literally delivered. In one respect it felt just like every other step along the way in this journey. Trust and things will fall into place. This seems like a simple little thing, but coincidences like that have always been prevalent in my life—but never as frequently or obviously as those that have been happening on this journey.

A short time later, a small gallery in town was opening a new art show. Against my better judgment I was convinced to include a piece or two in the exhibit. Remember my work never shows in this town. I exhibit all over the country, but not here. I certainly didn't give this gallery my new paintings. Those were being saved for my one-man show, being held at a different location several months out.

On the night of the opening I figured I'd go as a sign of support to the gallery. There was one pleasant surprise that night. Sandra was there. We were running into each other again. I first saw her as I approached the building. She was standing on the gallery front step. I recognized her from more than half a block away: A beautiful woman with long auburn hair. She was wearing a yellow patterned summer dress that moved so gently as the breeze brushed by. The closer I got the more attractive she looked. I remember thinking—I want to paint this woman. She needs to be the subject of my work. She's beautiful. As I passed her we each said a friendly hello and not much more. I went inside and she followed.

The exhibit was pretty much as I expected. It was much of the same thing that happens at openings all too often: There were paintings of images and subjects that had been done a thousand times before. People were drinking and talking about anything but the work. Everyone was trying to see and be seen. All my life it seemed to me that when it came to art openings, people attending cared more about themselves, who they talked to and were seen with, what food there was to eat and where the after-party was. Too often I saw the art taking a distant backseat. There wasn't a lot here that I was excited about. Well almost, I did keep running into Sandra.

If you total up the time she and I spent talking that night it would add up to less than an hour. But very little of it was for any continuous length of time. I kept getting pulled away to talk with someone else about my work, or the Amish, or having to take a phone call or something. I was even fielding phone calls that night about an ABC talk show crew coming to town. They wanted an interview about the new Amish school that was about to open. It was a whirlwind of a night. I remember standing at one end of the room while someone was talking on and on to me about something. I couldn't even tell you then what they were talking about, let alone now. That's not like me. I'm normally very focused and attentive when talking with people. I just remember watching Sandra across the room. Occasionally she'd be looking at the artwork with a friend or perhaps she was being approached by some other guy who wanted to talk with her. I remember wishing I was that guy talking to her. So eventually I would make my way back over there. Who was this woman? Why was I so attracted to her? I had met plenty of women, especially in this past year. None of them had affected me like this. Sure she was striking to look at, with a figure of classic beauty, the legs of a dancer and a smile that lit up a room. She was talented and intelligent. Her spirit was strong and independent. What man wouldn't be attracted to her? Even so, there was more going on here. There was an attraction that went beyond her physical attributes.

Like I said, I had met a lot of people along this journey: Many of them women and others telling me of women who I just had to meet . . . if you know what I mean. It seemed that several times a week I was told of a sister, or friend, or co-worker who I just had to meet. Lots of introductions, or potential introductions, came my way. But meeting a woman through introductions like that were the furthest thing from my mind just then. I was truly caught up in the moment of the incredible events in my life. In fact, there was this one time while I was out with a couple of neighbors, having a friendly birthday drink, when I encountered three, shall we say overly affectionate, young women. I didn't know them. But they knew me through various TV appearances and they weren't shy about letting me know it. To keep this story short, I'll simply say, one neighbor I was with looked at me and made a comment about just how interested in me these three were. I could tell and I knew what he meant. I was just out to have a quick birthday drink with friends and then head straight home. This happened at the end of a very long—a very trying day and I was exhausted. Going out for this drink was just being neighborly. So I excused myself and headed home as planned, alone.

My point here is that opportunities were presenting themselves frequently, to meet new women in my life. But my focus was on this journey and the reasoning behind it. A distraction like that I didn't need just then. Sandra was different somehow.

I just knew it. The same way I knew of other important developments in my life. During our lives, our paths cross with those of many other people. There are those that exist around us almost as undetectable as the air we breathe. Others hit you like a gale force wind. She was actually neither. Experiencing her was more like a warm summer breeze, welcome, refreshing and invigorating.

In our discussion Sandra told me of her American Indian heritage, which I found fascinating. She could trace her roots back directly to the specific tribe and individuals she had descended from. Lately, Native American culture seemed to be showing itself often in my life. Recently it was discovered that my great-grandmother was Native American. Stefan was very involved with the family history research. He was the person who spearheaded the tracking of that information. Not very long ago, as he and I were discussing this newly found Native American heritage, completely out of the blue, he asked me if I had met a special woman along this journey. Without laboring the point, he simply said that he had a feeling I might meet someone special. I told him of the many introductions and how none went much further than that. Very little else was said of it. Also, not so long ago (before I painted Kindness and Compassion) I was invited to participate in an Indian ritual that lasted several days. It was held out in the woods and steeped in Indian ceremony and ritual. It was based on the premise of doing good for others and spreading peace among people. Then there was the elderly Indian woman I met at the mud sale. The one who told me of the chief and holy man who want to meet with me. She said to me, "People don't meet by chance. They are supposed to meet. You should be watching for the people you are suppose to meet." All these things were running through my mind as I thought about our meeting and getting to know each other. There was more to this woman that I had yet to learn. I do think we were supposed to meet.

Realizing a few days later that Sandra and I hadn't yet discussed my helping her with her public speaking, I called her to set up a time to get together. She accepted my offer to come by for dinner and we could talk. From the moment she arrived at my house, from the time I saw her walk through my doorway, I experienced a feeling of comfort that lasted the entire evening. I barely even knew this woman, but the feeling of easiness and comfort was so apparent. I made some dinner. We got to talking. We discussed my work, her work, my life, and her life. I showed her the studio. We discussed everything but her public speaking, well almost. When I finally did ask her about it she answered with a bit of hesitation. Remember I told you how for the past two years I sensed she was always busy and preoccupied. I was about to find out why. She was about to share with me information about herself that very few people knew.

Sandra is a very private, single mom, who totally on her own is raising two boys. Her family lives halfway across the country and her interaction with them is minimal. She resettled here with the boys many years ago and made a life for them. Through her strength, creativity and love for them she found ways to make this their home, with virtually no outside help. Three years ago, just before I first met her at the art center opening, her oldest boy Ryan, was in a car crash. He was the victim of the actions of a drunk driver. Twenty years old at the time he got into a car with some friends only to find the girl behind the wheel had been drinking. After having made several attempts to have her stop the car, even offering to drive himself or be left out to walk home, she would not stop. Seconds later the horrific crash occurred. The car flipped over and spun upside down several times, tearing off the sunroof and demolishing the car completely. Ryan strapped in with his seat belt was the only person not thrown from the vehicle. As the car spun and rolled upside down, the impact that the exposed road through the sunroof had on his head, his brain, his entire body was beyond belief. Those few seconds changed the life she built for them, forever. Ryan was airlifted to a hospital in Philadelphia.

By the time the police collected enough information to contact Sandra, Ryan was already under the most intensive care that modern medical science could provide. In the rain and dark of night, Sandra fought through the tears to find her way, driving herself two hours to that hospital. Once there she received the worst news a mother could hear. The doctors told her that the damage to his skull, brain and spinal cord was so severe that he could be lost at anytime. In fact he had died in flight and was revived. They told her they had never seen a patient with so much brainstem damage and still be alive. At that moment all that was keeping him in this world was medical machinery. Essentially he was already gone. In fact they were so sure of this, that they told her he was a prime candidate to be an organ donor. This news would of course devastate any mother. She told me, "Everyone in that hospital that night heard the cries and screams of anguish from a mother losing her son."

In the middle of that hospital hallway she fell to her knees with her face against the cold floor. She prayed. She asked for guidance. She asked God for the life of her son. This woman, this parent, this mother, was having the life of her son ripped away from her by hands of another person. Much like the response of the Amish mothers, I would learn how she dealt with this tragedy by focusing on anything positive she could find in this time of darkness.

In a moment of clarity, against all that she was told by the doctors, against all that she heard was medically possible, against death itself, she knew he was still alive in there. She got up and demanded those doctors go back inside and do everything possible and more to help her son. This was not a begging plea from an emotionally hysterical mother. This was a demand from a woman of inspired vision. She knew he would live. The doctors on the other hand were certain his outcome would be death. They literally shrugged their shoulders and with no idea of how to treat someone in this bad of condition, went back inside. His injuries were so severe that everything they would do with Ryan from this point forward would be completely experimental . . . they were working in the dark. No one had ever been damaged this badly before and lived. But Sandra wasn't working in the dark. She knew down to the core of her being that this was not his death. This was not his time. He was going to live.

The details of her story are enough to fill her own book and someday they may. But I will tell you this, for the next two and a half years Sandra defiantly insisted those doctors keep working. She maintained her teaching schedule, her art, the everyday life of her other son Mark and still was vigilantly at Ryan's hospital bedside everyday.

Now more than three years later, Ryan has baffled the logic and reasoning of all medical science. Each day he miraculously showed slow signs of recovery. Every time he would reach a plateau that the doctors thought he would never rise above, he did. He surpassed being unable to see, unable to speak, unable to move, unable to eat, in a coma, loss of his memory, the loss of all emotions themselves (imagine that, not having the sense of emotions). From all of these enormously life-threatening challenges and so much more, even from being given a zero chance to live, he has nearly fully recovered and I do mean fully. I have since met him and he is a strong, active, intelligent, well-spoken young man. His motor skills have returned to the point where he even plays drums in a rock band . . . extremely well. Of course he still has a long way to go—but this young man is a walking miracle. He continues to completely baffle medical science.

As for those two years, when I thought Sandra seemed preoccupied, now I knew why. During those years, she told very few people how bad things really were. To greet her or encounter her, as she struggled through each day, all you would find from her were smiles and a positive attitude. Sandra is thought of by those who know her, as the woman to see if you need a lift to your day, or a level head to help with a problem.

Even through this dark time in her life, it was the kindness and compassion in her heart that she presented to everyone she met.

As for my helping with her public speaking: She and Ryan were about to begin speaking in different forums about the devastation drinking and driving can cause. Devastation not just to the immediate victim but also the turmoil and pain it causes to the entire family of the victim. They had already been included in a short film dealing with the hazards of drinking and driving. It was traveling the country being featured at high schools and colleges. Now they were going to be making appearances as well. I most certainly wanted to do whatever I could. I told you I thought this was a woman of strong character but I had no idea how strong until that night. That dinner and that evening is one I will never forget.

Over the course of the next few weeks we spent some wonderful times together: We went to a benefit art auction, which included both of our works; shared a dinner at her house; even went to hear Ryan's band play at a local club. My fondness for Sandra was certainly growing. But I truly couldn't tell if she felt the same for me. I now knew how good she was at keeping things to herself.

Then one night while teaching, I passed Sandra in the hallway or perhaps I should say she passed me. Hurrying by me with a very quick hello and barely even a glance my way was all she did to acknowledge me. It was much like the reaction I seemed to provoke from her for the past two years, pleasant but minimal. Something seemed wrong. That night I sent her an e-mail of concern, checking to see if she was all right. Her response came the next day and it was a letter I'll never forget.

She had opened up to me about Ryan's crash and now she was going to share something else. The e-mail was titled "Okay, here goes."

This is not a letter I am going to quote to you. But I will tell you that in it she expressed how she felt about me. She told me that her actions of hurrying by me and avoiding me in the hallways was due to the fact that she had trouble containing herself around me. For the past two years she found herself so attracted to me that she would shake or need to catch her breath. She told me that just seeing me, even from a distance, made it hard for her to form a sensible sentence. So she simply avoided me. She couldn't understand it. No one affected her this way.

Reading this and finding out I wasn't alone in my attraction to her was absolutely a thrill. It took my breath away to read that letter. I must have read it twenty times. Of course I saved it. In fact, I've saved every letter she ever wrote me, including the very first one about the documentary. How should I respond to this? I wanted to tell her that I had feelings for her as well. But, she apparently had a two-year lead on me in the area of being attracted. For two years she had been shall I say, noticing me from afar. Where as for me, this feeling was relatively new. What do you say to someone in that position? Not being completely sure how to handle this situation, I contacted her the way we contacted each other most often, e-mail. Okay, I admit, it wasn't the most romantic move on my part. It also wasn't my intent to keep her waiting for a response, but it took me more than a day and a half to put into words just what I wanted to say. But my words must have been appropriate. From that point on we were seeing each other, or at least talking daily. We inspired each other in our work and in our personal lives. We both felt right from the start, that we were positive influences in each other's lives. We were good for each other. I finally got around to helping her and Ryan with their speaking and Sandra was fast becoming my strongest advocate on this journey. I could only hope that I was having the same effect on hers. I saw her life as one filled with compassion and everyone who met her spoke of her abundant kindness.

Sandra knew people were asking me to write and tell this story. But she, more than all others, was the most supportive. The strength I was gaining from her being in my life was felt everyday. Mutually we found each other's lives to be fascinating, unfolding journeys. Our two lives together were becoming a powerful force. This was a very good thing that we found each other. We both felt it. No, this woman wasn't stealing my heart. She would never be so bold in matters of such emotion. The truth is, this was a woman one gives his heart to and hopes she accepts. That's what I found myself doing. Before too long I realized that the feelings in her heart were matching mine. We were falling in love.

As spring became summer we continued to grow closer, doing everything together. Through our closeness, Sandra was learning more details about my journey and experiences than anyone else. Her support of my work, in all its aspects, was overwhelming. The intermingling of our two journeys made each of us stronger. Wanting her to share in the experiences I was having, I invited her to visit the Nickel Mines area and visit with a few Amish families. In her gracious manner she nearly declined. She felt that was my journey, my life, my experience and it wasn't her place, or anyone else's, to intrude on that. But I could feel how important she was becoming in my life. I wasn't sure just how important, but I knew having her in my life was special.

Prior to the Nickel Mines trip, we set aside a special evening of intense conversations—an evening to specifically address any curiosities she had about my journey. It was a time for me to share detailed accounts of my experiences. We watched the DVDs of various TV media coverage: news reports, talk show interviews, things like that. We looked through the piles of newspaper articles, letters and photos and talked at great length about the uncommon and unusual experiences of this time. I told stories and she asked questions. We covered topics that night that no one had heard me speak of before . . . and may never again. This special night brought forth expressions of emotion ranging from laughter to tears. By that night's end, I felt as though I now had a companion like no other on this journey.

The next day, off we went to Nickel Mines. This day I would expose Sandra to some of the places and people that had become so important to me. We went to the site of the old school grounds. I showed her the area where gifts from around the world were placed for the girls; the scene where media madness was rampant; visited the new school; drove by the gunman's home; and I even took her shopping in the local general store that the Amish use daily. But perhaps more importantly we visited not just places, but people. Several Amish households were stops along our way. Not wanting to show up empty-handed, we prepared about thirty individual treat bags for the children. Each bag was filled with a variety of candies and sweet surprises. The kids loved when I, or anyone, stopped by with surprises. What kid doesn't? The parents were okay with it too.

By way of those visits Sandra and myself caught a glimpse of how these humble, gracious people were now doing. Arriving at each home unannounced, we had walked in on a variety of situations: Some were just beginning lunch. In one home we found some of the family napping. Others were working in the yard or field. As for the children, they were either helping their parents, or laughing and playing with friends who were visiting for the day. Sounds much like any of our homes, doesn't it? Please remember these are real people, with real lives of their own. These people are not a tourist attraction. There's real feeling, real emotion, real life here, with parents raising their children and those children becoming parents themselves one day. Aspirations like this, we very much share in common with these neighboring friends.

We found that nearly a year later some of the children were still having difficulty dealing with what they had been through. Of course when this tragedy happened, the physical injuries were treated immediately. Those injuries showed themselves without needing an effort to be seen. Injuries like that are visible with the naked eye. The internal, psychological, traumatic wounds are never as apparent. Some of the children were only now beginning to have their internal struggles surface. This would not be a short road of recovery. No one ever thought it would be. But these humble people were dealing with those challenges everyday. Through it all, they continued to hold focus on their values, and then initiate those values into daily lives that emulated their beliefs. Beliefs that included the importance of forgiveness, kindness and compassion toward others. These were families and individuals who didn't need or look for recognition for such noble actions.

They simply needed to live true to their hearts. The expression of that alone was reward itself. Holding in such high regard the expressions of this way of life is why they were so moved by the expression of the message associated with my painting. This is a message that will find its way through all turmoil to rise to the top. It will present opportunities in its own way; in its own time, for each of us to act upon it. Each of us at times will find ourselves needing to rise above the trials of our lives and choose actions that reflect the most humane expressions of ourselves. I saw this being done by the Amish community. I saw it being done by Sandra and I am sure each of you will find times in your lives, to rise to the top as well.

Having Sandra see these new friends pursue this honorable way of life firsthand (and now, through these writings, having all of you see that as well) is heartwarming. That day brought us closer together. Perhaps these words have brought you and I closer also. I see these people and their ways of dealing with this tragedy as an example to us all.

So now if I may, let me move forward on to where this journey was about to take me next. Through my telling you of mine and Sandra's dealing with the Amish, I don't mean it to sound like everything we did was focused on this journey. We were having plenty of good times together, unrelated to that. There were dinners, movies, family picnics, art openings and more. Our journeys were always there, in the background, but not always talked about. Antiques and flea markets were something we both enjoyed. One weekend we decided to go to a flea market that was featuring Native American displays. It so happened this was the same flea market where I bought the bell in my painting. I hadn't been back there since the day I bought it. This would be my first time back in almost a year. The day we went was beautiful and sunny. We wandered the grounds enjoying our time and searching for that day's perfect treasure. The Native American displays weren't as good as we hoped they would be. They were a main reason for us coming here, but they were a bit of a disappointment. Nevertheless we pushed on, going from stand to stand examining the tens of thousands of crafts and antiques.

When I turned a corner to enter the area of the next stand we approached, my eyes fell upon a sight that stopped me cold. I stood for a second just staring. I felt the blood rushing through my veins and my breathing get heavy. Then I pointed and said to Sandra, "Do you see that?" "Oh my God," she said as she looked where I was pointing. "That's exactly the same." Lying on the table in front of us was an identical bell to the one in my painting. I mean identical—the white porcelain bell, the black wrought iron hanger, the wooden clacker, even the same welds holding it together. This was a second *Kindness and Compassion* bell. Of all the things that could have been on that table, it was that bell. And of all the people who could have found it, it was me.

This wasn't the same stand where I found the first bell. It was at the extreme other end of the grounds. But it was the same flea market and it definitely was the same bell. Now there were two bells, found nearly a year apart, and I had found them both.

I picked it up and looked around as if this was some kind of practical joke, or almost to see if there was an angel watching over us or something. I wasn't sure what to do at first. I was so stunned that I remember even saying to her, "Do you think I should buy it?" "Of course you should buy it. How often does this happen? You should buy every one of these you ever find," she exclaimed. Then we both examined it further and asked the owner of the stand a few questions about it. He couldn't tell us much. He simply said a woman brought it to him, who had it hanging in her kitchen for years, and now she wanted to sell it. Odd, in my kitchen is where I have mine hanging.

Of course I bought it. The stand owner wrapped it up in newspaper and put it in a used paper bag. Just as the original was wrapped in old paper when I bought it, this one now had the same humble beginnings, as I became its new caretaker. We took that bag, carrying it in awe of the situation, and headed back to my car. Each step of the way, the two of us were either silent or could only bring ourselves to speak of this incredible find . . . nothing else. Now what? What did this mean? Was this a bend in the road on this journey? Where would this take me?

We got to the car and as I tried to start it found the battery was dead. All it did was weakly grind . . . then again . . . then nothing. It wouldn't start. Without a word from me, Sandra jumped out of the car and flagged down an older gentleman as he was passing by in his truck. Like some guy's not gonna stop if she's flagging them down. I know I would. I suppose in a way she already did flag me down. Anyway . . . she told him of the bad battery and he gave us a jump. It started and we were on our way.

Our first stop before going anywhere else would be the battery warehouse (that's the shop were I get batteries for mine and the kids' cars). This was a Sunday, so as we pulled up we found the entire lot was empty. They were closed. There was not another car in sight. I pulled up directly in front of the building, right to the front door. I wanted to read the sign that listed their hours. I stopped the car with it facing directly at the building. Only the sidewalk entrance separated us from the front door. As soon as the car was motionless, we both looked at each other and said, "Did you see that?" Yes, we agreed we both saw it. Without a further word to each other, we simultaneously jumped out of the car and ran around to the front. There, sitting on the sidewalk directly in front of my car, no more than a foot away, was a large black wrought iron bell. It was just like the bell for the new school. We shook our heads in disbelief. This can't be happening we thought . . . the same flea market, an identical bell, now minutes later a bell just like the new school bell.

I suppose curiosity got the best of me, or maybe I just couldn't believe my eyes. I actually needed to see if it was real. So I reached down and moved it. It was real all right. It was just as heavy as the one I photographed at John's house.

That bell we left sitting right were it was. We didn't know where it came from. We didn't know who it belonged to. But we didn't need to take it with us either. The "coincidental" act of driving directly from one location where we found the small bell, a place I hadn't been to in nearly a year, to stopping within a foot of this large bell, in a parking lot I maybe visit every other year, was more than enough at the moment. It didn't need to go with us. We got back in the car and before I even had a chance to pull away, Sandra said to me, "You know this means something. You've been looking for a sign to let you know if this message and this journey were to continue. A sign telling you that the story should be in writing. If you don't see these two bells as signs that you are suppose to tell this story, then what will it take? Two identical bells! You need to write this story."

She was right. She's right about a lot of things and never afraid to speak what's in her heart. Just then she was saying what was in mine as well. I had been struggling with the idea of writing. I was wondering whether or not this journey was over in some way, or coming to a close, or whether it needed to be told. I mean come on. This had to mean something, didn't it? Was I supposed to be writing or what?

My kids Tim and Molly, went to dinner with Sandra and I that evening. We talked of many things. Much of it the usual stuff—what to order, what the kids were doing with the rest of their night, how work was going for the two of them—just some time for us all to sit and catch up on the day's events. They asked what we had done that day. With smiles and not sure how to approach the answer to that question, we simply said, "We went to a flea market." "Oh what one? You find anything good?" Tim asked. I told them we had been to the market where I found the schoolhouse bell. That it was my first time back since then. Molly came back with the jokingly asked question, "So, what did you find another bell or something?" There was a pause at the table just then. Sandra and I looked at each other, smiled and then kind of laughed. We didn't even have to say anything. Molly exclaimed, "No way! You didn't! Really?" That's when we told them about our experiences of the day. Interestingly Molly had this comment, "Well dad the last time you found one, that Monday something terrible happened, the shootings. What's going to happen this Monday, tomorrow?" Oh man, everyone at the table felt a sense of pressure on their chest. I could see it, feel it and hear it in the gasps of reactions. But my feeling, the one I had since first having that second bell in my possession, one I hadn't spoken of, was one of moving forward. Moving on to the next step, a positive step—not backward to the negative. The first bell brought with it darkness, from which came light. This one represents spreading that light. Think what you will, but that's how I saw it. That's how it felt. This bell and message weren't done with me yet. That's what I told Molly and everyone at the table.

When trying to sleep that night my body couldn't stop buzzing. The rush of the day was overwhelming. Sandra was right. I had to tell this story somehow. I suppose writing a book would be the way, but I had never done anything like that before. I didn't even know where to begin or how to go about it. My God, I thought, how am I going to be able to do that? Then there was the ever present financial state I was in . . . not a particularly good one. With so much time dedicated to *Kindness and Compassion*, I already hadn't worked for most of this past year. I could end up losing everything if I do this. Even as that thought ran through my mind, I knew I would find a way. I knew there would be a way. I didn't know how. But it had to be done. I went to bed praying, looking, and searching for an answer. I vowed that if it could be done, if there could be a way for me to make ends meet, if somehow that could happen, then I would write this book.

The very next day I received a phone call from someone I hadn't heard from in four years. He is the administrator for a ranch in New Mexico. He purchased three of my paintings when last we spoke. He called to tell me that an extremely philanthropic gentleman had just donated a very large sum of money to the ranch. In return this gentleman was given one of my three paintings. The presentation of the painting and his donation was a lavish affair. The painting generated a tremendous amount of interest from everyone in attendance. Now this gentleman wanted to purchase a large quantity of high-end, limited edition prints of that painting. He wanted to purchase those prints from me.

Let me explain to you what that meant. Let me tell you just how important this was. In essence, I received a phone call (an answer to a prayer perhaps) from someone I hadn't talked to in four years delivering news to me that I was about to make the largest single sale of my career, totally out of the blue, and the sale was to a gentleman I hadn't ever met. Just like that, I had my funding to write.

The following day I began writing. More than eight months have passed since I wrote those first words. Not one time since that day was I drawn back to the easel. My creative energies found another outlet. The starkness of the blank, white page became my canvas.

Tomorrow I'll be back at the easel once again, painting.

Epilogue

ALTHOUGH THE STORYTELLING portion of this book is finished, because books do need an ending, the journey continues. It continues for all of us. The incredible experiences you just read, of this special time in my life, are but a snapshot of an ongoing, ever evolving process of life—both my life and those mentioned within.

During the eight months of writing this book, my journey and my life didn't just sit on a shelf, waiting to continue once I finished. There's no waiting for life or a journey to continue. It is always taking place. In fact, the writing of this book itself is part of that journey. All of the people mentioned on these pages and many more are now a part of my life. I will always think of them fondly. Most every one of them continues to be, at the very least, a friend. Day after day my life is filled with extraordinary events. So is yours. Take the time to notice them. Some of them go by in a flash and could easily be missed, if you're not aware. Some are more powerful. They come right up, look you in the eye and are big enough to stop you in your tracks. Each of the experiences we have, every one, big or small, is life changing in some way. Every experience we have gives us the opportunity to build, enhance, develop and mold our individual character.

With every experience comes a choice. I've heard people say about instances in their lives, "I didn't have a choice" or "I had no choice, I had to do that." No way. With every experience you encounter, you do have a choice. It may not be an immediately obvious one and once recognized, it may not be an easy one to make. The options presented may not be ideal. It may be a choice that forces you to question the very nature and structure of your beliefs. But there will always be a choice. Choosing your actions, your words, even your thoughts, are part of the process of developing your character. And your character is the physical expression of your being. With each choice made, comes the responsibility of accepting the consequences of it. That is yours to own. Choose wisely. Additionally, each of your choices presents those around you with their choices. Our lives and our paths, as individual as they seem, are continually overlapping and intersecting. No one is in this totally alone. Our actions influence and affect those around us. Nothing we do happens completely independently. All things are connected.

Take the word universe, for example. It is a word given to the idea of encompassing everything. Everything. It is the word given to the largest collection of, and expression of, anything and everything ever known to man. And the word itself means one verse, one song, all one. You see nothing exists truly independently. At the most basic level of existence, we are all one. So your actions, words and even thoughts are part of that collective. They matter. Make wise choices.

So I ask you, as you encounter those in your life, those intersecting your path, how would you like them to treat you? Would it be with cruelty, harshness, and malice? Or would you like to be treated with kindness? I believe your answer would be: I would like to be treated kindly. Who wouldn't? My guess is you're not longing to be treated with hostility or cruelty. No, and neither is that person crossing your path. Their actions will affect you. Your actions will affect them. And each of you, each of us, can make the choice to act kindly toward one another. Making that choice can make all the difference. I know it can. I see it. I live it.

I urge you, at each moment throughout your day, your week, your life, become aware of the choices you have. Realize your own divinity. Listen to the inspiration it provides. It is the language of the spirit. It speaks softly, providing you with the choices that will lead you, and those around you, to a higher level of consciousness. Act with kindness and compassion.